D1563953

MANAGEMENT DECISION METHODS

for Managers of Engineering and Research

MANAGEMENT DECISION METHODS

for Managers of
Engineering
and Research

by

Wm. E. Souder, Ph.D

Professor of Industrial Engineering,
Systems Management Engineering and Operations Research
University of Pittsburgh
Pittsburgh, Pennsylvania

VNR **VAN NOSTRAND REINHOLD COMPANY**
NEW YORK   CINCINNATI   ATLANTA   DALLAS   SAN FRANCISCO
LONDON   TORONTO   MELBOURNE

Van Nostrand Reinhold Company Regional Offices:
New York   Cincinnati   Atlanta   Dallas   San Francisco

Van Nostrand Reinhold Company International Offices:
London   Toronto   Melbourne

Library of Congress Catalog Card Number: 79-19213
ISBN: 0-442-27888-8

Manufactured in the United States of America

Published by Van Nostrand Reinhold Company
135 West 50th Street, New York, N. Y. 10020

Published simultaneously in Canada by Van Nostrand Reinhold Ltd.

15 14 13 12 11 10 9 8 7 6 5 4 3 2 1

Library of Congress Cataloging in Publication Data

Souder, William E
    Management decision methods for managers of
engineering and research.

    Includes index.
    1. Decision-making.   I. Title.
T57.95.S67   658.4′03   79-19213
ISBN 0-442-27888-8

This book is dedicated to my mother and father—
for their constant support and encouragement.

Preface

This is a book for practitioners of modern management. It brings together many quantitative and behavioral techniques for management decision making in individual, group and organizational settings. This book is especially dedicated to today's managers of scientific and engineering functions who are constantly frustrated by the many technical and societal uncertainties that surround them. The author hopes that the approaches presented in this book will help them.

Managers, students and teachers who are interested in the practical aspects of managerial decision making should all find this book useful. Most of the methods and techniques presented here have been tested and successfully implemented in real decision situations and organizational settings. Some of the techniques are well-suited for "back-of-the-envelope" applications where quick decisions are needed and very little information is at hand. Others are more appropriate when precise answers are needed for well-defined problems.

Many engineers, scientists and managers will find that this book is a useful handbook or practical reference work. It can provide many solutions, insights, approaches and hints for a wide variety of decision problems. And it can serve as a state-of-art catalog of available methods and techniques. Thus, this book is best used as a working reference or daily decision making companion. The author's objectives will be amply met and his ego will be gratuitously flattered if every copy of this book soon becomes dog-eared, underlined and well-worn from use.

This book is divided into fifteen chapters, which are grouped into seven parts. The chapters and their groupings parallel the general structure of a decision making process, as follows:

THE DECISION MAKING PROCESS	STAGES	RELEVANT PARTS AND CHAPTERS IN THIS BOOK
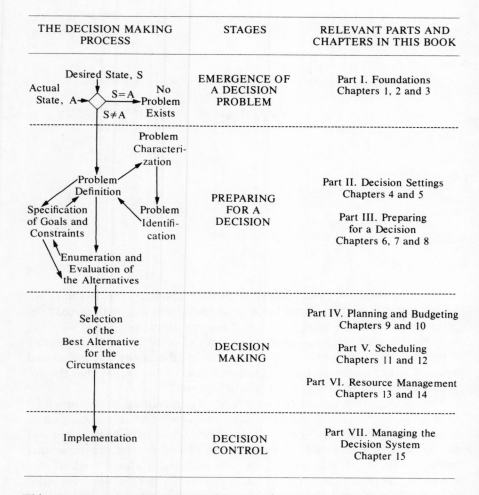	EMERGENCE OF A DECISION PROBLEM	Part I. Foundations Chapters 1, 2 and 3
	PREPARING FOR A DECISION	Part II. Decision Settings Chapters 4 and 5 Part III. Preparing for a Decision Chapters 6, 7 and 8
	DECISION MAKING	Part IV. Planning and Budgeting Chapters 9 and 10 Part V. Scheduling Chapters 11 and 12 Part VI. Resource Management Chapters 13 and 14
	DECISION CONTROL	Part VII. Managing the Decision System Chapter 15

This arrangement of the material makes this book well-suited for a one-semester graduate course in an engineering management or business administration program. The level of the material is generally appropriate for a beginning graduate student. However, some of the material in Chapters 8, 13 and 14 may be challenging for a beginning student. Because this book surveys and integrates many disciplines and techniques, it is also appropriate for a survey course, a graduate seminar course, or the last course in a degree program. Numerous realistic examples and illustrations are contained in each chapter, which facilitate the comprehension of the concepts. If this book is used in a beginning course, the instructor can use these examples as a point of discussion. In an advanced course, this book can be used as the basic materials and the instructor can devote the lecture time to more advanced examples and embellishments of these basic materials.

So many persons have contributed to this book in so many small but helpful ways that it becomes impossible to acknowledge all of them. The author is especially indebted to Dr. Albert G. Holzman, Chairman of the Department of Industrial Engineering, for his unwavering faith and support during my cantankerous periods. The secretarial staff, Penny Brown, Denise Rouse, Freda Stephen and Janice Dobrinski, deserve special plaudits for tirelessly typing and revising the manuscript. Special thanks go to my daughter Denneta for giving up part of her summer and her midterm college break to lay out the illustrations and do the line drawings. Last but not least, special thanks to my wife Edie and my other two daughters Dianna and Dorene for understanding the time I took away from them to complete this work.

WM. E. SOUDER
Mt. Lebanon, PA

Contents

MANAGEMENT DECISION METHODS

for Managers of
Engineering
and Research

Part I
Foundations

The three chapters that make up Part I provide some foundations and background for the remainder of this book. Chapter 1 examines the nature of modern-day management decision problems. It is concluded that a whole new approach to managerial decision making is needed in order to cope with the complexity of today's problems. A structured decision making system is outlined to fill this need. Chapter 2 discusses the structured decision making system and its various elements. Several inadequacies and deficiencies of typical management decision processes are examined. The ways in which the structured system overcomes these deficiencies are discussed. Chapter 3 presents several management science techniques which should be used within the structured system. Illustrations are given of the ways in which these techniques can improve the effectiveness of management decisions.

1

Management Decision Problems

1.0 INTRODUCTION

Modern management decision problems are very complex and far-reaching in their implications. Today's managers must make difficult choices and trade-offs between many different factors. Some of these are outside the manager's immediate control. Modern decision making methods and approaches are required in order to cope with these new challenges.

This chapter examines the nature of management decision problems and presents the need for a structured decision making process that will aid modern managers. A seven-step process is outlined and its application is briefly discussed. This process is shown to be especially useful for the technical manager, who must make combined decisions concerning technologies and people.

1.1 THE STRUCTURED DECISION PROCESS

"Why didn't I prepare for this?" I asked myself in disgust as I stood shivering at the bus stop. A mixture of rain and sleet was falling. A cold north wind was stinging my face and cutting through my lightweight jacket. Traffic was beginning to back up in typical Monday morning fashion. It began to dawn on me that my bus might be quite late. By the time it arrived, I could be thoroughly soaked and miserable. But I did not want to risk missing this last bus to my office while I raced home for warmer clothing.

My predicament was a direct result of my failure to use a structured decision making process earlier that morning. I could not hope to influence the weather, which was characteristically quick to change at this time of the year. But, by using a structured decision process I could have avoided a great deal of the discomfort I was now experiencing. In fact, I had not really used any decision process at all in preparing to leave for my office. Upon awakening, I casually glanced out the window and noticed the clear day that was dawning. I then set about getting ready to leave the house in my habitual pattern. However, the early morning appearance of the day was not representative of the weather that was shortly to appear. My failure to appreciate this was a direct consequence of my failure to use a structured decision making approach. I soon regretted the consequences of my failures.

1.1.1   Steps in the Process

The structured decision process is a logical, systematic procedure for selecting actions that will achieve one's objectives. It consists of the following seven steps:

1. Problem definition,
2. Specification of the goals to be achieved and their relative importance,
3. Enumeration of the decision alternatives,
4. Evaluation of each alternative,
5. Selection of the optimum alternative or alternatives,
6. Post-optimal analysis,
7. Controlled implementation.

Problem definition involves becoming fully aware of the existence of the problem and its larger context. I was insensitive to this larger context when I left for the bus stop on that Monday morning. I failed to carefully examine the situation, to note the changing weather patterns and to weigh the information in the morning weather forecast against my cursory observations.

The specification of the goals and their relative importance establishes the desired state of affairs. Had I stopped to consider my objectives on that Monday morning, I would have become more aware that comfort was my highest-valued goal. A little more thought might have caused me to dress more warmly, since I normally pay some attention to my highest-priority wants.

The enumeration of the decision alternatives establishes the various ways of achieving some or all of the goals. A careful consideration of my situation on that morning would have shown that I had several acceptable alternatives. I could have dressed in a variety of ways. Some of these ways would have protected me against a range of adverse weather conditions, without being especially burdensome under favorable weather conditions. For instance, I could have worn my lightweight raincoat and carried its zip-in lining in my briefcase. Then if the weather turned cold, I could have protected myself by zipping in the lining. I also had several alternative ways of getting to my office. I could have taken a cab, a trolley or a bus. I could have ridden with a friend or neighbor. Or I could have driven my own car and maximized my personal comfort. Better yet, I could have taken an earlier bus and been comfortably seated at my desk before the storm arrived. But, on that Monday morning I did not stop to consider any of these alternatives.

The evaluation of the alternatives determines their relative benefits, regrets and costs. For instance, the benefits from wearing a heavy topcoat in cold weather are very high. There is a large contribution to my personal comfort. But, in warm weather a heavy topcoat becomes a regret: it creates personal discomfort. A lightweight raincoat with a zip-in lining provides a great deal of flexibility for all weather conditions. But this increased flexibility comes at a cost and with some potential regrets. It gives less protection than a heavy topcoat in really bad weather (a regret). It costs more than a topcoat. And the zip-in lining takes up a lot of space in my briefcase (a regret) when I do not need to wear it. These kinds of considerations represent a very systematic and rational approach to analyzing the alternatives. I failed to carry out any such analyses.

Based on these kinds of analyses, I could have selected the best alternative clothes to wear and the best alternative mode of transportation to take. Wearing the raincoat with the zip-in lining and taking the early bus would have maximized the contributions to my goals of personal comfort, convenience and ease of commuting to my office. But I also need to consider the trade-offs between cost and contribution. For example, I may decide that the flexibility of having the zip-in lining raincoat is not worth its added cost if I establish a policy of always taking the early bus. The early bus is generally on time in even the worst weather because it is unencumbered by traffic tie-ups. Thus, with proper planning I can minimize the amount of time I spend waiting in the cold weather at the bus stop. Then I will not need a heavy coat at all. Or, I may decide to assume the risk of being uncomfortable. I shall simply try to match my clothes to the weather on the basis of careful attention to the available weather data and forecasts. This may be the optimum least-cost decision for me, given my personal goals and risk-taking propensities.

In the post-optimal analysis, the optimum decision is tested to determine whether or not it is the best choice under a wide range of possible circumstances. The results may suggest new combinations of several alternatives that should be taken as a hedge against some circumstances. The post-optimal analysis is one of the most important steps in the structured decision process. Yet it is a step that is often glossed over. For example, the probability that an extremely severe winter will occur is low in the region where I live. But, if a severe winter should occur, then not having a topcoat could be health-threatening. To hedge against all eventualities, I may need both the topcoat and the lightweight zip-in lining raincoat.

In the controlled implementation step the decision is carried out in such a way as to prevent any inadvertent consequences. These implementation methods often involve the use of behavioral techniques. For example, if my optimal decision involves taking the early bus, then I may have to retrain myself and modify my bedtimes and my early morning activities.

1.1.2   Applying the Process

In practice, the application of the structured decision process is usually a very dynamic and heuristic experience. It may involve a substantial amount of human interaction. The seven steps often overlap and they may not be performed in sequence. The decision maker may return to an earlier step at several points in the process. There may be considerable recycling through all seven steps before arriving at a final decision. Or, there may be some oscillation back and forth between the steps for some period of time. This does not mean that the structured decision process is not working. Rather, this is simply the nature of management decision problems and settings.

Management decision problems are usually so complex that they often don't become fully visible or understood until quite late in the structured decision process. Even then, the problem may not be equally perceived by all parties. This may pose considerable obstacles to a final decision. Evaluating alternatives, assessing the relative importance of goals and selecting the optimum alternative all involve personal value judgments. Individuals seldom have identical value systems. Thus, the results of these activities will often vary with the individual decision maker who performs them. The decision setting and environment can substantially influence the decision process and its outputs. Whether the decision maker is playing the role of an individual, a member of a group or an official in an organization will generally influence the decision behaviors, motives and perceptions. Information availability and data collection problems often arise in applying the structured decision process. There are few situations in which all the alternatives are known, and in which their effectiveness can be unequivocally determined. In the face of these uncertainties, some decision makers may be reluctant to make any decisions at all. Still others may be psychologically challenged to take the responsibilities for high-risk decisiveness.

Thus, the structured decision process must be thought of as a prescriptive guide. It cannot be rigidly applied to most management problems. And it certainly cannot be expected to make decisions for us. But it can be used to guide us through the often complex maze of real world decision making. It is a systematic process that forces us to consider all the aspects, in their proper order. It aids in sharpening decision making skills and analyses. It can point out otherwise hidden aspects and enlarge our awareness of the total decision system.

1.2 TECHNICAL vs. MANAGERIAL DECISIONS

1.2.1 Technical Decisions

Traditional engineering and scientific decisions primarily involve the application of established principles of physics, chemistry, mathematics and other sciences. Engineering and scientific problems are usually well-identified. The decision alternatives are usually fairly well-known. The performance data to evaluate the relative effectiveness of the alternatives is either at hand or obtainable through measurements and laboratory experiments. The data are objective and demonstrable. The optimum decision can be chosen on the basis of established physical laws and rational engineering calculations.

Today, technical decision making is much less straightforward. Society and technology are so interwoven that there is hardly any technical decision that does not have some effect on the quality of life. Today's technical decisions invariably involve some trade-offs between technical, economic and social factors. The choice of the optimum chemical process, the most effective design or the most marketable product can have many far-reaching legal, social and economic consequences. These consequences can affect many different parties, sometimes for many years into the future. Modern-day technical decision makers cannot afford to be insensitive to the systems aspects and the human impacts of their decisions. Engineers and scientists must be able to integrate human and nonhuman considerations into their decisions. Modern technical decision making involves a sensitivity to organizations, institutions, people and society as well as technology.

Thus, modern day engineers and scientists have a substantial need to rely on the structured decision making process, and to avail themselves of its benefits. Without the rigor and systematic procedures which the structured decision process supplies, it would be easy for modern engineers and scientists to lose their way in decision making. They must traverse a maze of decision factors, a variety of multiple goals and the often conflicting needs of safety, profitability and technical performance.

1.2.2   Management Decisions

Technical decisions primarily impact on things. Management decisions primarily impact on people. Moreover, management decisions characteristically involve large commitments of resources. Technical decisions are usually much more micro in their orientation. Management decisions are usually clouded by a great deal of uncertainty. Technical decision makers have relatively more information, concepts, theories and tangible foundations for their choices. Managers often deal with situations where information is almost completely lacking. A manager's decisions are usually risky, and they may have very long-lasting consequences.

Thus, large elements of judgment, intuition and experience characterize management decisions. Because of this, the manager's individual personality will often deeply influence the decision making style and the decision outcomes. However, an exclusive reliance on managerial personalities is a handicraft approach to decision making. This is precisely the approach that left this author shivering at the bus stop on a bleak Monday morning! A complete reliance on individual personalities would lead to uncoordinated chaos in organizational decision making. Thus, the further away we get from the well-ordered world of technical decision making and the closer we get to the less-structured world of managerial decision making, the more important it becomes to use the structured decision process. The structured decision process becomes all-important for focusing decision behaviors and controlling haphazardness in management decision behaviors.

1.2.3   A New Era

Today's managers face a whole new era of challenges. Government, labor unions, consumers, stockholders, suppliers and a host of other groups are all of concern to today's managers. Many different demands are placed on the modern manager in satisfying these groups.

Today's manager must thus play the role of an innovator, a negotiator, a fireman, a motivator and a resource-allocator in the decision making process. The innovator role demands that the manager lead the organization into new products, new fields and new technologies. As a negotiator, the manager must bargain, compromise and harmonize various groups and factions. As a fireman, the modern manager must be alert to small disturbances and be decisive in eliminating them. Today's manager must be able to motivate others to action. The successful manager is decisive in allocating resources to competing projects and effective in setting timely priorities.

Thus, today's manager must supplement experience and intuition with more powerful tools and processes. Organized and systematic processes are necessary in order to cope with the demands of this new era. The structured decision process and its associated techniques and methods can be a potent tool, especially when combined with seasoned judgment.

1.3 FROM SCIENTIST/ENGINEER TO MANAGER

1.3.1 Science *vs.* Management

Scientists and engineers are trained and sensitized to use methodical logic and objective thinking. They are trained to make conclusions and solve problems through the application of theorems and proofs. They are taught to seek unequivocal evidence before coming to a final conclusion. The formal training of a scientist or an engineer emphasizes an analytical capability and the scientific approach. The focus is on finding exact solutions to well-defined problems, by the use of objective data and established theories. Sound technical decision making depends on the ability to apply rigorous methods in searching out causes and solutions to problems.

By contrast, managerial decision making requires an ability to size up people and situations, with only a minimum of information about *symptoms*. An effective manager is able to diagnose a situation when only a very small amount of the problem iceberg is visible. This is in direct contrast to the scientific approach. The scientific approach to decision making uses a large volume of well-ordered information, which is sifted and evaluated in the light of established theories and concepts. By contrast, a manager may modify the theory with each new problem. Management theories are often nebulous and tentative, and are often based on a few individual cases. In effect, the manager has relatively few established rules and principles to rely on.

These differences may pose considerable problems for the young scientist or engineer who has just been advanced to a managerial level position. For others, the transition may be less difficult because they have a latent reservoir of managerial talents. This reservoir may be an inherited trait, it may be due to early experiences, or some combination of both. For most scientists and engineers, managerial abilities must be acquired. They can best be acquired through a combination of formal training in a university classroom and on the job experiences. This exposes the individual to a combination of theory and practice that reinforce each other. This combination of formal and experiential training is all the more important in today's complex society, where managers are confronted with a vast new era of challenges.

1.3.2   The Technical Manager

In today's new era of management challenges, there are ever increasing needs for individuals who understand technology and who can effectively manage human resources in harnessing that technology. Moreover, because we live in a management-class oriented culture, many engineers and scientists aspire to managerial positions. Thus, the technical manager has become a very important and prevalent member of today's management ranks.

A technical manager is an individual who manages research, development, engineering and other technological functions. The job may carry a title such as group leader, section leader, project manager, product manager, R&D manager or vice president of technology. The content of the function may be primarily technical, as in the case of a group leader. Or it may be primarily administrative, as in the case of a vice president of technology. All technical management functions are especially demanding and challenging. They require the individual to be both a capable technical decision maker and a capable manager. The successful technical manager must be able to partition technical and managerial skills, bringing them to bear on different problems at different points of time. The technical manager must recognize which skill is being demanded and when to draw on how much of each. The technical manager must be able to distinguish between a technical problem and a managerial problem, or a problem that is some combination of both. In short, the technical manager must be able to play both the role of the scientist or engineer and the role of the manager. A technical manager must have the ability to move between whichever role is demanded at that particular point in time.

Because the methods of science and management differ, the ability to move smoothly between these two roles is not easily acquired. In the technical role, the individual is inclined to seek out salient facts that lead directly to a solution. There is a strong inclination to seek exact conclusions to some particular portion of the overall problem. But most managerial situations require that the decision maker distinguish symptoms from causes and understand the *whole* problem, in its total setting. Satisfactory resolutions of the whole problem are sought by achieving some balance among the human and technical aspects.

When the structured decision process is properly applied, it can help the technical manager distinguish the technical and managerial roles. It can increase the effectiveness of management decision making by integrating some scientific methodologies with some judgmental approaches. As we shall see in subsequent chapters, the structured decision process is especially well-adapted to assist the technical manager.

1.4 SUMMARY

Today's managers are confronted with decision making challenges of unparalleled complexity. Society and technology have become so interwoven that the successful manager must be able to direct an entire system of human, political, economic, social, ethical, legal and technical factors. A large element of judgment is required in solving modern management problems. But reliance on judgment alone is not sufficient to cope with today's demands. A much more structured, more systematic and more powerful decision making process is needed. This book presents, discusses and illustrates that process.

1.5 BIBLIOGRAPHY

Badawy, M. K. "Easing the Switch from Engineer to Manager." *Machine Design,* May 15, 1975, pp. 66–68.

Braybrooke, David and Lindblom, C. E. *A Strategy of Decisions.* New York: Free Press, 1963.

Cleland, D. I. and King, W. R. *Management: A Systems Approach.* New York: McGraw-Hill, 1972.

Duncan, W. J. *Decision Making and Social Issues.* Hinsdale, Illinois: Dryden, 1973.

Ebert, R. J. and Mitchell, T. R. *Organizational Decision Processes.* New York: Crane, Russak & Company, 1975.

Estes, R. M. "The Business-Society Relationship: Emerging Major Issues," in *Selected Major Issues in Businesses' Role in Modern Society,* G. A. Steiner (ed.), Los Angeles, California: UCLA Graduate School of Management, 1973.

Hallenberg, E. X. "Dual Advancement Ladder Provides Unique Recognition for the Scientist." *Research Management,* **13,** No. 3: 221–227 (1970).

Handschumacher, A. G. "The Scientist: Is He Equipped for Managing?" *Office Executive,* April 1961, pp. 20–21.

Kimblin, C. W. and Souder, W. E. "Maintaining Staff Productivity as Half-Life Decreases." *Research Management,* **18,** No. 6: 29–35 (1975).

Simon, H. A. *The New Science of Management Decision.* New York: Harper & Row, 1960.

Sutherland, J. W. *Administrative Decision-Making.* New York: Van Nostrand Reinhold Company, 1977.

Tagiuri, Renato. "Value Orientations of Managers and Scientists," in *Administering Research and Development,* C. D. Orth, J. C. Bailey and F. W. Wolek (eds.), Homewood, Illinois: Richard D. Irwin, Inc., 1964, pp. 63–71.

Tartar, J. L. "MBO: Blue Collar to Top Executive." *The Academy of Management Review,* **4,** No. 2: 148–149 (1979).

2

The Structured Decision Process

2.0 INTRODUCTION

What, really, is a "decision?" Is it an event? An occurrence? A behavioral process? A mental process? These are surprisingly difficult questions to answer. A decision would seem to be all of these and more. Yet a precise definition is very elusive.

A decision is a very personal thing that occurs internally with each individual. Judgment and intuition are involved, as are sentiments and individual value systems. We never really get to see a decision. We only see its manifestations and effects. We can observe how individuals and groups go about making a decision. We can document their behavior patterns and the analytical methods used. We can describe the sequence of logic used, the factors influencing the decision and the rationale for the final choices that are made. But it can hardly be said that we have observed a decision. Rather, we have observed only the elements of a decision process. These elements consist of the behavior patterns, the analytical procedures and the sequence of logic used in making a decision. Thus, while a decision may be a mysterious thing, the elements of a decision making process are not. They are visible, tangible and controllable. And they can be structured in such a way that they constitute a highly objective and systematic approach to decision making.

2.1 ELEMENTS OF DECISION MAKING

2.1.1 Model of a Decision Process

Though decision processes usually differ with the nature of the problem, the situation and the individual decision maker, Figure 2.1 presents a

12

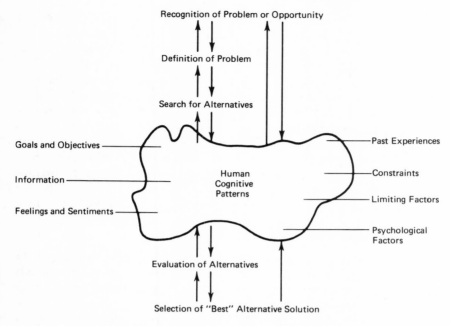

Figure 2.1. Elements of a decision making process.

general picture of most decision processes. This model depicts decisions as being precipitated by the recognition of problems or opportunities. If the problem or opportunity is perceived as routine, the decision maker may go immediately to the selection of the best alternative solution. If the problem or opportunity is familiar, then little time may be devoted to its definition. If the problem or opportunity is well-defined, then the search for alternative solutions or ways to take advantage of the opportunity may be brief. If the relative effectiveness of the alternatives are known, then very little time may be spent in analyzing and evaluating the alternatives and deliberating about the best one.

In terms of Figure 2.1, the nature of the problem may influence whether or not the decision maker moves through the process slowly or quickly. If the problem is a routine one that is solved by habit, then the decision maker may jump from problem recognition to the selection of the best alternative solution. If the decision is one that has been preprogrammed, then the decision maker may skip the problem definition and the search for alternatives. In a preprogrammed decision there are a finite number of alternatives with known effectiveness, and the decision maker must match up the appropriate alternative with the problem stimulus. An example is deciding what clothes to wear in the morning. The problem stimuli include the weather and the planned daily activities. Sunny, warm weather and recreational activities require one kind of wardrobe, while other weather and other activities require different appropriate dress.

If the decision problem is complex or poorly understood then the decision process may be quite lengthy and deliberative. As Figure 2.1 shows, there may be considerable recycling back and forth within the process. The search for alternatives may result in information that further clarifies the problem or suggests its redefinition. New alternatives may be discovered during the processes of evaluating and analyzing the original set of alternatives. The best alternative may not be apparent from the original set, and a new search for alternatives may be undertaken. Thus, the decision making process may be very heuristic and iterative in nature.

2.1.2 The Human Aspects

The model in Figure 2.1 depicts human cognitive patterns as being at the center of the overall decision making process. These patterns are largely unknown and unobservable to us. We know that personal values, goals and organizational objectives can strongly influence the decision maker. In part, these influences explain why two individuals may not perceive a problem in the same way, or may not select the same final solution. Goals and objectives, the level of available information, the individual's feelings, the individual's psychological make-up, and a host of other variables may deeply influence the perception of the problem, the evaluation of the alternatives and other elements of the decision making process.

Unfortunately, we cannot easily look inside human thought processes to see precisely how these patterns operate. Thus, attempts to directly improve actual human thought patterns are stymied. But, as Figure 2.1 shows, a substantial number of important elements in the overall decision making process are not locked up within the human cognitive area. These elements can be made more rational, systematic and complete through the direct application of improved methods and techniques. By improving these elements, human thought processes may then be indirectly impacted upon and improved.

2.2 THE STRUCTURED DECISION MAKING PROCESS

Figure 2.2 presents an algorithm for the structured decision making process. This algorithm describes the various steps that are performed within the structured decision making process, and shows the relationships between them. The algorithm builds on the model presented in Figure 2.1, and on the seven-step process outlined in Chapter 1.

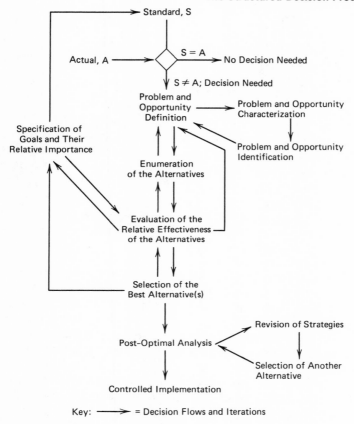

Figure 2.2. Algorithm for the structured decision making process.

This algorithm is a general one that applies to a variety of types of problems and situations. Let us examine each of the various steps within the algorithm and the procedures for carrying them out.

2.2.1 Recognizing a Problem or Opportunity

The first indication of the existence of a problem or an opportunity comes as a variance between the actual conditions and the established standards, or the desired conditions. If there are no standards, or if the standards are poorly established, then there is a good chance that the problem or opportunity may go unrecognized much longer than it should. This capability to have early warnings of pending problems or opportunities is perhaps one of the most convincing arguments for engaging in thorough planning and standard-setting. Early detection often makes the difference between success and failure in decision making. But if there are no plans or comparative standards, then one has no way of determining whether a problem or opportunity exists.

Problem and opportunity recognition is a highly personal and subjective process. It may be influenced by a variety of personal filters and barriers. Habits, past experiences, aspirations and many other personal behavioral variables can influence whether or not a situation becomes a part of an individual's cognitive awareness. These factors also influence whether or not the individual admits the situation into the cognitive list of important problems or opportunities. Thus, problem and opportunity recognition is a two-step personal process of seeing and admitting. I may see a problem, but I may not think it is important or significant. If I do not think it is important, it will not motivate me to action. The result will be the same as if I had not seen the problem at all.

Many problems and opportunities are not recognized in a timely fashion because the decision maker cannot discriminate between relevant and irrelevant information. Situations typically contain a great deal of information that is irrelevant to the real problem. To be effective, a decision maker must develop the skills to sort out important from unimportant information. The decision maker must also be alert and sensitive to the market, technological, economic, legal and political environments that surround the problem or opportunity. The market, economic and technological environments will determine whether or not the problem or opportunity is one that can wait or must be acted upon now. The legal and political environments will determine whether the event is a problem or an opportunity. For instance, antipollution laws are problems for some heavy industries, but they provide many opportunities for pollution control firms. Enterprising and alert organizations can often find creative ways to turn problems into opportunities if they can gain sufficient lead time by examining the emerging technical, social and political trends.

The setting in which the problem arises will often greatly influence its perception. An individual may perceive a problem that is not recognized by others. In an individual decision setting, action may be taken immediately. But in a group or organizational setting, this same problem might not be acted upon at all unless all the parties recognize it.

Thus, there are many individual, situational and environmental filters that can cloud the problem- or opportunity-recognition process. The alert decision maker will examine all variances between the actual conditions and the standard by asking the following four questions.

1. Is this a variance that could have major technical, social, legal, economic or political ramifications?
2. Could these ramifications produce either problems or opportunities for the organization, the decision maker, or other concerned parties?
3. Is the variance greater than the random variations that could normally be expected?
4. Is the variance likely to increase if no action is taken now?

If the answer to any of these four questions is "yes," then the decision maker cannot afford to ignore the variance. An in-depth analysis of the nature of the variance and its implications is warranted.

2.2.2 Problem and Opportunity Definition

Problems and opportunities almost never present themselves in a well-defined fashion. The first visible parts of the iceberg are the symptoms. But operating on symptoms will normally be ineffective. The decision maker must peel through the onion-like layers of symptoms until the real issues are confronted.

This is no easy matter. The available information will be a mixture of random facts, feelings, complaints, prejudices, inferences and opinions about the situation. During the early stages, it will be difficult to distinguish relevant from irrelevant information. But, as more information is acquired, this distinction will gradually emerge. The process of probing for more information and the sorting of fact from fancy will take time and require perseverance. The organizational climate must encourage and support these efforts, which will compete for the manager's limited time and energies. The entire process of problem and opportunity definition is often a very discontinuous, groping action. It requires patience and a belief in the potential payoff. But anyone who has attempted to treat symptoms knows from first-hand experience how important it is to get to the real problem.

The price for operating on symptoms can be a missed opportunity or an unsolved problem, on top of the wasted time and resources spent on ineffective treatments. It is nearly always cheaper in the long run to search out the real, underlying problems and opportunities. Few decisions fail because the wrong alternatives are chosen. But many decisions fail because the wrong problem was solved. An adequate investment in problem definition efforts is perhaps the highest payoff investment that can be made in the whole decision making process.

To assist the decision maker in defining the problem or opportunity, some characterization and identification procedures are available. However, these are only aids or guidelines. Their application requires a great deal of incisive inquiry and dogged detective work. Let us briefly look at these procedures.

2.2.2.1 Problem and Opportunity Characterization. Every variance should be characterized by its time and location of occurrence. Such when-and-where diagnoses help to distinguish what the problem *is* from what it *is not*. The decision maker should always ask "What is it *not?*" This helps to narrow down the possible list of problems or opportunities. The determination of the time and location of the variance tells us where to look for additional diagnostic information, and serves as a guideline in distinguishing relevant from irrelevant information. For example, suppose we can state that an observed difference between the actual and desired product performance has the following time and location characteristics. It seems to originate in the quality control department, it occurs only during the third production shift, and it never occurs on Tuesdays. These statements help to direct and focus the search for additional relevant information that will define and clarify the real problem or opportunity.

2.2.2.2 Problem and Opportunity Identification. This approach identifies the specific nature and properties of the variance. A written identification statement is developed that specifies:

1. the specific standard that has been violated;
2. the implications of this;
3. the potential and actual problems or opportunities which this creates;
4. the most serious, urgent, immediate or otherwise prominent problem or opportunity from the list of potential ones;
5. whose opportunity or problem it is, in terms of responsibilities and under what circumstances.

When these identification and characterization procedures are combined, they provide a comprehensive approach to the definition of the specific problem or opportunity. This definition includes an information base for further decision making, it identifies the person responsible for taking further actions and it provides some direction for this action.

2.2.3   Enumeration of Alternatives

The process of generating alternatives is seldom given the attention it deserves. Many decision makers spend a great deal of effort on the evaluation and selection of alternatives, and very little time generating alternatives. Because the quality of a decision can be no better than the quality of the alternatives that are available, it is important to devote an adequate amount of time to the generation of high-quality alternatives.

The development of alternative solutions is often a very heuristic process. It is also a very delicate creative process. Thus, the application of various creativity and idea-generating methods are often needed at this stage of the process. Experience shows that behavioral process controls and group management methods are also important, since ideas are more easily produced in a non-evaluative atmosphere. Combinations of alternatives should be sought, both as a springboard for generating more creative ideas and as viable combined solutions. Combined solutions are often needed when the problem is highly complex.

The "do-nothing" alternative is always an admissible policy. It should always appear in the list of possible alternative decisions. It may not turn out to be a viable alternative. But it should always be as painstakingly analyzed as any other potential action. The alternative of doing nothing is sometimes written off all too quickly, and the decision maker rushes into commitments that turn out to be much worse choices. The exercise of considering and analyzing the "do-nothing" alternative can lead to an enlightened picture of the decision problem, which may trigger the generation of other creative alternatives.

It should be noted that deciding to do nothing and procrastinating are two very different things. A decision maker who *decides* to do nothing has gone through a logical decision process. But a decision maker who has not gone through a decision process does not really know whether the "do-nothing" alternative is the best or the worst. Procrastination suggests that the decision maker is unskilled, indecisive and ineffective in decision making.

2.2.4 Specifying Goals

The goals which the decision maker wishes to achieve by solving the problem must be clearly stated at the outset. The goals represent the desired state of affairs. They serve as the basis for measuring the effectiveness of the alternatives. And they serve as indicators that tell us when the problem is solved. Quite simply, the problem is not completely solved until all the goals are achieved. If the best available alternatives cannot be expected to achieve all the goals, then more effective alternatives should be sought before the decision maker commits to a final decision.

The goals and the standards (see Figure 2.2) must articulate closely with each other. The standards are the specific, detailed benchmarks which translate the goals into measurable targets. The standard is the statement of the acceptable level of achievement of the goal. For example, if the goal is to maximize sales volume, then the corresponding standard should specify the level of sales volume targeted during some time horizon. If the standards are set too high this may lead to under achievements and to false signals of problems or opportunities when there are none. The failure to achieve a high standard may demotivate future achievements, and cause the standards to be set too low in the next planning cycle. This may result in the adoption of less ambitious goals. If the standards are set too low, then the system will never sense any problems or opportunities, even though they may abound.

Real goals are not always apparent, and hard thought is sometimes needed to develop a precise statement of the desired state of affairs. This is often the case in group and organizational settings, where the various individuals and departments may collectively have many dissimilar and conflicting goals. Even an individual decision maker may have multiple goals and several desired levels of achievements. A good starting point in ascertaining goals and standards is to simply ask the following two questions: "What is the desired state of affairs?" and "How would you know when the problem is solved?" This usually evokes a set of criteria which embody the goals and standards. For example, suppose the decision maker responds that the problem would be solved when sales return to the desired three billion dollar per year level. In this case, the three billion dollar level is both a goal and a standard.

2.2.5   Evaluating Alternatives

Each alternative must be analyzed and evaluated in terms of its value, cost and risk characteristics. The value of an alternative is measured in terms of its contributions to the achievement of each of the goals. The value of each alternative should be assessed in terms of the benefits that can be expected to result if it is chosen, and in terms of the regrets that can be suffered if it is *not chosen*. A focus on the regrets that may occur by not choosing a particular alternative can often be very revealing. In some cases, the regrets for not choosing an alternative may be so enormous that it must be chosen in order to protect the organization's current position.

The cost of each alternative must be carefully assessed in terms of its out-of-pocket costs, opportunity costs and follow-on costs. The out-of-pocket costs are the day-to-day expenses and capital outlays which the organization must pay to finance the alternative. Opportunity costs are hidden costs like the interest foregone on invested capital or other opportunities foregone because funds are invested in this alternative. The follow-on costs of each alternative should be very carefully examined. It is not unusual to find that an alternative, which looks inexpensive, may require massive capital at some later date to implement or maintain it.

The risk characteristics of each alternative should be carefully assessed, in terms of the likelihoods of achieving each of the goals. Some high-valued alternatives may have the potential to make very large contributions to the achievement of the goals. However, the likelihood that they will actually accomplish these potentials may be very small. Other, medium-valued alternatives may exhibit a high degree of certainty of making moderate contributions. Thus, when their risk characteristics are taken into account, the medium-valued alternatives may be the higher-contributing choices.

In most decision situations, multiple goals will exist. Some of the goals will be more important than others. These differences in importance need to be carefully expressed as a basis for distinguishing between the alternatives. An alternative that contributes to a highly important goal will generally be a higher-valued alternative than one that contributes to a less important goal.

2.2.6 Selecting the Best Alternative

Theoretically, the alternatives can be ranked from best to worst on the basis of some benefit/cost, regret/cost or risk/cost ratios. However, it is not possible to include all the relevant factors in such an index. Some of these relevant factors are: the efficiency with which the alternative solves the problem, the impact of the alternative on the various noneconomic organizational goals, the acceptability of the alternative to those who will implement and use it, the changes in behavior patterns required if the alternative is chosen, and the interrelationships between the alternatives. In group or organizational settings, there may be many different persons who are involved in the final decision. These persons may be suppliers of decision information, decision makers, or decision influencers. Thus, the selection process may be influenced by many behavioral factors.

Judgment, bargaining and analytical processes may often be used in selecting the best alternative. In the judgmental approach, an individual makes an intuitive choice from among the alternatives. The judgmental approach is often so intuitive that it is not easily documented or explained to another decision maker. Bargaining is a process by which a group of decision makers with conflicting goals exercise judgments, converse about them, and then trade off wants and desires until some agreement is reached. The analytical approach involves factual evaluations and rigorous comparisons of the alternatives on the basis of costs, benefits, regrets and other measures. The analytical approach includes a quantitative and procedural measurement of values and costs. Political activities may also occur. They generally manifest themselves in the use of bargaining routines by those who have some control over the choices. In organizational settings, the final decision may have to be approved by many different layers in the organization. Thus, there may be many opportunities for bargaining and political activities in an organizational decision making setting.

In the structured decision process, the best alternative is selected on the basis of the application of analytical models and techniques. Operations research and management science methods are used to help the decision maker select the optimum choice on the basis of economic considerations. Political activities are thus kept to a minimum by focusing on objective processes and rigorous analyses. However, systematic and controlled judgments are incorporated into the process at various points, in order to include non-economic and nonquantifiable considerations. Controlled bargaining may also be necessary at some points in order to arrive at a decision that balances all the various needs and desires. Sometimes a single best alternative may be chosen. Sometimes several alternatives may be found to be satisfactory. More often, no one alternative will be the best on all the criteria or under all the considerations. Then, a package of alternatives may be devised. Or several alternatives may be selected for implementation in a sequence of steps, ranging from the least risky to the most risky.

2.2.7   Post-Optimal Analysis

The best or optimum decision for the conditions confronting the decision maker may not be the best choice under some other conditions. Using management science models and methods, a post-optimal analysis can be made to check the sensitivity of the optimum decision to changes in the decision conditions. If the optimum decision is not found to be the best decision over the entire range of possible conditions, then several strategies are available. The post-optimal analysis may be used to find combinations of alternatives that are effective over the entire range of conditions. Contingency plans may be developed. Or a multiechelon decision approach may be taken, where various alternatives are implemented as the emerging conditions warrant.

The post-optimal analysis also provides an opportunity for the decision maker to review all the preceding steps in the structured decision making process. The logic chain and sequence of activities can be checked. And any new information or alternatives that may have arisen during the process can be taken into account at this time.

2.2.8   Controlled Implementation

A decision is absolutely worthless if it cannot be implemented. Anyone who takes the time and effort to make a decision that cannot be implemented may be worse off than if no decision had been made. Once the time, effort and funds have been expended the decision maker may develop an emotional attachment to the decision. It may then be difficult to convince the decision maker that this particular decision is impractical or unacceptable to those who must use it.

A decision is not complete until a plan for its implementation has been devised. The development of an effective implementation plan is every bit as important as the decision itself. This plan should specify the barriers and obstacles to the acceptance of the decision, and the ways in which these are to be overcome through motivational and behavioral changes. Because of the nature of people in general, abrupt changes in human behavior should not be expected. Thus, the implementation should be spread over a reasonable time span. In general, the most difficult decisions to implement are those which involve major changes in human behaviors, those which have uncertain effects and far-reaching implications, those which involve personal risks to the individual decision makers, or those which involve large commitments of resources. These are precisely the characteristics of most managerial decisions.

Implementation will be facilitated where the following three things are done. First, implementation should be considered during the evaluation and analysis of the alternatives. Any alternative that is not implementable should not be considered further. Any alternatives that are difficult to implement should be considered only as a last resort. Second, the implementation of any alternative will be improved where those who have to use it are participatively involved in its formulation. Not only will the users be more willing to accept something they have had a hand in, but the actual quality of the decision may also be improved. Finally, attention must be given to selling the alternative. Those who must accept and use the new decision must understand how it can help them, and they must be enthusiastic about it. The decision maker must always keep in mind the motives of those who are expected to adopt and use the decision.

2.3   SOME ROADBLOCKS

There are several human traits and proclivities that can diminish the effectiveness of the structured decision making process unless they are carefully guarded against. By being aware of these roadblocks, the decision maker will be in a better position to avoid them.

2.3.1   Jumping from Problem to Solution

It is human nature to jump from problem to solution, and to circumvent an explicit algorithmic process. We all have a proclivity to rely on our innate abilities. There is a tendency to feel that reliance on any decision models or algorithmic aids somehow diminishes our own personal abilities. But intuitive processes do not give any assurances that some information or some alternative has not been missed. To be sure that "all the bases have been touched," an explicit algorithm like the structured decision process must be followed.

2.3.2   Premature Evaluation

When first confronted with a problem, it is human nature to want to immediately search for causes and solutions. But, it is usually more important to search for more information about the problem itself. An expanded diagnosis of the what, when, where, how and why of the problem is necessary before an enlightened search for causes and solutions can occur. Otherwise there is a very great danger of solving the wrong problem.

2.3.3   Over-Reliance on Experience

Most of us have experienced the *déjà vu* phenomenon of having "been here before." As our experiences grow and we become successful in decision making, many elements of the new situations we encounter are indeed much like some we have encountered before. This can be a dangerous trap. It encourages us to apply old solutions that have succeeded in the past. The danger is that all of us suffer from incomplete recall. And the new situation is often just enough different that the old solutions do not apply. Thus, what seems like an old problem may mysteriously fail to respond to our tried and proven ways. This is a very great danger for the decision maker who becomes complacent and overconfident as a result of past successes.

2.3.4   Premature Commitment

Finding a satisfactory solution too early in the process can blind the decision maker to better solutions. This is especially the case where the problem appears to be a familiar one. The decision maker may become so emotionally committed to this one satisfactory alternative that others simply do not penetrate this blind commitment. Maintaining an open mind and a healthy skepticism toward older, well-tried solutions is a protection against this roadblock.

2.3.5   Confusion of Problems and Symptoms

There is a natural human tendency to deal with problems at face value. Consequently, many symptoms are mistaken for problems. The decision maker should always maintain that a hidden agenda exists, under the layers of first impressions and awarenesses. It is always more costly in the long run to overlook a problem. Looking for a hidden problem and being disappointed is seldom a great waste of effort or funds, relative to the enormous regrets that can result from failing to look.

2.3.6   Focusing on One Solution

Most real problems are a complex bundle of interrelated smaller problems. Thus, it is unlikely that a single alternative solution will be completely effective. A combination or system of articulated solutions is usually needed. This salient fact is often overlooked. Many decision makers seek the unreachable, all-purpose single solution. This is usually unrealistic.

2.3.7   Overlooking Implementation

There is a tendency to gloss over the implementation aspects. The fact that no solution implements itself is often overlooked. Frequently, more time and effort are needed in implementing the solution than it takes to find and develop it. A sensitive and realistic decision maker is aware of the natural human resistances to change, and these considerations are taken into account in the choices and actions.

2.4   SUMMARY

A decision involves many intuitive and deep-seated cognitive mechanisms that cannot be observed or directly influenced. What can be influenced are the behavior patterns, the analytical procedures and the sequences of logic that are followed in making a decision. These are the elements of the decision making process.

The elements are often haphazard, unsystematic, inefficient and ineffective. Improvements may be sought through the application of the structured decision making process. Improvements can be expected in the following eight areas. One, more timely sensing and recognition of emerging problems and opportunities will result. This will enable the decision maker to have more time to devote to the problem and to take earlier actions. Two, a greater depth of comprehension and a more accurate identification of the real problems and opportunities will result. Thus, the chances of operating on false symptoms or solving the wrong problems will be reduced. Three, more logical and higher quality alternative decision choices and strategies will result. Since the quality of the final decision is limited by the quality of the available alternatives, improvements in the alternatives will translate directly into improvements in the final decision. Four, a detailed specification of the articulated goals and standards will be developed. This will tie the problem-solving activities closely to the organizational or individual goals and the long range plans. Five, a comprehensive evaluation of the benefits, costs and regrets of each alternative will be undertaken. The resulting expanded information base will permit the decision maker to exercise more enlightened judgments. Six, intuition, bargaining and political processes will be reduced in favor of more rigorous, systematic comparative analyses as the basis for selecting the overall best alternative. Seven, contingency plans and other preparations will be more effectively developed. Eight, through the use of behavioral techniques and group methods, the chances that the decision will be implemented will be increased. The remainder of this book focuses on the techniques for achieving these eight kinds of improvements.

2.5 BIBLIOGRAPHY

Ackoff, R. L.; Gupta, S. K.; and Minas, J. Sayer. *The Scientific Method: Optimizing Applied Research Decisions.* New York: John Wiley & Sons, Inc., 1962.

Braybrooke, David and Lindblom, C. E. *A Strategy of Decisions.* New York: Free Press, 1963.

Dewey, John. *How We Think.* Boston: D. C. Heath & Company, 1933, pp. 106–118.

Edwards, Ward and Tversky, Amos. *Decision Making.* Middlesex, England: Penguin Books Ltd., 1967.

McKeney, J. L. and Keen, G. W. "How Managers' Minds Work." *Harvard Business Review,* **52,** No. 2: 79–90 (1974).

Raiffa, Howard. *Decision Analysis.* Reading, Massachusetts: Addison-Wesley Publishing Co., Inc., 1970.

Souder, W. E.; Maher, P. N.; Baker, N. R.; Shumway, C. R.; and Rubenstein, A. H. "Methodology for Increasing the Adoption of R&D Project Selection Models." *R&D Management,* **4,** No. 2: 75–83 (1974).

Sutherland, J. W. *Administrative Decision-Making.* New York: Van Nostrand Reinhold Company, 1977, pp. 51–107.

Ward, Barbara. "Progress for a Small Planet." *Harvard Business Review,* **57,** No. 5: 89–93 (1979).

3
Management Science
Decision Techniques

3.0 INTRODUCTION

The preceding two chapters have presented the structured decision making process. This chapter presents several management science decision making techniques which may be used at various points within the structured process. When combined with informed judgments and systematic analyses, these methods can provide powerful assistance to the management decision maker. This chapter presents the most useful and effective management science approaches for assessing the relative values of decision alternatives, rating the relative importance of decision making goals, and assessing risks and outcome likelihoods.

3.1 VALUE AND BENEFIT ASSESSMENT

The need to make value assessments and benefit measurements occurs at two points in the structured decision making process (see Figure 2.2 in Chapter 2). These two points are: the specification of the relative importance of the goals and the evaluation of the relative effectiveness of the alternatives.

Value is ultimately an intuitive, personal concept. The old saying that value is in the eye of the beholder does not seem to be far wrong. The management science approach accepts the idea that value is basically an intuitive concept. But it does not accept the idea that value must be *measured* intuitively. The management science approach combines the application of rigorous measurement methods with systematic judgments and subjective assessments.

Four different types of management science methods exist for making value and benefit assessments. These four are: sorting, ranking, rating and scoring methods. The choice of one type of method over another depends on the user's needs and the nature of the circumstances.

Sorting methods categorize the items, thereby creating a discontinuous nonnumerical scaling. No distinctions are made between the items within a category, so that they are assigned the same value. Though numbers may be assigned to the categories, the crudeness of measurement severely restricts the arithmetic operations that may be performed on them. However, sorting methods are very natural and easy to use, they are the only methods capable of handling large populations of items, and they lend themselves well to group and organizational decision settings.

Ranking methods result in a unique numerical value assessment for each item. These methods are rather natural and easy to use. But they are not capable of handling large populations of items. Though numbers result, they are rank order numbers. Thus, only limited arithmetical operations can accurately be performed with them.

Rating methods give a more precise measurement and they result in numbers which can accurately be subjected to most arithmetic operations. However, these methods cannot handle some kinds of items and they may not meaningfully apply to some situations.

Unlike the other three methods which provide only comparative measurements of value, scoring methods provide absolute measurements of the value of each item. A further advantage of scoring methods is that they can explicitly handle multidimensional situations, where the total value of an item is a result of several attributes. However, these methods are especially difficult to perfect and use with accuracy. The amount of data required also severely limits their applicability.

3.1.1 Sorting Methods

Though many ways of sorting may be devised, the Q-sort method is one of the most useful. As outlined in Table 3.1, the mechanics of Q-sorting are relatively simple. An individual is given a deck of cards, with each card bearing the name and identification of one of the items to be sorted. The individual is then asked to successively sort and re-sort the cards into several predesignated categories, according to a predefined criterion like "worth" or "priority." The definition of this criterion is purposely kept vague, in order to permit the individual's own personal definitions and perceptions to shape the results. The resulting categories may contain any number of cards, including none.

The Q-sorting procedure thus results in a distribution of items, arrayed according to how the individual "feels about them." The choice of the

Table 3.1. The Q-sorting procedure.

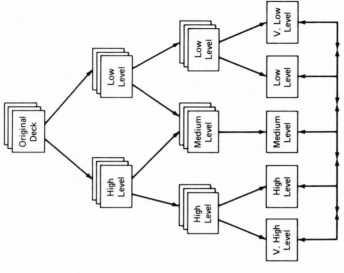

RESULTS AT EACH STEP

STEPS

1. An individual decision maker is given a deck of cards, each card bearing the name, title or other identification of one item. A vaguely specified criterion (e.g., "worth") is the basis for the sorting.

2. Divide the deck into two piles, one representing a high level of the specified criterion, the other a low level. (The piles need not be equal.)

3. Select cards from each pile to form a third pile representing the medium level of the criterion.

4. Select cards from the high level pile to yield another pile representing the very high level of the criterion; select cards from the low level pile to yield another pile representing the very low level of the criterion.

5. Finally, survey the selections and shift any cards that seem out of place until the classifications are satisfactory.

number of sort categories is based on a consideration of the number of items to be sorted, the nature of the distributions sought and the felt naturalness of the process. Generally, an odd number of sort categories is required by the sequential procedures outlined in Table 3.1. However, the sorting could be terminated at the end of three categories, or it could be continued beyond the five categories illustrated in Table 3.1.

The Q-sort method has been found to lend itself quite well to group and organizational decision making settings, where the results may be statistically analyzed for interindividual similarities and group consensus. The mechanics of the method are simple and the results provide a great deal of information to stimulate group discussions and exchanges of perceptions. In hierarchical organizational settings, two or more levels of organizational representatives may individually carry out Q-sorts which can then be compared and discussed. Differences in perceptions may thus be highlighted as a basis for subsequent resolution and consensus.[1,2]

Sorting methods have the advantages of simplicity, naturalness and ease of use. A very large number of items, even as many as 400 or 500 items, can be assessed without great difficulty.[3] The results may be used as a scale to measure the value of any new item by simply comparing the new item to those that are already sorted. The disadvantages of sorting methods lie in the nature of the accuracy of their outputs. No attention is given to measuring the magnitudes of the differences between the categories. We can only say that "high" is higher than "medium," etc. We cannot say by how much. The outputs are not numerical. Though numbers could be attributed to the categories (e.g., "very high" = 1, "high" = 2, etc.), this could easily lead the user to impute greater accuracy to the numbers than is warranted. Sorting methods do not result in a unique value for each item. Though categories are distinguished, the items within a category all have the same value.

3.1.2   Ranking Methods

The simplest ranking approach is to intuitively rank a set of items first, second, third, etc. However, there is no assurance that any systematic procedures are employed in an intuitive approach. The most systematic approach is an exhaustive comparison, in which every item is compared with every other item. However, if there are many items, the meaning of the label "exhaustive" will quickly become apparent to the user of this method!

The paired comparison method has been found to be a simple and effective method for obtaining unique rankings. Since every item must be compared to every other item, the total number of comparisons can become quite large. However, the process is considerably simplified if the items are presented in a paired comparison matrix instrument like the one illustrated in Figure 3.1. To use the instrument, the items to be ranked (A, B, C and D) are listed as column headings in any order from left to right in the matrix. The items are also listed as row headings, in the same order from top to bottom in the matrix. All pairs of items can then be judged in their permuted combinations, by sequentially comparing each column item to each row item. A "+" is scored where the column item is judged more important, and a "0" otherwise. The item with the highest number of "+"'s (column marginal total) is assigned a rank of "1," the next highest is ranked "2," etc., as illustrated in Figure 3.1.

The symmetry of the matrix instrument around its diagonal provides a check on the user's logic. A completed matrix should have offsetting "+" and "0" entries across the diagonal. This means that the column and row totals should be identical. If not, then the user has an inconsistency in logic in at least one pair of items. Each inconsistency can be found by isolating every pair of items that does not have offsetting "+" and "0" scores. Nonoffsetting scores indicate that the user preferred one of the paired items at one point in the matrix and subsequently reversed the preference at some other point. Such inconsistencies often mean that the individual finds it difficult to distinguish the items, perhaps due to a lack of complete information. If any ties exist in the row totals or in the column totals after all the inconsistencies are removed, then the user has an

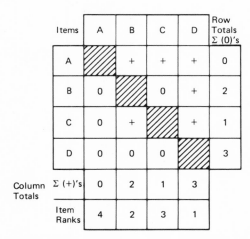

Key to Symbols: + = column item is preferred to row item
0 = column item is not preferred to row item

Figure 3.1. Illustration of paired comparison instrument for four items.

intransitivity. An intransitivity is a complex inconsistency involving three or more items. Figure 3.2 illustrates a situation in which the preferences are all intransitive. All three preference orderings cannot be correct. The user must sort out the correct one by reexamining each preference ordering. The frequency of occurrence of inconsistencies and intransitivities has been found to be reduced if the user Q-sorts the items into high, medium and low value categories prior to recording them in the paired comparison instrument.[4]

The paired comparison matrix instrument has been found to be effective and useful for soliciting value judgments in individual, group and organizational settings. It is sufficiently rigorous that it forces careful thinking about value judgments and perceptions. Inconsistencies and intransitivities normally occur in all decision making situations. The paired comparison approach makes them visible, pointing out otherwise hidden anomalies in logic and identifying points where decision making information may be deficient. Resolving the inconsistencies and intransitivities forces the user to seek out additional information, to more carefully think through the logic patterns, and to make careful distinctions that might not otherwise be made. The paired comparison method has thus been found to be quite valuable in eliminating irregularities in decision making processes. Unfortunately, the method can become cumbersome to use for

Items	A	B	C	Σ (0)'s
A		0	+	1
B	+		0	1
C	0	+		1
Σ (+)'s	1	1	1	

Conclusions from:

1st column: A is preferred to B; A is not preferred to C
2nd column: B is not preferred to A; B is preferred to C
3rd column: C is preferred to A; C is not preferred to B

Inferences from:

1st column: C is preferred to A is preferred to B
2nd column: A is preferred to B is preferred to C
3rd column: B is preferred to C is preferred to A

All three preference orderings cannot be correct. Hence, there is an intrasitivity somewhere.

Figure 3.2. Illustration of an intransitivity.

items in excess of about a dozen, or where there are many intransitivities.[4, 5]

The paired comparison and other ranking methods result in a unique value assessment for each item. Thus, the value scale that results from a paired comparison exercise is a more accurate and useful yardstick than the scale that results from a Q-sort exercise. However the numbers that result from a ranking method are only rank order numbers. Like the sorting methods, the differences between the numbers are meaningless. We do not know anything about how close the second-ranked item is to the first-ranked item, etc. Thus, mathematical operations are limited to those that are appropriate for rank order data.

3.1.3   Rating Methods

Rating methods assign unique numerical values to each item in such a way that the differences between the numbers are meaningful.[6, 7] The successive ratings method illustrated in Table 3.2 is an example of one of the simplest rating methods. In this method, the items are first ranked from highest to lowest value. Q-sorting, paired comparison or other sorting and ranking methods may be used for this. The ranked items are then entered into the successive ratings form illustrated in Table 3.2. The numbers 100 and 10 in the boxes in Table 3.2 are a prerecorded part of the standard successive ratings form. Each lower-ranked item is then successively compared to the highest-ranked item and a number corresponding to its relative value is assigned. For instance, the number 60 for alternative B in Table 3.2 indicates that it is perceived to have 60% of the value of alterna-

Table 3.2. Illustration of successive ratings method.

	ALTERNATIVES	COLUMN 1 Compare to Most Preferred	COLUMN 2 Compare to Least Preferred	COLUMN 3 Compare to Most and Least Preferred
Highest Rank	Alternative A	100	120	100
	Alternative B	60	70	65
	Alternative C	30	20	25
Lowest Rank	Alternative D	20	10	10

tive A. Similarly, alternative C is perceived to be 30% as valuable as alternative A, and alternative D is 20% as valuable as alternative A. When column 1 is filled in, the comparison process is reversed to obtain the data in column 2. For example, in Table 3.2 alternative C is judged to be twice as valuable as alternative D, alternative A is twelve times as valuable as D, etc. Finally, in column 3 a set of numbers is produced that reconciles the ratings in columns 1 and 2. Each number in column 3 should reflect the values of the alternatives relative to both the highest- and the lowest-ranked items.[8]

Rating methods result in numbers whose differences are meaningful, and which are anchored at both ends of the value scale. Thus, most arithmetical operations are permissible. However, only relative value numbers are created and the value scale is arbitrary. For instance, the value of alternative B is only measured relative to alternatives A and D, for which the respective values 100 and 10 were arbitrarily assigned.[6, 8]

Table 3.3. Illustration of a scoring model analysis of bulk hauling Vehicle A.

PERFORMANCE CRITERIA AND WEIGHTS	CHARACTERISTICS		SCORES
Economy $W_1 = 3.0$	Low Outlay Cost		0
	Low Operating Cost		1
	Low Upkeep Cost		1
	Total Dimension Score	=	2
	Relative Score, R_{1A}	=	.67
Durability $W_2 = 2.0$	Short Distance Use		1
	Long Distance Use		0
	All-Weather		1
	Heavy-Duty Service		0
	Total Dimension Score	=	2
	Relative Score, R_{2A}	=	.50
Driver Comfort $W_3 = 1.0$	Short Distance Use		1
	Long Distance Use		1
	Full-Load Conditions		1
	Total Dimension Score	=	3
	Relative Score, R_{3A}	=	1.00

$$T_A = W_1 R_{1A} + W_2 R_{2A} + W_3 R_{3A}$$

Total Value of Vehicle A = 3.0 × .67 + 2.0 × .50 + 1.0 × 1.0
= 4.01

3.1.4 Scoring Models

Scoring models consist of absolute scales for scoring the worth of each item relative to several desired characteristics. These characteristic scores are then collapsed into a single value number. A typical scoring model is

$$T_j = \sum_i W_i R_{ij} \qquad (3.1)$$

where T_j is the total value of the jth alternative or item, W_i is the relative importance value or weight of the ith performance criterion, and R_{ij} is the relative performance score. The magnitude of R_{ij} is given by

$$R_{ij} = \left(\sum_k s_{ijk} \right)/N_i \qquad (3.2)$$

where s_{ijk} is the dimension score of the jth alternative (or item) on the kth characteristic, and N_i is the number of characteristics within the ith criterion.

An illustration of the application of this model is provided in Table 3.3. The illustration is for a bulk hauling vehicle, vehicle A, which is being evaluated relative to several other alternative vehicles. The vehicles are all being evaluated on the basis of three performance criteria: economy, durability and driver comfort. The criteria are fully defined by the various characteristics listed in Table 3.3. The importance weights W_1, W_2 and W_3 were determined in a paired comparison exercise. The s_{ijk} scores are all either "1" or "0" respectively, depending on whether or not vehicle A possesses that particular characteristic. For instance, vehicle A is not judged to have a low outlay cost, so it is scored "0" on that characteristic. It is judged to have high durability in short distance use, so it is scored "1" on that characteristic. Detailed engineering and economic analyses were used as the bases for these judgments. The "0"'s and "1"'s are summed to obtain a total dimension score, which is normalized by dividing it by the total number of possible "1" 's (i.e., a perfect score). The resulting relative scores, the R_{ij}'s, are multiplied by the appropriate weight and summed to obtain the total value of the vehicle. Vehicle A's value score of 4.01 can be compared with similarly determined scores for the other alternative vehicles.

This is a relatively simple scoring model, in terms of the scaling methods used. Here, the basic measurements are either "0" or "1." In more sophisticated models, the characteristics may be importance-weighted and performance distributions may replace the dichotomous 0-1 scoring procedures. Examples and illustrations of these types of methods are given in Chapter 9.

Scoring methods result in the highest levels of numerical measurement, and the numbers may legitimately be subjected to all arithmetic operations. However, scoring models usually require a great deal of data and they may be tedious to apply if there are many characteristics or many alternative items. The development of accurate measurement scales and procedures for unequivocally determining the s_{ijk} scores can sometimes be quite difficult.[9, 10]

3.2 RISK ASSESSMENT

The relative likelihoods that the various alternatives will achieve the desired goals must usually be assessed as a part of most decision processes. Probabilities are used to express these likelihoods.

3.2.1 Subjective *vs.* Objective Probabilities

An objective probability is the proportion of times an event has occurred out of the total number of times it could have occurred. Historical analyses may be used to establish frequency counts of past events, which may be converted to proportions or probabilities of occurrence. If history is anticipated to repeat itself, then the objective probability may be used as the predicted probability of future occurrence. In other cases the probability of occurrence of a particular event may be estimated by enumerating all the outcomes. For instance, the probability of drawing a king on a random draw from a normal deck of 52 playing cards is 4/52 or .0769.

The subjective concept of probability has become quite commonplace during the last decade. A subjective probability is an index of personal belief. For instance, a subjective probability number of .60 simply means that the individual feels the odds are 6 to 4 that this event will occur. This need not relate to any objective probability whatsoever. The individual may or may not have been influenced by some observed frequencies. In many cases where subjective probabilities are used the particular event may be a unique one-time happening that has not yet occurred. Based on personal experience and insights, the individual makes a judgment call. The subjective probability number is an index, on a scale from 0.0 to 1.0, that reflects the individual's felt judgment that the event will occur.

3.2.2 Solicitation Methods

Many different methods have been devised for soliciting subjective probabilities. These methods may be broadly classified as either direct query or indirect methods of solicitation. In indirect methods, the probabilities are deduced from observations of a subject's decision behaviors. The choice of one method over the other will depend largely on whether or not the subject feels comfortable with it, the time and costs to train personnel in the use of the method, and the subject's depth of knowledge.

The most common direct solicitation method is to ask the subject to estimate the odds of a particular event. The odds are then converted to a subjective probability number. Other methods include the successive divisions, area approximations, hypothetical sampling and mean-variance methods. In the successive divisions technique, the subject is asked to state the most optimistic and pessimistic outcomes that would be likely to occur no more than one in ten times for the particular situation being examined. Then, the subject is asked to identify the outcome that has a 50-50 chance of occurrence. This divides the outcome space into two segments, which can then be further successively divided by reapplying the above procedures. The area approximations method is similar to the successive divisions approach except that areas under the normal curve are used. In the hypothetical sampling method, the subject is asked to specify the number of trials and the sample sizes required to achieve at least one success. The mean-variance approach asks the subject to estimate the mean and the variance of the distribution of outcomes for the particular situation being examined. The probability distribution of the outcomes can then be constructed by fitting a normal curve to these estimates.[11, 12, 13, 14]

The most common indirect methods place the subject in some hypothetical gambling situation where probabilities can be inferred from the bets and gambles. Sophisticated lotteries, indifference methods and betting situations have all been devised.[15, 16] However, it is difficult to devise theoretically correct gambles that are valid for all subjects.[17] And, since the probabilities must be inferred by a party other than the actual subject, the chance for interpretive errors is introduced.

There is not a great deal of evidence to date to indicate that indirect solicitation methods give superior results to direct methods. Direct methods have given some remarkably accurate results under real situations.[18, 19, 20]

3.2.3 Probability Concepts

The following probability concepts are frequently used in decision making analyses. Some controversy still surrounds the question of whether or not these concepts are equally meaningful for objective and subjective probabilities. However, the general practice is to apply these concepts to either subjective or objective probability numbers.

The probability of occurrence of event e is denoted by $p(e)$. The probability that independent events $e_1, e_2, e_3, \ldots e_n$ will occur simultaneously is computed from $p(e_1) \times p(e_2) \times p(e_3) \times \cdots \times p(e_n)$. The probability that

e_1 will *not* occur is given by $1.0 - p(e_1)$. The probability that at least one of the events e_1 or e_2 will occur is given by:

$$1.0 - ([1.0 - p(e_1)] \times [1.0 - p(e_2)]). \tag{3.3}$$

For instance, let $p(e_1)$ and $p(e_2)$ be the respective success probabilites of two projects. Then $1.0 - p(e_i)$ is the probability of failure of project i, and Equation (3.3) gives the probability of at least one of the projects being successful.

The conditional probability that event e_2 will occur if e_1 occurs is denoted by $p(e_2|e_1)$. The joint probability of occurrence of two events e_1 and e_2 is $p(e_1,e_2)$ or $p(e_2,e_1)$, where

$$p(e_1,e_2) = p(e_1|e_2) \times p(e_2). \tag{3.4}$$

The probability that the value of event e_i will be at least equal to some number x is $p(v_i \geq x)$, where v_i is the value of event e_i.

3.2.4 Expected Values, Losses and Regrets

Suppose the value of an event is V and its probability of occurrence is .70. Then let us assume that $V = 0$ when the event does not occur, and its probability of nonoccurrence is $1.0 - .70 = .30$. From a frequency standpoint, the average value that accrues over 100 trials is $(70(V) + 30(0))/100 = .70V$. This is the expected value. The expected value is thus the long run average value. In general, the expected value of the ith alternative EV_i is given by

$$EV_i = p_iV_i, \tag{3.5}$$

where V_i is the value of the ith alternative if it occurs, and p_i is the probability that the ith alternative will occur. The expected value of n alternative outcomes is given by

$$EV = \sum_{i=1}^{n} p_iV_i. \tag{3.6}$$

Equation (3.6) says that the expected value of n outcomes is the sum of the weighted values of the outcomes, where the weighting factors are the respective probabilities of occurrence. Since the probability p_i is the proportion of times the ith outcome occurs, then the expected value EV_i is simply the mean of the distribution of values of outcome i.

In general, if c_i is the cost of the ith alternative then its net expected value, NEV_i, is given by

$$NEV_i = p_iV_i - c_i. \tag{3.7}$$

Net expected values are often used in analyzing and comparing alternatives.

The expected opportunity loss is another concept that is often used in comparing alternatives. To illustrate the expected opportunity loss ideas, suppose I can invest in either of two alternatives, A_1 or A_2. If I invest in A_1, I anticipate with a .30 probability that I will receive a \$10,000 reward. If I invest in A_2, I anticipate with a .70 probability that I will receive a \$5,000 reward. My expected reward from A_1 = \$3,000 and my expected reward from A_2 = \$3,500, so that A_2 is the better alternative. In fact, if I select A_1 I will lose the opportunity to receive an additional expected reward of \$3,500 − \$3,000 = \$500. This is the expected opportunity loss of alternative A_1. In general, the expected opportunity loss of the ith alternative, EOL_i, is given by

$$EOL_i = p_k V_k - p_i V_i, \tag{3.8}$$

where $p_k V_k$ is the largest alternative expected value. The expected opportunity loss concept is simply another way of looking at the comparative value of an alternative, relative to the others that are available.

The expected regret measures the expected total losses that could occur under an adverse outcome. For example, suppose it will cost me \$500 in fees to invest in A_2 and I anticipate that there is a .30 probability that the investment will yield \$0 return. Then my expected regret is .30 × \$500 = \$150. In general, the expected regret of the ith alternative is given by

$$ER_i = q_i R_i, \tag{3.9}$$

where R_i is the regret amount under the worst outcome, and q_i is its probability of occurrence. A regret is quite different from an opportunity loss. An opportunity loss results from an opportunity foregone. It is a relative concept only. It measures the relative difference between two alternatives. On the other hand, a regret is the total cost, the total amount lost, the total wasted, the total amount given up, etc., if the worst should happen. The regret is for that alternative. Of course, in some situations, ER_i and EOL_i may produce the same numbers. But the concepts are different.

3.2.5 Bayesian Analyses

Using the Bayesian approach, "prior" probabilities may be updated to obtain "posterior" probabilities. This revision allows the decision maker to take changing circumstances into account and to accordingly update the decisions. In general, Bayes' theorem is given by

$$p(S_i|X) = \frac{p(X|S_i)(p[S_i])}{p(X)} \tag{3.10}$$

where there are $i = 1, 2, \ldots, k$ mutually exclusive and exhaustive states, and where X is the most recent event. The probabilites $p(S_i)$ are called "priors," and the probabilities $p(S_i|X)$ are called "posteriors." A posterior probability gives the likelihood of outcome S_i given that new information shows X to exist.

As an example, suppose the introduction of a particular new product could result in an \$8M increase in profits if a competitor does not introduce a similar product (state S_1). However, if the new product is introduced and the competitor also introduces a similar product (state S_2), then an opportunity loss of \$4M could result. Let the respective priors be $p(S_1) = .3$ and $p(S_2) = .7$, based on the best judgments possible. Then, on an expected value basis, the new product *should not be* introduced because $EV = (.3)(\$8M) + (.7)(-\$4M) = \$-.4M$. Now let us assume that some time has passed. Suppose that an empirical evaluation of the competitive patterns of the industry suggests that an \$8M increase in profits will occur with 8 to 2 odds when competition does not come in, and with about even odds when it does. Let the event $X = \$8M$. Hence, it now looks as if $p(X|S_1) = .8$ and $p(X|S_2) = .5$. Should the priors or the posteriors be used in making the new product entry decision? Bayes' theorem says that both sets of data are valid and they should be "averaged" by applying equation (3.10). Applying this equation we obtain the data and results in Table 3.4. Now the investment *should be* undertaken because $EV = (.406)(\$8M) + (.593)(-\$4M) = \$+.87M$.

Bayes' theorem specifies the theoretically correct way to update an older set of probabilities when new information arises, as illustrated above. The theorem is also useful for "averaging" data or judgments from two sources or two parties. For instance, the sales department may supply the priors based on their best judgment and prior experiences in the marketplace. The marketing research department may then subsequently supply the posteriors based on more recent information and data. The priors and posteriors may then be "averaged" with Bayes' theorem.

3.2.6   Binomial Probabilities

Many occasions will arise in which a decision maker is confronted with a series of trials where each trial has only two outcomes. For example, the

Table 3.4. Application of Bayes' Theorem.

S_i	$p(S_i)$	$p(X|S_i)$	$p(X|S_i) \times p(S_i)$	$p(S_i|X)$
S_1	.3	.8	.24	.24/.59 = .406
S_2	.7	.5	.35	.35/.59 = .593
			$p(X) = .59$	

outcomes might be either accept or reject, success or failure, good or bad, etc. When the probability of the success (accept, good, etc.) outcome is the same on each trial the situation is called a Bernoulli process. The binomial distribution gives the probability of r successes in n trials of a Bernoulli process. This distribution is given by

$$p(r|n,q) = C_r^n q^r (1 - q)^{n-r} \tag{3.11}$$

where r is the number of successes in n trials, each of which has a probability of success q. The variable q is called the trial probability. Here, $C_r^n = \dfrac{n!}{r!(n-r)!}$, which is the number of combinations of n things taken r at a time. Then the probability of at least r successes in n trials is given by

$$p(X \geq r) = \sum_{j=r}^{n} C_j^n q^j (1 - q)^{n-j} \tag{3.12}$$

where X is the number of successes.

As an illustration of the application of the binomial distribution, suppose it is desired to estimate the number of drug compounds to be screened in order to find one that is "active." Given this estimate, the time and cost of the screening project can then be budgeted. Let us assume that, on the average, about one out of four compounds screened in the past has been active. Thus, the trial probability $q = 1/4 = .25$. A sometimes mistaken interpretation of this situation is that a success can be achieved with certainty on four trials. This is not the case at all. Rather, the probability of at least one success in n trials is given by $1 - p(r = 0|n,q)$, where $r = 0$ represents no successes. Then, to be 95% confident of obtaining at least one success, $.95 = 1 - p(r = 0|n,q)$. And when $q = .25$, then:

$$.95 = 1 - (.25)^0 (.75)^n. \tag{3.13}$$

Solving gives $n = 11$. That is, eleven trials are necessary to be 95% certain of getting at least one success. Note that Equation (3.13) is an exponential equation. For instance, if a confidence level of 90% is desired then $n = 8$, and for a 99% confidence level $n = 16$. For a 100% confidence level (or certainty) n is infinity.

3.3   COST ASSESSMENT

The cost of each alternative must be assessed as part of the measurement of its net effectiveness. There are several techniques and concepts that are helpful in making cost estimates.

3.3.1 Ratios, Factors and Models

Cost ratios are useful rules of thumb which relate the cost of an activity to some other characteristic of that activity. Structural ratios can often be found between the cost of an item and its achievement potentials, its sales potentials, etc. An example is the common practice of estimating overhead costs as a percentage of total variable costs. Another example is the use of cost-size models.

One commonly used cost-size model is

$$C_B = C_A \left(\frac{S_B}{S_A}\right)^x \tag{3.14}$$

where C_A and S_A are the respective cost and size at one level of achievement, C_B and S_B are the respective cost and size at another level of achievement, and x is the cost-size factor. Values of x are available from published sources, by a historical analysis of completed projects, or by a rule of thumb. For example, if doubling the achievement increases costs by about 1/2, then substituting into Equation (3.14) gives $1.5 = 1 \times (2/1)^x$, and $x = .585$.

When adequate historical data are available, cost estimating relationships (CER's) may be devised. A simple CER can be developed by making scatter plots of historical costs and noting the apparent relationships that are depicted. A more precise approach is to apply multiple regression techniques to the historical data, to develop equations which accurately define the apparent relationships. In this way, equations can be developed for predicting the cost of an item from a knowledge of its design and performance specifications. However, since CER's are based on historical costs, great care may have to be taken to insure that these older cost structures are still relevant. In periods of inflation and price increases, cost adjustment indexes should be used to update the data.

A cost adjustment index is a dimensionless number for a given year that shows the cost at that time relative to a particular base year. In general, the present cost C_p can be computed from

$$C_p = C_r\left(\frac{I_p}{I_r}\right), \tag{3.15}$$

where C_p is the present cost, C_r is the original or reference cost, I_p is the value of the cost index at the present time and I_r is the index value at the time the reference cost was obtained. A cost index is usually a composite of n items, e.g.,

$$I_p = \frac{(C_{11}/C_{01}) + (C_{12}/C_{02}) + \cdots + (C_{1n}/C_{0n})}{n} \tag{3.16}$$

where C_{ij} is the cost of the jth item in the ith year, with $i = 0$ being the base year and $i = 1$ being the current year. A variety of indexes and sources are available to help the cost estimator. Some common indexes are the series of wholesale, retail and consumer price indexes that are published monthly by the *United States Bureau of Labor Statistics,* the *Chemical Engineering Index,* the *Construction Index* and the *McGraw-Hill Index.*

3.3.2 Learning Curve Models

Since it was first noticed in aircraft manufacturing, the learning curve concept has been widely applied in contract negotiations, purchasing and cost estimating. The basic idea is that repetition results in less time or effort expended with each repetition. This observed performance is called learning and it can be quantitatively modeled.

In the most general case, the amount of time or effort needed to complete a unit of product will decrease by a constant percentage each time the production quantity is doubled. A common percentage is 20%. This establishes an 80% curve, which means that the time or cost to complete the second unit will be 0.80 times that required for the first, the fourth unit will require 0.80 times that required for the second, etc. A negative exponential model is often used to describe this phenomenon. This model is:

$$E_i = (k)(i)^f, \qquad (3.17)$$

where E_i is the effort required to produce the ith unit, k is a constant and f is the learning factor. The value of k is set to the effort required for the first unit, and the value of f is set to $f = (\log \phi / \log 2)$, where ϕ is the learning curve slope parameter. When $\phi = 1.0$ there is no learning, and when $\phi = 0.0$ there is perfect learning. For an 80% curve, if the first unit required k man hours, then the man hours required for the fifth unit would be calculated from Equation (3.15) as $E_5 = (k)(5)^{\log 0.8 / \log 2}$. The total cost of an entire job consisting of repetitive operations to produce n units can be computed by simply aggregating the E_i values over all n units. If the learning rate increases or otherwise varies with different units, then the corresponding E_i values are computed with the appropriate varying ϕ values.

The basis for the learning curve phenomenon is largely intuitive, though many empirical studies have verified its existence. The learning effect is more pronounced during the earlier units, and it trails off to near zero as more units are produced and the maximum learning is achieved. The effect is influenced by many variables, such as the amount of training and previous experience with like items, leadership styles, the complexity of the technology, the organization of the shop and the type of incentive plans in effect. Thus, the selection of the particular model form must be determined empirically for each shop, each organization or each technology. Cost estimators, purchasing agents, and contract negotiators have made extensive use of learning curves in negotiating contract fees, prices, target dates and performance conditions.[21]

3.3.3   Life Cycle Costing and Design to Cost

In life cycle costing (LCC), all present and future costs during the complete evolution of the product are estimated. For instance, in applying LCC concepts to the purchase of an automobile, one would consider the original purchase price, the interest on the loan and all the operating costs during the life of the automobile. A comparison of two alternative automobiles on an LCC basis might result in a different preference ordering than a comparison based on simply the purchase price. It is always wise to estimate the LCC of the alternatives. Some may have very large add-on or operating costs beyond their initial development costs.

In recent years the design-to-cost (DTC) concept has become prominent in government contracting work, as well as industrial applications. In this concept, the market price of a substitute or a like item is the starting point for analysis. Working backward from this price by the use of industry markup ratios, learning curve analyses, or LCC considerations, the development cost of the item is deduced. This is taken as the base cost to design for zero performance improvements. The cost of designing for a 10%, 20%, etc., improvement can then be estimated from this base cost number.[22]

3.3.4   Error Analyses

Estimating the accuracy of a cost estimate is largely a judgmental process. However, errors that are introduced by mathematical operations can be precisely calculated. When two or more numbers are added or subtracted, the errors will tend to cancel out. The result will have a lower error than any of the other numbers. But the errors are magnified when numbers are multiplied or divided. Specifically, the resulting error from adding numbers that each contain an error e_i is $\sqrt{\Sigma e_i}$. The resulting error from multiplying two numbers together is $\sqrt{e_1^2 N_2^2 + e_2^2 N_1^2}$, where N_i is the number being multiplied. To illustrate, when the numbers 80 ± 16 and 50 ± 15 are added the result is $130 \pm \sqrt{16 + 15} = 130 \pm 5.57$. When these two numbers are multiplied the result is $4,000 \pm \sqrt{(16)^2(50)^2 + (15)^2(80)^2} = 4,000 \pm 1,442.2$.

3.4 SUMMARY

Several management science methods are available for use at various points within the structured decision making process. These methods enable the application of rigorous mathematical models to be combined with systematic judgments and subjective assessments. The methods are directly applicable to determining the relative importance of goals and objectives, assessing the relative value of alternatives and estimating risks and costs.

This chapter has presented and discussed the most useful management science methods for decision making. Each method has been detailed and illustrated. Some ways in which the methods can be used within the structured decision making process have been demonstrated.

3.5 REFERENCES

1. Souder, W. E. "Field Studies With a Q-Sort/Nominal Group Process for Selecting R&D Projects." *Research Policy,* **5,** No.4: 172–188 (1975).
2. Helin, A. F. and Souder, W. E. "Experimental Test of a Q-Sort Procedure for Prioritizing R&D Projects." *IEEE Trans. on Eng. Mgt.,* EM-21, No. 4: 159–164 (1974).
3. Kerlinger, F. N. *Foundations of Behavioral Research.* New York: Holt, Rinehart and Winston, 1976, pp. 581–598.
4. Souder, W. E. "Achieving Organizational Consensus With Respect to R&D Project Selection Criteria." *Management Science,* **21,** No. 6: 669–691 (1975).
5. Souder, W. E. "Effectiveness of Nominal and Interacting Group Decision Processes for Integrating R&D and Marketing." *Management Science,* **23,** No. 6: 595–605 (1977).
6. Churchman, C. W.; Ackoff, R. L.; and Arnoff, E. L. *Introduction to Operations Research.* New York: John Wiley & Sons, Inc., 1957, pp.136–154.
7. Fishburn, P. C. *Decision and Value Theory.* New York: John Wiley & Sons, Inc., 1964, pp. 77–130.
8. Easton, Allan. *Complex Managerial Decisions Involving Multiple Objectives.* New York: John Wiley & Sons, Inc., 1973, pp. 138–219.
9. Souder, W. E. "Project Selection, Planning and Control," in *Handbook of Operations Research: Models and Applications,* J. J. Moder and S. E. Elmaghraby (eds.), New York: Van Nostrand Reinhold Company, 1978, pp. 301–344.
10. Souder, W. E. "A Scoring Methodology for Assessing the Suitability of Management Science Models." *Management Science,* **18,** No. 10: 526–543 (1972).
11. Winkler, R. L. *An Introduction to Bayesian Inference and Decisions.* New York: Holt, Rinehart and Winston, 1972.
12. Winkler, R. L. "The Quantification of Judgment: Some Experimental Results." *Proceedings of the Am. Stat. Assoc.,* **62,** No. 4: 386–395 (1967).
13. Savage, L. J. *The Foundations of Statistics.* New York: John Wiley & Sons, Inc., 1954, pp. 127–136.
14. Schlaifer, Robert. *Analysis of Decisions Under Uncertainty.* New York: McGraw-Hill, 1969, pp. 24–125.
15. Raiffa, Howard. *Decision Analysis.* Reading, Massachusetts: Addison-Wesley Publishing Co., Inc., 1968.

16. Hillier, F. S. "The Derivation of Probabilistic Information for the Evaluation of Risky Investments." *Management Science,* **10,** No. 2: 105–118 (1963).
17. Becker, G. M. "Decision Making: Objective Measures of Subjective Probability and Utility." *Psychological Review,* March 1962, pp. 136–148.
18. Souder, W. E. "The Validity of Subjective Probability of Success Forecasts by R&D Managers." *IEEE Trans. on Eng. Mgt.,* **EM-16,** No. 1: 35–49 (1969).
19. Balthasar, H. U.; Boschi, R. A.; and Menke, M. M. "Calling The Shots in R&D." *Harvard Business Review,* **16,** No. 6: 151–160 (1978).
20. Rubenstein, A. H. and Schroder, H. H. "Managerial Differences in Assessing Probabilities of Technical Success for R&D Projects." *Management Science,* **24,** No. 2: 137–148 (1977).
21. Conway, R. W. and Schultz, Andrew, Jr. "The Manufacturing Progress Function." *Journal of Ind. Eng.,* Jan–Feb, 1959, pp. 39–53.
22. Eaton, E. P. "Let's Get Serious About Total Life Cycle Costs." *Defense Management Journal,* **13,** No. 1: 2–11 (1977).

3.6   BIBLIOGRAPHY

Ackoff, R. L. (ed.) *Progress in Operations Research.* Vol. I. New York: John Wiley & Sons, Inc., 1961, pp. 3–32; 37–59.

Blanchard, B. S. *Engineering Organization and Management.* Englewood Cliffs, New Jersey: Prentice-Hall, Inc., 1976, pp. 171–194.

Bock, R. D. and Jones, L. V. *The Measurement and Prediction of Judgment and Choice.* San Francisco: Holden-Day, Inc., 1968.

Fisher, G. H. *Cost Considerations in Systems Analysis.* New York: American Elsevier Publishing Co., Inc., 1971.

Feller, William. *An Introduction to Probability Theory and Its Applications.* New York: John Wiley & Sons, Inc., 1957, pp. 104–223.

Goldberg, Samuel. *Probability: An Introduction.* Englewood Cliffs, New Jersey: Prentice-Hall, Inc., 1960, pp. 158–267.

Kelley, C. W. and Peterson, C. R. *Probability Estimation and Probabilistic Procedures in Current Intelligence Analysis.* New York: International Business Machines Corporation, 1971.

Lee, Wayne. *Decision Theory and Human Behavior.* New York: John Wiley & Sons, Inc., 1971.

Mosteller, Frederick; Rourke, R. E.; and Thomas, G. B. *Probability With Statistical Applications.* Reading, Massachusetts: Addison-Wesley Publishing Co., Inc., 1961, pp. 19–284; 360–402.

Pessemier, E. A. *New Product Decisions: An Analytical Approach.* New York: McGraw-Hill, 1966.

Schlaifer, Robert. *Probability and Statistics for Business Decisions.* New York: McGraw-Hill, 1959, pp. 2–486.

Souder, W. E. "Management Science and Budgeting–Quo Vadis?" *Budgeting,* **16,** No. 2: 1–8 (1968).

Souder, W. E. "What Can O.R. Contribute to Market Planning and Budgeting Decisions?" *Management Decisions,* **2,** No. 1: 16–19 (1968).

Part II
Decision Settings

Given the same facts and information, a single individual, a small group and a large organization may come to very dissimilar conclusions. The following two chapters discuss why this can happen. Different kinds of variables and factors are brought into play in each setting. These variables and factors can dramatically influence the decision processes, and the resulting decisions which are produced. Chapter 4 presents and illustrates several different types of individual decision making processes, which may be taken by a single individual who is uninfluenced by others. Some of these processes are shown to be more rational than others. The structured decision making process is shown to be the most rational and effective of all. Chapter 5 shows how the need for the structured decision making process becomes even greater in group and organizational settings, where many behavioral factors may impede rationality. Chapter 5 also shows how the structured decision making process must be modified and combined with other group management methods, in order to achieve its greatest effectiveness in group and organizational settings.

Part II
Decision Centers

4

Individual Decision Settings

4.0 INTRODUCTION

In the individual setting, the individual's own personal value systems, objectives and perceptions guide the decision making process. The individual's past experiences, existing needs, expectations, motivations and aspirations influence how the problem is viewed, the alternatives that become visible and the choice of a "best" solution. In the individual setting, one's personal proclivities and orientations are the most determining and influential factors. This chapter discusses these factors and the ways in which they influence individual decision processes. Four models of individual decision making behaviors are discussed: the economic model, the strategies model, the satisficing model and the behavioral model.

4.1 THE ECONOMIC MODEL [1, 2]

This model is based on the following five assumptions. One, all the decision alternatives can be identified and enumerated. Two, all the possible outcomes from these alternatives can be identified and enumerated. Three, explicit decision goals or objectives exist. Four, the value or worth of each alternative can be specified, in terms of the outcomes and goals. Five, the decision maker wishes to select the one alternative that maximizes the total value or worth achieved (or some function of value, such as value divided by cost, value minus cost, etc.).

Thus, the economic model views the decision maker as a shrewd, logical calculator, with all the information needed to rationally pick the goal-maximizing decision. Three environmental situations are possible within this model: decision making under certainty, risk, and uncertainty.

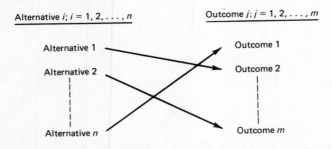

Decision Rule: Select that alternative which leads to the highest-valued outcome.

Figure 4.1. Decision making under certainty.

4.1.1 Decisions under Certainty

The certainty environment is characterized by the following three conditions. One, each alternative leads to a single unique outcome. Two, the choice of alternative i neccessarily leads to a corresponding outcome j. Three, the corresponding value V_j will necessarily result.

Figure 4.1 illustrates this environment. The choice of alternative 1 necessarily leads to outcome 2, and the corresponding value V_2 will result from this decision. The choice of alternative 2 will necessarily lead to value V_m, etc. Under this environment, decision making involves finding the highest-valued outcome, and then selecting the alternative which leads to it.

As an illustration of decision making under certainty, suppose a decision maker can invest in either stock A or stock B, or hold cash. Suppose the respective outcome values for these alternatives are $50, $40 and $0. Then stock A is clearly the optimum choice, since it leads to the highest-valued outcome.

4.1.2 Decisions under Risk

The risk environment is characterized by the following four conditions. One, some alternatives may lead to more than one outcome. Two, some outcomes may have more than one alternative. Three, for each ith alternative, the likelihood or probability that it will lead to any j^{th} outcome can be specified as p_{ij}. Four, if alternative i is selected and if it leads to outcome j then the corresponding value V_j will result.

Figure 4.2 illustrates this environment. Alternative 1 may lead to either outcome 1 or outcome 2, with the respective likelihoods p_{11} and p_{12}. Alternative 2 may lead to either outcome 2 or outcome m, with respective

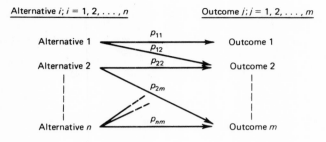

Alternative i; $i = 1, 2, \ldots, n$ Outcome j; $j = 1, 2, \ldots, m$

Decision Rule: Select that alternative which leads to the highest total expected outcome values.

Figure 4.2. Decision making under risk.

likelihoods p_{22} and p_{2m}, etc. Under this environment, decision making involves selecting that i^{th} alternative having the highest total expected outcome value, EV_i. In general,

$$EV_i = \sum_j p_{ij} V_j. \qquad (4.1)$$

Table 4.1 presents an example in which there are three alternatives: purchase stock A, purchase stock B or hold cash. The respective outcome values are gains of \$50, \$40 and \$0. The respective probabilities or likelihoods that the various alternatives will lead to each of these outcome values are shown in Table 4.1. As shown in the calculations at the bottom of Table 4.1, stock A is the alternative with the highest expected value (\$44). It is therefore the optimum choice. Thus, it may be seen that decision making under certainty is a special case of decision making under risk. In particular, it is the special case where one of the p_{ij} values equals 1.0 for every alternative.

4.1.3   Decisions under Uncertainty

This circumstance is the same as decision making under risk, except for one very important difference. The difference is that the p_{ij} values are all *unknown*. The decision maker cannot specify the probability with which any i^{th} alternative will lead to any j^{th} outcome. Thus, expected value calculations cannot be carried out.

There are, however, several other possible analyses that may be carried out. One approach is to carry out an indifference point analysis. In such an analysis, the decision maker computes the values of the probabilities that would cause one to be indifferent between the alternatives. Then a

Table 4.1. Example of decision making under risk.

ALTERNATIVES	LIKELIHOODS, p_{ij}	OUTCOME VALUES, V_{ij}
$i = 1$, Stock A	$p_{11} = .40$	$V_1 = \$50$
	$p_{12} = .60$	$V_2 = \$40$
	$p_{13} = .00$	$V_3 = \$0$
$i = 2$, Stock B	$p_{21} = .10$	$V_1 = \$50$
	$p_{22} = .80$	$V_2 = \$40$
	$p_{23} = .10$	$V_3 = \$0$
$i = 3$, Hold Cash	$p_{31} = .00$	$V_1 = \$50$
	$p_{32} = .00$	$V_2 = \$40$
	$p_{33} = 1.00$	$V_3 = \$0$

$$EV_i = \sum_j p_{ij} V_j$$

$$EV_1 = (.40)(\$50) + (.60)(\$40) + (0.0)(\$0) = \$44$$

$$EV_2 = (.10)(\$50) + (.80)(\$40) + (.10)(\$0) = \$37$$

$$EV_3 = (.00)(\$0) + (.00)(\$0) + (1.0)(\$0) = \$0$$

judgment is made about whether or not these indifference values are near the actual values. If they are, then the decision maker is indifferent and it does not matter which alternative is chosen. In this case, the best alternative can be selected by simply flipping a coin. The indifference point is computed as follows. At the indifference point:

$$EV_i = EV_{i+1} = \cdots = EV_n, \text{ or} \tag{4.2}$$

$$\sum_j p_{ij} V_j = \sum_j p_{i+1,j} V_j = \cdots = \sum_j p_{nj} V_j. \tag{4.3}$$

Then, knowing that all the probabilities must sum to unity, that is,

$$\sum_j p_{ij} = 1.0, j = 1, 2, \ldots, m, \tag{4.4}$$

the indifference values p_{ij}^* may be found by the simultaneous solution of Equations (4.3) and (4.4).

As an illustration, assume the likelihoods in Table 4.1 had been unknown. Then the indifference point is given by:

$$\$50 p_{11} + \$40 p_{12} + \$0 p_{13} = \$50 p_{21} + \$40 p_{22} + \$0 p_{23} \tag{4.5}$$

Equation (4.5) has an obvious solution:

$$p_{11}^* = p_{21}^* \text{ and} \tag{4.6}$$

$$p_{12}^* = p_{22}^*, \tag{4.7}$$

where p_{ij}^* is an indifference value. (Note that in this problem the $p_{i3}V_3$ terms are all zero, and are therefore not included in Equation [4.5]). Hence, the decison maker will be indifferent between stocks A and B only when their likelihoods of achieving the $50 and $40 gains are the same. If the decision maker feels that this is in fact the case for stocks A and B, then either one can be selected as the best alternative, since they both yield the same expected values. Otherwise, this analysis shows that the decision maker is definitely not indifferent, and more information should be sought in order to further clarify the differences between stocks A and B.

In the more usual circumstances, the alternatives will not lead to the same values. This case is illustrated in Figure 4.3. The indifference point for the data in Figure 4.3 is given by

$$\$50p_{11} + \$40p_{12} = \$60p_{21} + \$30p_{22}. \tag{4.8}$$

Substituting $p_{11} + p_{12} = 1.0$ and $p_{21} + p_{22} = 1.0$ into Equation (4.8) and solving gives

$$p_{22}^* = (1 + p_{12})/3. \tag{4.9}$$

Equation (4.9) tells us that, for the data in Figure 4.3, the decision maker will be indifferent between stocks A and B when p_{22} is one-third of the quantity $1 + p_{12}$. There are many values of p_{12} and p_{22} that satisfy Equation (4.9). Thus, there are many instances in which the decision maker may truly be indifferent between the alternatives. One such instance is when $p_{12} = .8$ and $p_{22} = .6$ (where $EV_1 = EV_2 = \$42$).

In situations like this, where there are multiple alternatives and multiple outcomes, there may be a large number of indifference points. If any of these indifference points have p_{ij} values that are judged to be close to the actual likelihoods, then the decision maker may truly have an indifferent situation. In this case, it doesn't matter which alternative is chosen. They all lead to the same expected value results. The best alternative can be

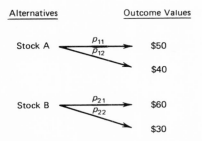

Figure 4.3. Illustration of a case of different valued outcomes.

chosen at random. Thus, before agonizing over a difficult decision, the decision maker should always check the indifference points. It may be that there really is no decision to agonize over. Given the available information, the *best alternative* may be *chosen at random!*

Another very useful method for coping with decision situations under uncertainty is the dominance analysis. In a dominance analysis, the relative performance of each alternative is analyzed over all possible outcomes. These outcomes include the indifference points. Then, these results are examined to see if one alternative is dominant over the other, in the sense that one is preferable over a wider range of outcomes. If one alternative is indeed dominant, then it is the best choice. So as not to complicate the illustration of the dominance concepts, let us take the following simple example. Assume a decision maker can select either alternative 1 or alternative 2. Alternative 1 can result in net gains ranging from $10,000 to $50,000. Alternative 2 can result in net gains ranging from $30,000 to $40,000. The probability that alternatives 1 and 2 will lead to any particular values within these ranges is unknown.

Figure 4.4 presents the dominance analysis for this example. In this analysis, p_i is the probability that the small gain will result if the ith alternative is chosen. The net expected gain of any i^{th} alternative is given by $p_i G_{iS} + (1 - p_i)G_{iL}$, where G_{iS} and G_{iL} are the respective small and large gains, e.g., $G_{1S} = \$10,000$, $G_{2S} = \$30,000$, $G_{1L} = \$50,000$, $G_{2L} =$

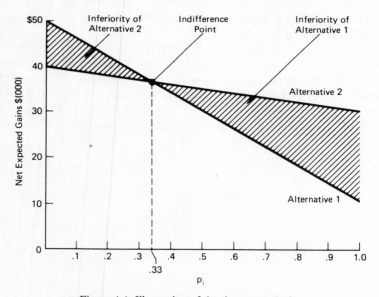

Figure 4.4. Illustration of dominance analysis.

$40,000. To develop Figure 4.4, p_i was permitted to take on all values $0 \leqslant p_i \leqslant 1.0$. The corresponding net expected gains were computed for each alternative, and the results were graphed as the performance lines for the two alternatives in Figure 4.4. These performance lines show that alternative 2 is dominant over 67% of the outcome range. It yields the highest net expected gain over two-thirds of the range: from $p_i = .33$ to $p_i = 1.0$. On the average, the decision maker can expect to achieve higher gains by selecting alternative 2. In fact, if alternative 2 is selected, the odds are 67:33 that higher gains will result.

Where there are multiple alternatives and multiple outcomes, then multidimensional dominance analyses become necessary. Since any problem with more than two dimensions is usually not easily solved by hand nor easily represented graphically, computer programs have been developed for these situations. The multidimensional cases usually involve many intersections of the performance lines for the alternatives, thus leading to multiple indifference points.

4.1.4   Using the Economic Model

The economic model can be used in several ways. One useful application is to use it as a prescriptive straw man; e.g., take the position that if the world were perfect this is the way decisions should be made. The results from this perfect case may then be compared to the actual decision which management seems to favor. If the economic decision and the actual decision are not in close proximity, then interesting and useful questions can be asked. One such question is: What assumptions of the economic model do not hold in this actual case, that account for the differences in results? If no answer can be found, then the actual decision is suspect and it should be carefully scrutinized.

Another useful application of the economic model is to use it as a prescriptive control model. The economic model determines the best decision if we want to maximize economic values. There may be real reasons for selecting a noneconomic alternative. But the economic model will show us how much we are deviating from the economically best decision. This deviation is something all managers should be aware of.

In any decision situation where there are multiple alternatives leading to multiple outcomes, the decision maker should be aware that there will be many indifference points. Some of these indifference points may have p_{ij} values that are very close to the likelihoods which might reasonably be expected to exist. Thus, it may be that the best decision does not require any deliberation: it can be selected by flipping a coin. This is the lesson brought out by the economic model. The more complex the decision situation, the larger the number of indifference points. This is a very revealing result for a decision maker who might agonize over some complex decision under uncertainty. The economic model tells us to look for indifference points before we needlessly agonize. It may be that, given the limited information available and the decision maker's objectives, the decision maker is truly indifferent between the alternatives. In that case, any deliberation is redundant. The optimum decision can be selected at random from the indifferent alternatives.

Of course, it is difficult for most decision makers to accept the idea that a random choice may be as good a decision as one that is deliberated and agonized over. Indeed, it may not be as good. The lengthy deliberation may clarify some otherwise unknown values in the uncertain situation. Or, by procrastinating, some new information may emerge. But deliberation and procrastination can have many costs and risks, in terms of the time and effort expended and the possibility of missed opportunities. Whether or not to make a random choice of an alternative or wait for more information to emerge must be determined on the basis of the significance of the relative rewards and regrets for each policy.[3]

4.2   THE STRATEGIES MODEL[1, 2, 4]

The value-maximizing economic approach may be inconsistent with the personalities of some decision makers. These individuals, instead of maximizing economic values, may be more interested in pursuing purposive strategies. We shall look at three such strategies: the maximax strategy, the maximin strategy and the minimum regret strategy.

4.2.1   The Maximax Strategy

In this strategy, the decision maker examines the outcome values and selects the maximum payoff set. From this maximum payoff set, the decision maker then selects the maximum single outcome value, or the maximax value. The corresponding alternative, the maximax alternative, is selected as the best choice. This is illustrated in Table 4.2, using the data from the example in Figure 4.4. A strategies decision maker would look at this situation as consisting of two alternative outcomes, Outcome A and Outcome B, for each decision alternative. Either alternative may be chosen, and either outcome can result. The maximax strategy is to choose that alternative which has the maximum value within the maximum payoff set. From Table 4.2, the maximax strategy is to choose alternative 1.

The maximax strategy is superbullish. It yields the largest gain under the most favorable conditions. But it may yield the worst gain under unfavorable conditions. For instance, Table 4.2 shows that the decision to

Table 4.2. Analysis of strategies.

	VALUES $(000)	
	OUTCOME A	OUTCOME B
ALTERNATIVE 1	Maximum of the Maxima = Maximax Value — $50	$10 — Minimum Payoff Set
ALTERNATIVE 2	$40	$30
	Maximum Payoff Set	Maximum of the Minima = Maximin Value

commit oneself to alternative 1 yields only $10,000 if some adversity should happen and Outcome B should result. Thus, the maximax strategy is a risky strategy that is only appropriate for the gambler mentality.

4.2.2   The Maximin Strategy

In this strategy, the decision maker examines the outcome values and selects the minimum payoff set. The decision maker then selects the maximum single outcome value from this set. This is the maximin value. This is illustrated in Table 4.2. Alternative 2 is the maximin strategy choice. The maximin strategy is a superconservative position. It is only appropriate for the risk-avoiding decision maker. Alternative 2 yields the least objectionable of all the outcomes. It protects the decision maker under adversity. On the other hand, in selecting a maximin strategy the decision maker gives up the chance to gain $50,000.

4.2.3   The Minimum Opportunity Loss Strategy

Table 4.3 presents an opportunity loss analysis for the two alternatives. The values in the matrix represent the opportunities foregone if a particular choice turns out to be wrong. For instance, if alternative 1 is chosen and Outcome A occurs, nothing is foregone. There are no better opportunities than alternative 1 under Outcome A. But if alternative 2 is chosen and Outcome A occurs, then a difference of $50,000 − $40,000 = $10,000 has been foregone. Similarly, selecting alternative 1 when Outcome B

Table 4.3. Minimum opportunity loss strategy.

	OPPORTUNITY LOSSES $(000)	
	OUTCOME A	OUTCOME B
ALTERNATIVE 1	0	$20
ALTERNATIVE 2 *	$10	0

* Minimum opportunity loss strategy.

occurs leaves the decision maker $30,000 − $10,000 = $20,000 worse off than if alternative 2 had been selected. Selecting alternative 2 when Outcome B occurs carries no opportunity losses. It is the optimum choice under Outcome B.

The minimum opportunity loss strategy is alternative 2. It protects the decision maker from suffering large opportunities foregone. Of course, the choice of the minimum opportunity loss strategy also limits the potential gains. We cannot have it both ways. The minimum opportunity loss strategy is appropriate for the decison maker who wants to cut the losses and who is willing to accept moderate gains in return for this protection.

In the example used here, the maximin and minimum opportunity loss strategies just happened to be the same alternative. In the more general case, where there are three or more alternatives, the maximax, maximin and minimum opportunity loss alternatives will usually differ. However, when one alternative is the best choice under two or more strategies this can be a very fortuitous result for the decision maker. It means that two or more strategies can be pursued simultaneously by selecting that alternative.

4.2.4   Other Strategies

In the example in Table 4.2, $40,000 is the minimax value and $10,000 is the minimin value. Alternative 2 and alternative 1 are thus the corresponding minimax and minimin strategies. It is worthwhile for a decision maker to keep these strategies in mind as the ones to be generally avoided. A rational decision maker would never purposely set out to achieve the lowest gains within either the maximum or minimum outcome set. There should always be a better strategy. Of course, an alternative can represent more than one strategy, as the above examples have shown. And a selected alternative may turn out to be the maximin or minimin strategies, in addition to others. But no alternative would purposely be selected because it is either the minimax or minimin value strategy.

The above discussions hold only for value maximizing decisions. If the objective is cost minimization, and if the numbers in Table 4.2 are costs instead of values, then the minimax and minimin strategies are viable. For cost minimization, the minimax and minimin strategies respectively replace the maximin and maximax strategies that are employed in value maximization.

Two-tiered and hedging strategies may be devised by appropriately combining alternatives. For example, a two-tiered strategy would be to implement both the maximax and the maximin alternatives in Table 4.2. The added cost of implementing both alternatives would be offset by the assurance that at least the maximin value would be achieved. A hedging strategy would be to implement both the maximin and the minimum opportunity loss strategies. This would provide a floor on the losses while simultaneously offering a chance at a larger gain.

4.2.5 Using the Strategies Model

The strategies approach is in some ways a much simpler approach than the economic model. The decision procedures focus only on the outcome values. Difficult to estimate data on p_{ij}'s and other aspects are not needed. Thus, this approach is highly appropriate for handling decision making under uncertainty.

The strategies approach assumes that all decision makers have a fundamental decision psychology that causes them to be either risk-takers or risk-avoiders. The strategies approach allows each decision maker to look at the alternatives in terms of what they imply for purposive strategies. Then, the alternative that "fits" the decision maker's psychology can consistently be selected. The strategies approach provides an opportunity for the decision maker to think through each alternative in terms of its strategic risk contents.

4.3 THE SATISFICING MODEL [5, 6]

The economic and strategies models have often been criticized on the grounds of unrealistic assumptions about information availabilities and human information processing behaviors. In the satisficing model, the decision maker searches only until a satisfactory alternative is found. The decision maker does not search beyond this point. This model depicts the decision maker as being content with a solution that is "good enough." Having the best solution is not necessary.

Why would a decision maker behave in this way? One answer has to do with the assumption of perfect information. A decision maker might satisfice if all the alternatives are not known. If the alternatives cannot all be set forth at the start, then there is no way of knowing which one of them is the best. Another answer has to do with the costs and benefits of continuing to search for a better alternative. Eventually a point may be reached where the cost of continuing to search exceeds the benefits derived from this last effort. Beyond some point, one may search for many hours to find an alternative that is only a little bit better than the best one found to date.

Thus, like the economic and strategies models of decision making, the satisficing model views the decision maker as a calculating person. Alternatives are sought, analyzed and compared on the basis of their costs, expected values or other relevant criteria. But in the satisficing model, these processes are much more abbreviated. Instead of choosing the optimum solution, the satisficing decision maker simply accepts the first feasible solution that is encountered. Empirical studies indicate that such decision behaviors are realistic and rational when there is great uncertainty or urgency in the decision making.[6]

4.4 THE BEHAVIORAL MODEL

4.4.1 Aspirations and Needs

In this model, the decision maker is guided and driven by aspirations, motivations, needs and other intrinsic behavioral forces. This model assumes that:

1. the decision maker has very sketchy information about alternatives, outcomes and values;
2. new alternatives may be suggested during the process of enumerating alternatives and analyzing the problem;
3. new outcomes may crop up at any time, often after the decision has been made;
4. the decision maker often relies on hunch, judgment, intuition and emotion;
5. the decision maker will search more or less diligently for alternatives, depending on the level of the decision maker's aspirations;
6. the decision maker will take greater or lesser risks depending on the decision maker's relative level of needs and aspirations;
7. the decision maker will make decisions on the basis of expected utility, a measure that combines several psychological and rational dimensions.[6]

In this model, if the decision maker is satisfied with the status quo, then no search is made for more alternatives or better strategies. This model holds that decision makers search for new alternatives only if they are dissatisfied with the present outcomes. The more the decision maker is dissatisfied with the present outcomes, the greater are the search efforts for better alternatives. The individual's aspirations and needs control the level of dissatisfaction. A needy individual with high aspirations will search for better solutions. But a needy individual with low aspirations will not. The behavioral model views aspirations as influenced by individual psychological variables, as well as the available rewards. For example, the presence of highly-valued outcomes may raise one's aspirations, thereby stimulating dissatisfactions with the status quo and a consequent search for a better decision.

Another important idea in the behavioral model is that decision makers will use the most convenient and least expensive information. In pricing decisions, for example, the decision maker may simply use the manufacturer's suggested retail price. This, of course, is an example of satisficing. But when the decision maker's needs and aspirations are high, the manufacturer's suggested price may not be satisfactory. Then a higher (more satisfactory) level of prices may be sought.

In the behavioral model, the decision maker copes with uncertainty by building contingency plans and flexibility into the decision. This means that most decisions consist of multiple strategies and multitiered policies. Collectively, these strategies and policies are designed to hedge against potential adversities and take advantage of several opportunities.

The behavioral decision maker is not a value-maximizer or an expected value-maximizer. The behavioral decision maker may be a satisficer, but a behavioral decision is not based exclusively on objective values. Rather, the decision is based on the utility of the alternative. "Utility" is a measure of the subjective worth that an individual places on an item. The utility concept is thus a highly personal or individualistic measure. The ideas behind the utility concept are simple, and yet they are rather abstract. The basic idea is that the worth of an item depends on the individual's intrinsic perception of its value. For example, to a pauper, a $1 bill may be worth a great deal. To a wealthy man, a $1 bill may be worth much less. Thus, it may be said that the $1 bill has relatively greater utility to the pauper. In short, a dollar is not a dollar. Subjectively, the dollar is worth a great deal more to the pauper. In the behavioral model, utility and expected utility respectively replace the concepts of value and expected value in the other models.

To date, methods for measuring utility have only been partially developed and much more research is needed. However, studies show that utility measures can be rather accurate portrayals of some actual decision making processes.

4.4.2 Using the Behavioral Model

The behavioral model is often a more accurate description of individual decison processes than the other models. However, the economic model will usually result in better decisions than the behavioral model, in terms of the total value or utility achieved. The problem is that because of its data needs and restrictive assumptions about human behavior, the economic model is seldom applicable. Thus, the decision maker is forced to fall back onto the behavioral model.

The behavioral model suggests some ways to encourage risk-taking and to stimulate searches for higher-valued alternatives and improved decisions. Needs and aspirations are the keys. For instance, a manager who knows how to raise the aspirations of subordinates can motivate a higher level of searching and decision making efforts. This will result in a potential increase in the quality of the decision outputs. But, on the whole, the behavioral model is not highly prescriptive. It does not provide many guidelines on how decisions ought to be made. It does not tell a decision maker very much about how to make better decisions. The decision maker who follows the behavioral model is behaving like the average decision maker. Thus, the resulting decisions cannot be expected to be any better than average.

4.5 SUMMARY

The settings can dramatically influence the nature of the decision making process and the resulting decision. In the individual setting, the individual's own personal values, perceptions and aspirations largely control the decision making. The individual is free to act at will.

Economic, strategies, satisficing and behavioral approaches may be taken to decision making in the individual setting. The economic approach presumes that the decision maker has perfect information, and can compute the statistically best decision choice. Though these assumptions seldom hold in most real situations, the economic model contains many useful analytical techniques and some important lessons for the individual decision maker. Indifference point and dominance analyses are very useful general techniques that can help clarify the decision maker's options. One of the important lessons is that a random choice of alternatives may be just as good as any other choice.[3] The strategies approach sensitizes the individual decision maker to the fact that particular decision choices reflect different risk-propensities and value-orientations. This approach permits the decision maker to select a blend of alternatives that achieves a desired level of risk-reward trade-offs. The satisficing and behavioral models show how the individual's level of needs and aspirations can influence the search for better decision alternatives.

Each model is appropriate for handling different situations, and the most effective decision maker recognizes when to use each one. In general, various elements and aspects of each model can be mixed together and used to provide a powerful combined approach.

4.6 REFERENCES

1. Savage, L. J. *The Foundations of Statistics.* New York: John Wiley & Sons, Inc., 1954, pp. 57–93.
2. Heinze, David. *Statistical Decision Analysis for Management.* Columbus, Ohio: Grid, Inc., 1973.
3. Souder, W. E. "Utility and Perceived Acceptability of R&D Project Selection Models." *Management Science,* **19,** No. 8: 907–923 (1973).
4. Ebert, R. J. and Mitchell, T. R. *Organizational Decision Processes.* New York: Crane, Russak & Company, 1975, pp. 99–161.
5. March, J. G. and Simon, H. A. *Organizations.* New York: John Wiley & Sons, Inc., 1958, pp. 56–108.
6. Simon, H. A. *The New Science of Management Decision.* New York: Harper & Row, 1960.
7. Ebert, R. J. and Mitchell, T. R. *Organizational Decision Processes.* New York: Crane, Russak & Company, 1975, pp. 55–66.

4.7 BIBLIOGRAPHY

Carter, E. E. "Project Evaluations and Firm Decisions." *Journal of Management Studies,* **7,** No. 3: 253–279 (1971).
Emory, C. W. and Niland, Powell. *Making Management Decisions.* Boston: Houghton Mifflin Company, 1968.
Heinze, David. *Management Science.* Cincinnati: South-Western Publishing Company, 1978, pp. 39–94.
Mintzberg, Henry; Raisinghani, Duru; and Theoret, Andre. "The Structure of Unstructured Decision Making." *Administrative Science Quarterly,* **21,** No. 2: 246–274 (1976).
Newell, Allen and Simon, H. A. *Human Problem Solving.* Englewood Cliffs, New Jersey: Prentice-Hall, Inc., 1972.
Shore, Barry. *Quantitative Methods for Business Decisions.* New York: McGraw-Hill, 1978, pp. 46–143.
Souder, W. E. and Zeigler, R. W. "A Review of Creativity and Problem Solving Techniques." *Research Management,* **20,** No. 4: 34–42 (1977).
Tichy, N. M., Tushman, M. L., and Fombrun, C. "Social Network Analysis for Organizations." *The Academy of Management Review,* **4,** No. 4: 507–519 (1979).

5

Group and Organizational
Decision Settings

5.0 INTRODUCTION

In the group decision setting, significant influence may be exerted by
other individuals. The way the individuals perceive each other, the levels
of peer respect accorded each other, the felt competitiveness among
them, differences in their individual value systems, whether one is a subordinate or a boss of another—and many other factors can influence the
interpersonal interaction patterns in a group setting.

Decision making behaviors can become even more complex in an organizational setting, where individual and group actions are shaded by
organizational roles and perceptions. Company policies and procedures
may become influential. Loyalties to departments may arise. The general
financial health and the risk-taking posture of the organization may influence the decision behaviors of individual members. The ways in which
responsibilities are structured within the organization will also influence
the decision process. But perhaps one of the most unique aspects of the
organizational setting is its impersonal nature. No individual is likely to
have the same type of emotional commitment to an organizational problem that they often have with a personal problem. Thus, just as the group
setting is a hierarchy or coalition of individuals, the organizational setting
is a coalition of groups and individuals. It has all the facets of individual
and group settings, overlaid with several unique facets of its own.

This chapter discusses these aspects of group and organizational settings. Some methods for increasing the effectiveness of group and organizational decision processes are presented and discussed.

5.1 THE GROUP SETTING

A group is a collection of individuals in a social setting who have status and role interrelatedness. Many individual decision models may apply in a group setting, since a group is a collection of individuals. But, a group is not a collection of *independent* individuals. In a group setting, the individuals are interdependent and interrelated. By myself, I can make whatever decisions I want. But in a group setting, this is seldom the case. Other members may not see the problem the way I do. Other members may not share my value system, so they do not rank the alternatives the same way I do. My best choice may be their worst choice. Our self-interests may differ. What is in my best self-interest may not serve anyone else. Other members may see alternatives I do not, and vice versa. Similarly, we may have different perceptions of the outcomes and their relation to the various alternatives.

Groups may behave in many different ways. For instance, group decision making may be by consensus, by acquiescence, by whatever the strongest member says, by fiat, by deference, by bargaining, by exchange, or by default. In the default mode, the group just lets the matter drift and they never come to any decision. In effect, the decision resolves itself. In the acquiescence process, the deliberations may be strong and heated. But in the end, some or all members simply "throw up their hands" and acquiesce to the strongest member or to some position. In bargaining, the parties engage in exchange. Each gives a little in return for some concession from another. One person's loss is another's gain, but each receives something from the other. As a result, all move closer together.

There are many phenomena which influence and control group decision behavior processes. Some of these are leadership, specious persuasion, bandwagon and snowball effects, cliques and factions, and risky shift phenomena. Let us now look at these aspects.

5.1.1 Leadership Forces

The presence of a strong personality in any group can dramatically influence its behavior. A formally appointed leader may or may not be a strong power center. If the formal leader has a strong personality, then the combination of the strong personality and the legitimization of the formal leadership role may provide a potent power center.

The success of a leader may depend greatly on the leader's style. Depending on the other personalities present within the group, an autocratic style may be more or less effective than a democratic style. Current research generally indicates that the most successful leaders are those who supply some structure, goals and objectives. But the successful leaders also allow all the members to play a major role in the actual decision processes of suggesting and debating alternatives, and in the selection of the final decision. In general, research indicates that the more technologically complex the decision task and the more highly trained the group members, the greater the autonomy and participation expected by the members.

5.1.2   Persuasion Effects

Most of us have had the experience of going to a group meeting with preconceived notions, and then finding that these notions have been greatly altered by the meeting. The exchange of information, the sharing of perspectives and the logic of the other members impacted on us and changed our notions. But how much of this impact was due to an objective display of the information and issues? And how much of it was due to the persuasiveness and salesmanship of the individuals who were there? These are difficult questions to answer. But both experience and controlled research show that persuasion and salesmanship can play a significant role in changing people's minds.[1,2]

5.1.3   Bandwagon and Snowball Effects

Anyone who has observed groups knows that it is not unusual for the entire group to suddenly accelerate toward a final decision. After some period of discussion, the group may begin to establish some progress toward consensus. Then, suddenly, the amount of agreement among the members may increase. Like a snowball rolling down a hill, members become caught up in the action and enthusiasm. Such effects are often sparked by some simple act, such as two of the members agreeing strongly on some issue and announcing their agreement. Suddenly, others get on the bandwagon and the group closes on a decision. Some very poor decisions can result from a bandwagon effect. It is largely an emotional phenomenon, and the swiftness with which it spreads often precludes real discussion, debate and analysis of the issues. Members may leave with a false sense of having engaged in an in-depth analysis, whereas they really only scratched the surface of the real issues and engaged in a very cursory analysis.[1,2]

5.1.4   Cliques and Factions

Though groups are seldom homogeneous in member orientations, the basic human need for affiliation drives individuals to band together. This need does not guarantee that all the group members will in fact band together. Dyadic (or two-person) and triadic (or three-person) interrelationships are the most stable. Maintaining more than one or two relationships with others becomes a psychological strain for most of us. Hence, it is not uncommon to find that a large group will splinter into two- person and three-person cliques. Figure 5.1 illustrates homogeneous and factioned groups. In the homogeneous group A, all members talk with, interact with, freely share information with, and exchange opinions with each other. Each has a relationship with the other. In group B, two factions have emerged. One is a triadic (three-person) clique, and the other is a diadic (two-person) clique. Many other possibilities exist, one of which is illustrated by group C. Here, individual number 3 is attempting to affiliate with individuals 1, 4 and 5, who are ignoring him. Individuals 4 and 5 have a clique. Individuals 2 and 4 have another clique.

Many factors can create such factions: weak leaders, lack of mutual interest in the decison problem, interpersonal frictions and dislikes for each other, dissimilar perceptions, polarized positions on the issues, etc. Once such factions occur it may be very difficult to bring them together again. The usual solutions are to either use some group-building processes, or to reconstitute the group under a strong leader. But neither of these solutions may be effective. The most effective practice is to take proper actions to prohibit the formation of factions, by properly constituting, training and organizing the groups.[1,2]

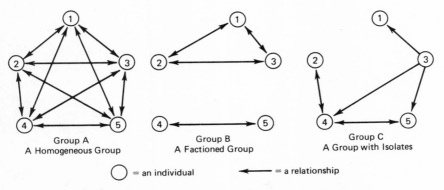

Figure 5.1. Illustration of homogeneous and factioned groups.

5.1.5   Risky Shift

The typical finding is that an individual's willingness to take risks increases in a group setting. This change is usually referred to as risky shift. This is contrary to what one might expect, given the usual group pressures to conform. The risky-shift phenomenon has been replicated many times. Professional groups, senior executives, management trainees, male subjects, female subjects—all have been found to show the risky-shift phenomenon.[3]

One reasonable explanation for the risky-shift phenomenon is that the group setting diffuses the individual's feelings of responsibility and exposure. This enables them, psychologically, to make riskier decisions. This explanation suggests the following causal chain. First, group discussion creates bonds between the members. Second, these bonds permit a diffusion of felt responsibility. Third, the diffusion of responsibility reduces the fear of failure. Fourth, the reduced fear of failure produces the risky shift. The practical implication here is that a group discussion may help to produce conditions through which the group is willing to take greater risks. If, however, it is the lessening of fear that results in the risky shift phenomenon, then groups are only one of many ways of achieving risk-taking decision behaviors. Anything that reduces one's fear of the consequences of a wrong decision may encourage risk-taking. This conclusion has many implications for managers in setting the climate for risk-taking.[4, 5]

5.2   IMPROVING GROUP PROCESSES

Group decision making tends to be a very heuristic process. Goals, constraints, objectives and decision criteria often unfold and become crystallized as a part of the process. This occurs as information is exchanged and sorted, and as issues are discussed.

Group decision processes often start with vague feelings and highly subjective opinions. This is usually followed by a period of introspection, dialogue, discussion or an exchange of thoughts. It is only after these preliminaries that the individuals may become aware of their own true feelings, perceptions and positions on the issues. This involves a self-realization and self-awareness of one's own inner value system of feelings and sentiments. Sometimes, communications with others are required before a person can truly know one's own sentiments.

Thus, group processes can be potent forces that provide many vital ingredients for effective decision making. It is important for these processes to be properly managed and energized.

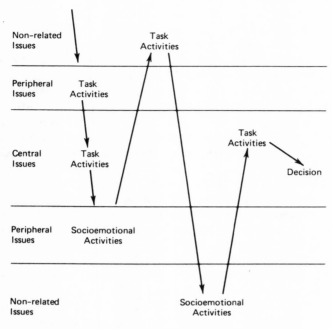

Figure 5.2. Illustration of cycled group process activities.

5.2.1   Managing Group Phases [2, 4, 5]

Groups generally cycle through two distinct phases: task-oriented and socioemotional-oriented. These two phases are usually not entirely separate and distinct. Often, what is happening represents various degrees of each, and the phases overlap and merge into each other. In the task phase, the group devotes its attention to decision issues. In the socioemotional phase the group lets off steam, dissipates tension and engages in social conflict.

Figure 5.2 illustrates a typical pattern of task and socioemotional activities. The group may start out on a task orientation, on some peripheral issues. Then, the focus may shift to the central issues, perhaps with help from the group leader. But, then some conflicts will often develop. Or some members will need reassurance about whether or not the group is doing what it is chartered to do. This will open up a socioemotional period. As the socioemotional needs are gradually met, the group becomes ready to handle another task-oriented period. The focus may return to either the mainstream issue or move on to some peripheral issues. Eventually, as the socioemotional needs are met a stronger task focus gradually emerges, and the mainstream tasks are more highly emphasized. Less time is spent on peripheral issues. Eventually, the group converges on a decision.

During a socioemotional phase, it is essential that orientation-giving, opinion-giving and suggestion-giving occur. The group leader may do this. But it is more effective if this comes from the other members. These are the positive socioemotional forces that balance off the negative forces of tension, uncertainty and antagonism that may arise. Tension release activities are also a necessary positive force. Joking and laughter are essential tension releasing activities, and a clever group leader makes sure they occur.[2]

What happens if the socioemotional phase is not permitted? The socioemotional phase involves the resolution of basic sociopsychological and human needs. This phase is an essential part of any group process. The decision making group cannot function when basic human needs are not met and when basic psychological questions are not resolved. If the socioemotional phase is not permitted to occur, an inferior decision is the best that can be expected. And no decision at all is likely. Without the socioemotional phase, the group cannot achieve closure on all the issues. Some members will not be completely satisfied, because their socioemotional needs will not be completely met. These unfulfilled members will attempt to continue the discussions, perhaps dragging out the deliberations until the other members are dissipated and the initial agreements come apart. If the unfulfilled members are in the minority, then they may be overruled by the majority or they may acquiesce to the pressure to conform.

5.2.2   Using Consensus Methods

Group decision consensus is a desirable quality. Decisions arrived at by consensus imply a strength of individual commitment to follow through. Parties that come to consensus can usually be expected to maintain an allegiance that is essential for the implementation of the decision.

Decision making styles and consensus methods vary from one culture to another. For example, the Japanese approach to decision making is characterized by a series of round robin presentations and a sharing of perspectives. All members are given a chance to offer an opinion and others have a chance to reflect on these. The Amish experiences are still another example. Their processes are characterized by lengthy periods of discussion. The discussions may continue for a very long time period. Closure occurs when each member senses that consensus has been arrived at, and when the decision appears to serve the good of the community.[1,4]

5.2.3 The Nominal-Interacting (NI) Process [6,7]

Figure 5.3 presents an outline of the nominal-interacting (NI) process. This process has been found to be highly effective in managing decision making groups. It provides a forum for exchanging feelings and opinions which helps the individuals to increase their self-awareness and build teamwork.

The NI process begins with a nominal period in which each individual in the group silently and anonymously completes an individual decision making exercise. This exercise may consist of ranking, listing, Q-sorting, etc. These individual results are then tallied in charts and displayed to the entire group. The focus is on the group agreement/disagreement statistics, while preserving individual anonymity. The group is then given a period in which they can interact and discuss the results. In this interacting period, the discussions are fully controlled by the participants: they may share opinions, exchange data, challenge each other, negotiate, remain placid, etc. The anonymity of the tally charts permits members to take the easy

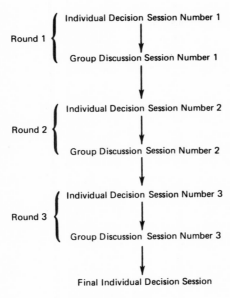

Figure 5.3. The NI procedure.

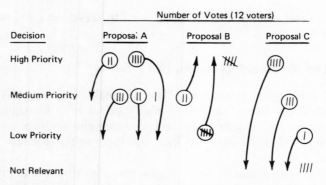

Figure 5.4. Distribution of votes in two rounds of an NI process.

choice of not responding to threatening or vituperative questions about who voted for what. Minority opinions may thus be preserved because they are not subject to specious group persuasion. Experience shows that the unstructuredness of the group permits the underlying sociometry and influence centers to emerge naturally, so that the group may work out its own opinion modification and accommodation patterns. To help guide these accommodation patterns, the group's effectiveness and growth patterns (e.g., hedonic tone, potency, trust, cohesiveness etc.) are periodically measured and fed back to the group.[7, 8, 9]

This sequence of an individual period (the nominal period) and a group discussion period (the interacting period) can be repeated for several rounds. Experience shows that two to three rounds are needed to stimulate complete information exchange, but more than four rounds dissipates the subjects. The first nominal period permits individuals to document their own thoughts and value judgments. The subsequent first interacting period confronts the group with a diversity of opinions to be resolved. The second nominal period permits each individual to privately restructure their thoughts. The second interacting period provides an opportunity to refine opinions and work toward consensus. A third nominal period provides the environment for closure and consensus. A consensus will usually emerge as the members adopt ideas and opinions from each other, acquire more information and interpersonal understandings, or become influenced by the enthusiasm of the group. The feelings of group identity, the loyalties, and the partnerships developed during the exercises are also very important. Experience shows that they can lead to a strong team identity.[7, 9]

Figure 5.4 is an illustration of the results from two successive rounds of an NI process which was used to assist a twelve-member council in a small community. Three proposals, proposals A, B and C, were put before the council. A secret-ballot vote was taken on the three proposals at the end of round 1 and again at the end of round 2 of an NI process. The arrows in Figure 5.4 show the changes in the votes from round 1 to round 2. At the end of round 2, as Figure 5.4 shows, the council had achieved a consensus decision to fund proposal B as soon as funds became available. A consensus decision was also made to postpone proposal A and to reject proposal C, as Figure 5.4 shows. As in most experiences with the NI process, consensus was achieved very rapidly and the participants felt the process aided them in arriving at a decision which they all generally agreed to.[7, 8, 9] A more detailed illustration of the NI process is presented in Chapter 9.

5.3   ORGANIZATIONAL SETTINGS

Organizational settings are perhaps the least-understood of the three decision settings. Organizational settings are extremely complex. In addition to group phenomena, organizations often have intergroup phenomena that cut across the groups. On top of this, there are the formal subordinate-superior relationships.

We sometimes say that organizations "make" decisions. Yet when we attempt to pinpoint exactly where in the organization these decisions are made we may fail completely. Often, it appears that decisions seem to just evolve. There does not seem to be any particular point in the organization where decisions are made. This is a result of the splintered responsibilities and the diffuseness that accompany most organizations, which create several loci of decision power.

5.3.1   Diffuseness and Splinteredness

Real world organizational decision environments are often characterized by splintered responsibilities and a diffuseness of organizational power. In splintered responsibilities, the objectives are selected and assigned priorities at one level of the organization while the resources to achieve these goals are assigned to them at a different level of the organization. Since the two organizational levels may have different viewpoints of the prevailing objectives and constraints, this confounds the possibilities for achieving an overall optimum. For example, it is not uncommon for the long range planning function of an organization to establish the acceptable programs, from which the operating departments may select particular projects. However, a hierarchy of budgets comes into play in determining the fundings for these projects. Divisions have total budgets. Departments within these divisions have budgets. And projects within divisions also have budgets.

Diffuseness refers to the fact that decisions may naturally occur at many different points in an organization. The decisions can be highly uncoordinated with each other. At the policy level, e.g., the corporate planning level, there may be a selection among alternative disciplines, technologies or product areas. At the operational level, e.g., the departmental level, a similar selection process may go on with respect to alternative methodologies for carrying out the project. At both levels, it is likely that many different persons will be involved in the project selection decision making. Many different persons will supply information to the process, e.g., the marketing personnel may supply information about the potential market returns from the project, the engineering personnel may supply cost data, etc.

5.3.2 Behavioral Obstacles

It should be clear that a variety of difficulties, both behavioral and logistical, can be encountered in assembling interdepartmental decision data. There may be a felt proprietariness about sharing information. Unless a sound relationship of trust and openness has been established between the parties, one or the other may hold a fear of revealing too much information too soon or of letting themselves open to criticism or ridicule from the other. As a case in point, the author recalls an experience in which a market research person was reluctant to communicate his intuitively based sales forecasts to the design engineers, though this information was absolutely essential and vital to the success of the design. He feared that the quantitatively-trained engineers would ridicule his "data" and embarrass him professionally. Thus, he told them very little, although they clamored for his information. The situation escalated to the point where the design could not be completed because the engineers refused to go ahead without the "data." They did not want to accept the responsibility for a design that had not been guided by market data. Consequently, marketing and engineering blamed each other for the design failure. And this incident added to the growing barrier between them.

Another illustration is the tendency for research departments to closet their work until it is completely finished. Details are sometimes purposely protected and kept secret from the marketing personnel. The logic of this is based on a premise that marketing may "run with the product" too soon. Thus, it is clear that information sharing barriers may exist.

5.3.3 Organizational Joint Problem Solving (OJPS)

In the traditional or classical approach to organizational decision making, individuals are assigned problems. The individual then either solves the problem or delegates it to a staff person or a subordinate. The top level of the organization retains the final authority for implementing the solution, and for making the final decision on the basis of the completed staff work. This approach is not suitable for handling complex problems where dynamic interaction is required. The alternative approach is to assign the problem to a group and to appoint a leader to provide the final say and give the group some direction. However this approach is subject to all the problems with groups and group management outlined above.

Organizational joint problem solving (OJPS) combines both of these approaches. It sets up a number of centers which are linked together to deal with a problem. A search for a solution is initially conducted at the highest level of the organization to establish goals for the second level. The centers then search within their own components to meet these goals. The plan of action developed by any center and the rationale for it is then broadcast to the other centers in the system. This permits inconsistencies between the components to be resolved. The processes of searching and broadcasting are coordinated and iterated until an overall solution is found which is as close to the objective as the centers can come. With this method of search it is not necessary for any one center or all centers to understand the whole problem. Instead, each need only interact with the others at the interfaces between them. Thus, OJPS is very amenable for use in organizations which are using project management or matrix management systems.[11, 12]

5.3.4 Evaluation Teams and Taskforces

The use of problem study teams, committees and evaluation task forces can help to break down the natural interdepartmental barriers and cultural separations that often arise in organizational settings. For example, appointing a study committee with members drawn from across several departments provides an opportunity to bridge these separations. Project management and task-focused matrix organization structures have also been successfully used to temporarily link various decision making centers.[12, 13] Though these linking arrangements provide the structure and climate for interaction, a very heterogeneous group is thereby created. Thus, in order to activate the group and create an effective decision making environment, the group dynamics controls and process management methods discussed above must be used.[7, 9, 13]

5.4 SUMMARY

In a group setting, individual actions may be constrained by a variety of interpersonal pressures and group dynamics. In an organizational setting, many complex forces may influence the decision making. In addition to group phenomena, organizational settings exhibit intergroup interaction phenomena and formal subordinate-superior behavior patterns. Organizational settings are also characterized by diffuseness, splinteredness and information-sharing barriers that may block the decision flow. Thus, different approaches are needed in order to achieve an effective decision in these different settings.

Leadership failures, specious persuasion, bandwagon and snowballing effects, and the tendency for groups to break into small factions are major obstacles to effective group decision making. Proper training and process management of decision making groups is needed if these obstacles are to be overcome. Several process management methods are available for increasing the effectiveness of decision making groups. These methods include the nominal-interacting decision making format, techniques to insure that the group cycles through the task and socioemotional phases, and feedback methods that guide the accommodation and maturation of the group.

The opportunities for factions, coalitions, bargaining, power plays, and politics are greatly increased in organizational settings. An organization consists of many different overlapping groups that are held together by a mutuality of interest and a formal structure of superior-subordinate relationships. This mutuality of interest is often very tenuous. Each group or formal department may have basically dissimilar goals and desires. The formalization of these groups into departments and divisions enhances a spirit of noncooperation and separateness. The application of organizational joint problem solving methods, task force study committees and group process management methods can overcome some of these problems.

Group settings can benefit greatly from the application of the structured process. The structured process can help to focus and channel the group behavior patterns, thought patterns and analyses. However, the structured process must be used in combination with group consensus and group management methods like the NI process, in order to handle group interaction and interpersonal dynamics phenomena. The organizational setting can similarly benefit from the application of the structured decision making process. However, structured decision making cannot be effectively used unless it is combined with organizational joint problem solving methods and task forces or other linking arrangements. These methods are needed to cope with the diffuseness, splinteredness and behavioral barriers that usually characterize organizational settings.

5.5 REFERENCES

1. Gibson, J. L; Ivancevich, J. M; and Donnelly, J. H., Jr. *Organizations: Behavior, Structure and Processes*. Dallas: Business Publications, Inc., 1976, pp. 147–224; 341–368.
2. Zaleznik, Abraham and Moment, David. *The Dynamics of Interpersonal Behavior*. New York: John Wiley & Sons, Inc., 1964, pp. 179–407.
3. MacKenzie, K. D. "An Analysis of Risky Shift Experiments." *Organizational Behavior and Human Performance*, **6**, No. 3: 249–266 (1971).
4. Hellriegel, Don and Slocum, J. W., Jr. *Organizational Behavior: Contingency Views*. New York: West, 1976, pp. 157–243.
5. Tosi, H. L. and Carroll, S. J. *Management: Contingencies, Structure and Process*. Chicago: St. Clair, 1976, pp. 96–116; 234–274.
6. Delbecq, A. L.; Van de Ven, A. H.; and Gustafson, D. H. *Group Techniques for Program Planning: A Guide to Nominal and Delphi Processes*. Glenview, Illinois: Scott, Foresman and Company, 1975, pp. 7–10, 17–18.
7. Souder, W. E. "Effectiveness of Nominal and Interacting Group Decision Processes for Intergrating R&D and Marketing." *Management Science*, **23**, No. 6: 595–605 (1977).
8. Souder, W. E. "A Group Process Model for Portfolio Decision Making in Organizations." *Proceedings of the American Institute of Decision Sciences, Western Regional Conference*. March 17–18, 1977.
9. Souder, W. E. "Achieving Organizational Consensus With Respect to R&D Project Selection Criteria." *Management Science*, **21**, No. 6: 669–691 (1975).
10. Shumway, C. R.; Maher, P. M; Baker, N. R.; Souder, W. E.; Rubenstein, A. H.; and Gallant, A. R. "Diffuse Decision Making in Hierarchical Organizations: An Empirical Examination." *Management Science*, **21**, No. 6: 697–707 (1975).
11. Swinth, R. L. "Organization Joint Problem Solving." *Management Science*, **17**, No. 1: B68–B79 (1971).
12. Cleland, D. I. and King, W. R. *Systems Analysis and Project Management*. New York: McGraw-Hill, 1975, pp. 183–298.
13. Souder, W. E. "Effectiveness of Product Development Methods." *Industrial Marketing Management*, **7**, No. 5: 12–28 (1978).

5.6 BIBLIOGRAPHY

Cyert, R. M. and March, J. G. *A Behavioral Theory of the Firm*. Englewood Cliffs, New Jersey: Prentice-Hall, Inc., 1963.
Ebert, R. J. and Mitchell, T. R. *Organizational Decision Processes*. New York: Crane, Russak & Company, 1975.
Elbing, Alvar. *Behavioral Decisions In Organizations*. Glenview, Illinois: Scott, Foresman and Company, 1978.
Gibson, J. L.; Ivancevich, J. M.; and Donnelly, J. H., Jr. *Organizations: Behavior, Structure and Processes*. Dallas: Business Publications, Inc., 1976.
Green, T. B. "An Empirical Analysis of Nominal and Interacting Groups." *Academy of Management Journal*, **18** (1975), 63–73.
Souder, W. E., et. al. *An Exploratory Study of the Coordinating Mechanisms Between R&D*

and Marketing as an Influence on the Innovation Process. National Science Foundation Final Report, Grant 75–17195, August 26, 1977.

Souder, W. E. "Effectiveness of Nominal and Interacting Group Decision Processes for Integrating R&D and Marketing." *Management Science, 23,* No. 6: 595–605 (1977).

Van de Ven, A. H. "Group Decision-Making and Effectiveness: An Experimental Study." *Organization and Administrative Sciences, 5,* No. 1: 1–110 (1974).

Van de Ven, A. H. "Nominal Versus Interacting Group Processes for Committee Decision-Making Effectiveness." *Academy of Management Journal, 14,* No. 2: 203–212 (1971).

Williams, J. C. *Human Behavior in Organizations.* Cincinnati: South-Western Publishing Company, 1978, pp. 49–92; 302–345.

Zmud, R. W. "Perceptions of Cognitive Style: Acquisition, Exhibition and Implications for Information System Design." *Journal of Management, 5,* No. 1: 7–20 (1979).

Part III
Preparing for a Decision

The care and preparation that a decision maker takes before actually making a decision can largely determine the quality of that decision. No decision can be any better than the analyses on which it is based. If the problem is poorly defined, or if only weak solution alternatives are devised, then the decisions will be equally poor and weak. The three chapters that make up this part of the book focus on preparing for a decision. Chapter 6 discusses methods for defining problems, opportunities and alternatives. Chapter 7 presents and illustrates various approaches to the economic analysis and evaluation of alternatives. Chapter 8 discusses the use of decision trees and fault trees to analyze alternatives.

6

Defining Problems, Opportunities and Alternatives

6.0 INTRODUCTION

A great volume of literature exists on the topics of analyzing alternatives and selecting the best one. But far too little has been said and written about defining problems, opportunities and alternatives. These are critical elements. An inadequate definition of the decision problem or the available opportunities and alternatives will necessarily lead to an inadequate decision. Even the best techniques for analyzing and selecting alternatives will not help a decision maker who has failed to pay attention to these critical elements. Solving the wrong problem, failing to perceive an opportunity or not developing good alternatives almost always leads to worthless decisions.

The previous chapters have presented and discussed the structured decision process and its application within various settings. This chapter focuses on the three critical elements within the structured decision making process: defining problems, opportunities and alternatives. Methods for identifying opportunities and clarifying problems are discussed. Several techniques for defining creative decision alternatives are presented and illustrated.

6.1 IDENTIFYING PROBLEMS

6.1.1 The Exception Principle

It is often difficult to know whether one is dealing with a real problem or merely the symptoms of a problem. One way to define a problem is by the *exception principle*. In this approach, a problem is any significant deviation from the standard or plan. To use this approach, the manager must have previously established a plan or a standard. Hence, planning becomes a fundamental and essential prerequisite to the ability to recognize a problem. This is perhaps one of the strongest cases for planning. It must be noted, however, that once the manager has defined an expected standard of performance, the accepted levels of achievement must then be defined. For example, if a 10% defect rate is the standard of performance, is 12% a problem? This may be well within the expected day-to-day variations. Thus, the manager must be careful to establish the long run or average performance that is desired, along with some control limits.

The exception principle or the *management by exception principle,* as it is also known, is widely used by many successful managers. Yet it has some theoretical and practical inadequacies. First of all, it tacitly assumes that the degree and type of significant problems which may arise can be anticipated. Second, the exception principle lulls the manager into a false sense of lethargic security. The idea behind the exception principle is that action is only taken when there is a significant deviation. No action is taken at any other time. Thus, a manager who blindly relies on the exceptions to energize actions may become unresponsive at other times.

6.1.2   The Deviation Check Approach

The deviation check approach is only a partial way around some of the above objections to the exception principle. In this approach, the manager begins by asking what is different, what is new or what is changed. These questions are asked periodically, so that there are multiple standards and base points. For instance, in making a quality deviation check, the manager would compare today's output to yesterday's, last week's, etc. The deviation check is purposely broad, unstructured and open. Any and all deviations are recorded. Then, for each deviation, the following detective work is carried out. The deviation is fully located, identified and described in terms of its time, place and extent. What sets the deviation apart from the usual situation is described by searching out and recording its distinguishing characteristics. The potential causes of the deviation are sought by searching for some distinctive feature, some mechanism or some condition that accompanied the deviation which is not normally present.

The deviation check approach avoids the biasing influence of prior standards. It seeks out and records any and all deviations—not just those that violate an established standard. Thus, it is an improvement over the exception principle. But this is also a deficiency in the method. Without prior standards, it is difficult to distinguish real problems from normal variations and inconsequential deviations. The deviation check approach is generally very costly, because all deviations must be sought out and analyzed. Some of these may be important, but most will be unimportant. However, if the nature of the situation is not well-known, or if it is important to have a fail-safe situation, then the cost of continuous deviation checks can be warranted. For instance, deviation checks are continuously run in nuclear research and development work. There, new and unexpected problems may occur at any time and all problems have the potential to escalate into very serious situations.

6.1.3 Management Audits

A management audit is a deliberate search for potential problems and opportunities. It is different from both the deviation check and the exception principle, in that emerging and potential problems are sought. A management audit is somewhat like a physical checkup in this respect. The basic health of the organization or system is evaluated in an attempt to locate weaknesses or faults that might develop into problems at some later date.

A management audit consists of a great deal of measuring, probing, evaluating and analyzing. Interview methods, statistical techniques, financial audit methods and industrial engineering techniques may all be used in a management audit. The established performance standards will be used as focal points for the audit, but many other aspects will also be covered. To successfully carry out an audit, management must thoroughly understand the characteristics of a healthy system and the early warning signs of pending diseases. Because audits usually require a specialized expertise, and because an outsider's viewpoint is likely to be less biased, most managers call on outside consultants for an audit.

6.1.4 The Pro-active Approach

The management audit method reflects an aggressive philosophy of seeking out potential problems before they actually occur. This is a pro-active approach. The exception principle and the deviation check method are reactive approaches. Reactive approaches reflect a passive orientation of waiting until the problem has begun to show up in some tangible fashion. No action is taken until there is a visible deviation or decline in product quality, organizational effectiveness or other achievements. In today's rapid-change society, effective managers cannot afford this kind of reactive posture. There is the ever-present danger that by the time the problem manifests itself it will already be too late for any effective action. Admittedly, pro-active problem identification is expensive. And its methods are relatively imprecise. But the long run regrets from *not* taking a pro-active posture can far outweigh its expense and its disadvantages.

6.2 IDENTIFYING OPPORTUNITIES

A pro-active posture is essential to achieving and maintaining a leadership position. No firm or organization can be number one if it does not aggressively search out problems and opportunities before they become visible to others. Seeking out and identifying opportunities is especially critical to achieving a leadership position. The old saying that opportunities wait for no one is literally true. Moreover, a pro-active posture of finding opportunities before they become apparent to others may go a long way toward avoiding problems. The forward-looking organization that forecasts, plans ahead and seizes on emerging opportunities will usually have a better-managed and more problem-free environment.

6.2.1 Environmental Monitoring

In this pro-active approach the economic, social, political and technological trends are constantly monitored and systematically studied. Table 6.1 lists some common information sources that can be consulted as part of

Table 6.1. Some information sources for environmental monitoring.

Thomas' Register of American Manufacturers. New York: Thomas Publishing Co.
Washington Information Workbook. Washington: Washington Researchers.
Business Trends and Forecasting Information Sources. Detroit: Gale Research Institute.
Statistical Abstract of the U.S. Washington: U.S. Government Printing Office.
The Economic Almanac. New York: National Industrial Conference Board.
Survey of Current Business. Washington: U.S. Office of Business Economics.
Economic Indicators. Washington: U.S. Government Printing Office.
Predicasts. Cleveland: Predicast, Inc.
U.S. Industrial Outlook. Washington: U.S. Government Printing Office.
Census of Business. Washington: U.S. Bureau of Census.
Census of Manufacturers. Washington: U.S. Bureau of Census.
Quarterly Financial Report for Manufacturing Corporations. Washington: U.S. Federal Trade Commission.
Moody's Handbook. New York: Moody's Investor Service.
Wall Street Journal Index. New York: Dow-Jones.
Business Week Index. New York: McGraw-Hill.
Business Week. New York: McGraw-Hill.
The Wall Street Journal. New York: Dow-Jones.
Barrons. New York: Dow-Jones.
Forbes. New York: Forbes, Inc.
Fortune. New York: Time, Inc.
Dun's Review. New York: Dun and Bradstreet, Inc.

an environmental monitoring program. A comprehensive monitoring program would include information searching, data collection, data reduction, trend analyses, correlational analyses, and the application of other methods for relating the observed variables and factors.

The technology scanning method is an example of environmental monitoring. In this method, a grid is drawn up to display the components of the system being monitored and their potential impacts or outcomes. The socioeconomic impacts of each component are then rated by a panel of experts. Another group of experts rates the goals of mankind, against which the elements of the grid can be arrayed. The data may then be combined to show which system components are most likely to emerge. Table 6.2 presents an illustration of a technology scanning exercise for a new aircraft flight control method, where options A, B and C are different configurations of emerging technologies.

Some other examples of environmental monitoring techniques are the relevance tree method,[1] the cross-impacts method [2] and QUEST.[3] In the relevance tree method, each technology that appears to be relevant to the solution of a particular problem is mapped against the states-of-the-arts in the underlying science and engineering disciplines that support it. Developments in these states-of-arts are then monitored for changes which may suggest that one or the other of these technologies is likely to emerge as a solution. The cross-impacts method examines the interactions among a series of events, using probabilistic techniques and Bayesian statistical methods. By tracking and analyzing these events over time, insights can

Table 6.2. Example of technology scanning.

NEW FLIGHT CONTROL TECHNOLOGY

COMPONENTS	IMPACTS GRID		GOALS OF MANKIND	
	SOCIAL	ECONOMIC	GOALS	RATINGS
Option A	High	Low	Safety	1st
Option B	Low	High	Timeliness	2nd
Option C	High	High	Cost	3rd

Impacts—Goals Array

Conclusion: Option C is the most likely technology to emerge.

be gained into those technologies and factors that are most likely to emerge. In the QUEST approach, basic trends in the sciences and scientific disciplines are analyzed and rated for their criticality in supporting existing technological needs. Current social and political trends are then factored into these analyses to develop a picture of the emerging sociotechnical climate.

6.2.2 Technological Forecasting

Basic changes in technology are the roots of many significant opportunities. If these basic changes can be identified, then many opportunities may be forecasted and deduced from them.

Technological forecasting is an attempt to identify potential changes and events in technology, as a basis for identifying opportunities. It is not an attempt to predict coming future events or the advent of a new technology with great accuracy. Rather, technological forecasting attempts to identify those periods of time when a new technology may be needed or when the circumstances are most favorable for its emergence. Technological forecasting is concerned with magnitudes and directions rather than precision and accuracy. It is based on the premise that the decision maker only needs to know the fundamental direction of a change in technologies in order to formulate contingency plans and decision alternatives. Thus, technological forecasting methods are especially appropriate for the preparation stages of the decision making process, where the emphasis is on defining and analyzing the available alternatives and contingent actions.

Technological forecasting techniques are a combination of analytical methods and systematic judgments. The specific techniques range from highly analytical methods like curve-fitting to highly judgmental methods like genius-forecasting.

6.2.2.1 Curve Fitting. Figure 6.1 presents the three basic types of curves that can be used for trend extrapolation forecasting. The linear curve would be chosen only where the forecaster has reason to believe that the change in y per each change in x is expected to be constant. Otherwise, either the quadratic or the exponential functions would be used. If a quadratic is used, then either some drag (curve a) or some synergistic effect (curve b) is being assumed. The exponential curve assumes that y follows a growth-decay phenomenon. The particular form of the exponential shown here is the logistic function or "S"-shaped forecasting curve. The constant e is the natural logarithm base ($e = 2.71828$), the constant a is the y intercept and the constant b fixes the slope of the curve. To use

Equation	Curve

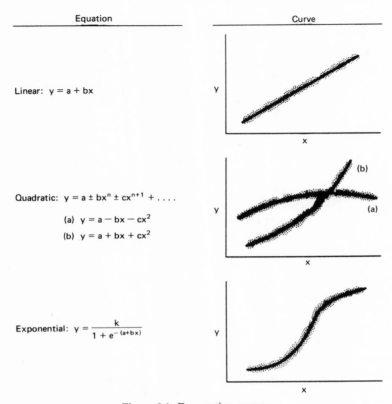

Linear: $y = a + bx$

Quadratic: $y = a \pm bx^n \pm cx^{n+1} + \ldots$

    (a) $y = a - bx - cx^2$

    (b) $y = a + bx + cx^2$

Exponential: $y = \dfrac{k}{1 + e^{-(a+bx)}}$

Figure 6.1. Forecasting curves.

this function, corresponding values of y and x are given and a and b are determined by regression for parametric values of k, where k is the upper asymptote of the curve.[4]

6.2.2.2 Modeling. The growth and spread of a technology can often be modeled by analogy to other natural processes. For instance, the news of an innovation often seems to spread though a community in a pattern that is analogous to osmosis, the gradual mixing of two liquids in a bottle, or the diffusion of a gas. Since these natural processes are described by well-known formulas and models, these same formulas are often applied by analogy to forecast the spread of a new technology.

Contextual chain models are often used to forecast the growth-chain of events when the previous patterns are well-established. For example, in aircraft flight control systems, there was a gradual evolution from manual to integrated systems, which then evolved into the automatic guidance controls of the 1960's and '70's. The advent of new electronic data processing units from outside the guidance control field led to further advances in central command systems and on-board solid state computers during the late 1970's. This chain suggests that the next generation of flight control systems will involve the use of computerized feedback control technologies from the macroprocessor industries.

The cross-industry diffusion and trickle-through of technologies and know-how can be modeled by the use of input-output (I/O) methods. The general idea behind I/O methods is that every industry is both a producer and a user of its own and of other industry's technologies. Statistics on the percentage use that one industry makes of another's outputs and technologies are generally available for constructing I/O models.[5]

Dynamic forecasting models allow the forecaster to model individual effects, interaction effects and feedback effects.[6] For instance, in forecasting the diffusion of new coal mining technologies, the influence of rising wage rates, the energy crisis, early successes and failures with related technologies, and the supply/demand factors may be fed into a dynamic forecasting model.[4] Such models are often more accurate because they are able to capture the total system of influences.

6.2.2.3 Expert Groups. Collective wisdoms are sometimes superior to individual viewpoints because a variety of perspectives can be collected and analyzed, bringing a total picture to bear on the issue. The opinions of several experts and knowledgeable persons can sometimes be "averaged" to cancel out the errors of individual predictions.

A poll or sampling of informed opinions may indicate the directions in which informed scientists are thinking. Indeed, such forecasts may be self-fulfilling: if enough people believe in something they can often make it happen. Thus, wide-based polls and samples may prove to be important barometers of future events. A panel or small group of informed experts who are brought together as a committee may also prove useful. The panel member's opinions are solicited in each other's presence. They are permitted to dialogue, debate and exchange views as they please. Consensus is not necessary. Rather, what is sought is a diversity of viewpoints, perspectives and predictions which can be further refined.

The Delphi method is a panel in which opinions are solicited under controlled conditions. The group is controlled in such a way that bandwagon effects, personality influences, repression, social group pressures and specious persuasion are minimized. This is done by insulating the members from each other, so that the opinions and identities remain anonymous. The forecast is then arrived at through repeated rounds or solicitations. In the first round, the panel of experts is interrogated through a questionnaire. For example, the questionnaire might ask the expert to specify a particular date when an event would come to pass. In addition to supplying the date, the expert is usually asked to write a short paragraph describing the basis or rationale for the prediction. The questionnaires are then collected and analyzed for statistical consensus. The mean and the standard deviation of the population of responses are computed. The short paragraphs are assembled into synopses that obscure the identities of the authors. These statistics and synopses are then reported to the panel, and their predictions and opinions are again sought in a second round of questionnaires. These rounds are repeated until consensus occurs. In most cases, if consensus does not occur within four or five rounds, then the method has failed. Figure 6.2 presents some typical results. Note the wide swings of opinions for Mr. C, Mr. D, Mr. E and Mr. F. In contrast, Mr. A never waivered in his opinion. The Delphi method in no way guarantees consensus. Nor does it guarantee that if consensus is reached the consensus will be correct. Mr. A could turn out to be right and all the others wrong.

The Delphi is thus a method for the systematic solicitation of informed opinions. The method replaces direct debate with indirect anonymity. The controlled exchange of information stimulates the participants to consider opinions, reasons and information they might otherwise ignore. But, there are some situations where the Delphi method may fail. It may fail because the participants need face-to-face contact, or they need to question each other in depth, or because the Delphi does not allow group spontaneity and creative interaction.[7] In these cases, the NI process described in

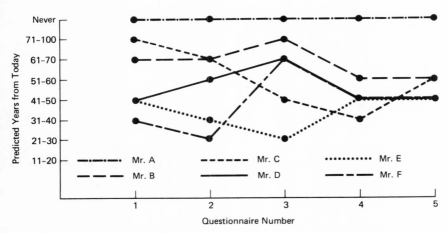

Figure 6.2. Delphi Results for: "When will the world run out of fossil fuels?"

Chapter 5 is a superior approach. In general, where there is a great deal of uncertainty, or where there are polarized opinions, or where there are few facts and much of the information is opinion-based, then the NI group process is likely to be superior to the Delphi method.

6.2.2.4   Intuition and Judgment. Intuitive or genius forecasting involves the nonsystematic sampling of learned persons. Indeed, some well-known persons have demonstrated an unexplainable and uncanny ability to predict events and occurrences. Perhaps these persons have a kind of extrasensory perception. Or perhaps they simply have a better grasp of the facts, a superior comprehension of events and a better awareness of human behaviors.

It is clear that learned judgment does have a place in forecasting. In any forecasting exercise, the forecaster must constantly ask whether or not the results are consistent with common sense and other knowledge. There is no substitute for the highly-informed individual who comprehends the technology and the envirosystem that surrounds it. Curve fitting methods, correlational analyses and analytical models are only techniques to aid the forecaster in utilizing informed judgments.

6.3   GENERATING ALTERNATIVES [8]

The explicit definition of the problem or opportunity may itself suggest one or more alternative solutions. However, this can be a tender trap. Solutions that seem "obvious" on the basis of a clear statement of the problem often prove to be only superficial palliatives. Yet these "obvious" solutions are seductively appealing. Unless a decision maker carefully guards against it, an awareness of an "obvious" solution can easily blind one to better alternative solutions. A decision maker who accepts the "obvious" solution is short-circuiting the structured decision making process. Without the benefit of the full process, one can never know if better alternative solutions were missed.

Two kinds of methods are available to help the decision maker generate alternative problem solutions. There are analytical methods and creativity methods. The analytical methods are not devoid of creativity, and the creativity methods are not bereft of analyses. The differences between the two types of approaches are more matters of degrees and orientations.

6.3.1   Analytical Methods

As the name implies, analytical methods consist of logic-based procedures for deducing new alternatives. These procedures involve a variety

Table 6.3. Illustration of morphological analysis.

		ALTERNATIVES				
PARAMETERS	TWO BUSES	AUTO AND BUS	TROLLEY	AUTO	TROLLEY AND TRAIN	BUS AND TROLLEY
Timeliness	Bad	Good	Good	Good	Bad	Bad
Cost	Good	Bad	Good	Bad	Bad	Good
Comfort	Good	Good	Bad	Good	Bad	Bad
Reliability	Bad	Bad	Good	Bad	Good	Bad
Transit Time	Bad	Bad	Good	Bad	Good	Good
Idle Time	Bad	Bad	Good	Bad	Good	Bad

of listing and comparing exercises that stimulate the decision maker to think of new extensions and combinations of solution alternatives.

6.3.1.1 Morphological Analyses. A morphological analysis is a way to visualize all the possible combinations of means to the solution of a particular problem. To carry out a morphological analysis, the parameters of a solution are first identified, then the alternatives are exhaustively generated by a combinatorial analysis. Table 6.3 illustrates a morphological analysis for the problem of commuting to and from work. The parameters represent the desired characteristics of a solution. All the single alternatives and their combinations are then listed and evaluated against these parameters. The process of structuring the approach in this fashion stimulates the decision maker to think through, develop and analyze all the available alternatives.

6.3.1.2 SAMM Approach. The SAMM (Sequence Attribute Modification Matrix) approach applies in sequential situations where the activities can be listed logically and explored for possible modifications. An illustration of the SAMM technique is provided in Table 6.4. The activities that can be modified are each checked for various possible modifications. These alternatives may then be subjected to a more rigorous analysis. Note that the SAMM approach does not specify how the modifications are to be made. It simply identifies those alternatives that are possible.

6.3.1.3 Attribute Listing. In attribute listing, the properties or basic characteristics of a product or situation are listed and reviewed with an eye toward improving them. For example, to use this method for improving a picture frame one could consider alternative shapes (round, oval, three-dimensional, etc.) or alternative materials (wood, plastic, metal, etc.).

Table 6.4. Example of the SAMM approach.

SEQUENCE/ATTRIBUTE DESCRIPTION	MODIFICATIONS				
	Eliminate	Substitute	Rearrange	Enlarge	Reduce
Roll Size				X	X
Spreader Speed					X
Final Press	X	X			
Initial Feed Action	X	X			
Feed Configuration	X		X		
Width of Stock				X	X

A related technique is the checklist approach. In this method, the problem is analyzed against a prepared list of attributes. Typical lists contain such attributes as how to make it longer or stronger, how to rearrange it, how to reverse it, how to change its form, etc. In general, attribute listing and checklists seem to be most effective when applied to problems and situations that are at least partially familiar to the decision maker.

6.3.1.4   Means-Ends Analysis. Nearly every program, alternative or planned action can be viewed as a means to some goal or end. And nearly every goal can be visualized as a means to some higher goal or end. To reveal each respective goal or end, the following question is repeatedly asked: "Why do I want this particular means, action, program or alternative?" To reveal each respective means, the following question is repeatedly asked: "What stops me from achieving this end, goal or objective?" The repeated asking and answering of these two questions provides a means-ends chain. Every end in this chain is a means to a higher end. And every means in this chain is an end for a lower means. Figure 6.3 presents an illustration of the means-ends logic process.

The means-ends technique captures the real dynamics of the iterative process of generating alternatives. In reality, the decision maker often oscillates between problem statements and potential alternatives before settling on a final list. This process often results in some refinement of the original problem statement. In fact, means-ends trees are ideal for redefining problems that are not clear. This is done by a means-to-ends approach of working upward by asking question 1 in Figure 6.3. New restatements of the problem should evolve from this approach. The trees are also useful when several problems seem to be interdependent. By asking question 2

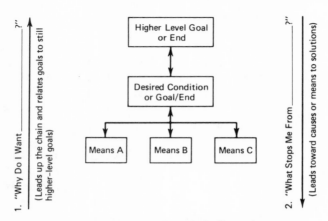

Figure 6.3. Means-ends analysis illustration.

in Figure 6.3, we may find that some of the problems are the means for one central problem. A third use of the trees is to iterate through questions 1 and 2 to elicit potential improvements in means and problem statements. Sometimes it is useful to "step-up" a level in the tree when it seems that the analysis is becoming bogged down. It may be that the lower-level problems are not the real ones. Thus, stepping up to a higher level in the tree forces one to focus on the more system-wide oriented goals. Once one has stepped up, then question 2 may be asked in order to generate system-wide types of solutions.

The means-ends approach diagnoses the decision problem within its total environment of higher and lower level problems, goals and alternatives. And this is often a more realistic picture than focusing on an isolated problem. By examining the higher and lower level surroundings of the problem, the decision maker is provided with a broader perspective for distinguishing symptoms from real problems. For instance, the problem may appear to be in department A. But if the decision maker steps up to a higher level it may be seen that the real problem is inimical to the whole organization. Thus, organization-wide solutions are actually necessary.

How far should one run the chain? Clearly, it could go on almost forever. There are three general rules: stop when the goals begin to exceed the manager's level of authority; stop when the means begin to exceed the available resources to implement them; stop when the magnitude of the analysis exceeds the time available. The first rule may be modified by the manager's degree of influence in the organization, or the ability to interest other higher-level managers in the analysis.

6.3.2 Creativity Methods [8]

Analytical methods stress the use of conscious, logic-based processes. By contrast, creativity methods stress the use of subconscious, fanciful and illogical processes. Creativity methods take the viewpoint that many innovative thoughts and decision alternatives arè locked up in the decision maker's subconscious mind. These methods are aimed at unlocking these innovative thoughts and solutions.

6.3.2.1 Brainstorming. The objective of this "group-think" technique is to generate the greatest number of alternative ideas from uninhibited responses. Nothing is rejected or criticized. Any attempt to analyze, reject or evaluate ideas is prohibited during the brainstorming process. Free wheeling is desired and combinations or extensions and improvements of ideas are encouraged during the session. The group is instructed to strive for a large quantity of ideas rather than high quality ideas.

The maximum size of a brainstorming group is about seven. Any larger-sized group does not allow every member to participate equally. Ideally, the group should be heterogeneous in member backgrounds and personalities. Careful group management is usually required in order to maintain the effectiveness of the group. The group leader must be sure that no one stops to evaluate the ideas as they are generated. If this happens, it usually shuts off the further flow of ideas.

Reverse brainstorming may be useful preparation for a brainstorming session, or it may be used in conjunction with it. This approach consists of purging or tearing down the ideas. This sometimes prepares the group for serious efforts at innovative thinking. A typical reverse brainstorming session would begin by listing all the things that are wrong with an operation, process, system, product or entity. Then each flaw is systematically examined for ways to overcome, improve or correct it. This part of the exercise is run as a brainstorming session. In using the reverse brainstorming technique, great care and sensitivity is required of the group leader. The negative ambience of the tearing-down process may completely override the group's optimism and sap their effectiveness.

6.3.2.2 Association Methods. In the free association method the subjects freely jot down ideas, pictures or symbols as they come to mind. The session begins with a problem statement and a list of problem characteristics or attributes. Then, the subjects have a timed session in which they intensely write down as many thoughts as they can. This is followed by a session in which they exchange and discuss what they have written and list their results for all to see. Then a second writing period is undertaken in which the subjects build upon their previous results. Any number of cycles of written and discussion periods may be conducted. If only one subject is carrying out the exercise, then either the discussion session is abandoned or the ideas can be discussed with a panel of colleagues. This method is also called "brain-writing."

In the forced association approach, a chain of ideas is sought through the rigid application of a three-step process. In the first step, the elements of the problem are isolated and the basic dimensions of the problem are listed. In the second step, the relationships (similarities, differences, analogies or cause-effects) are sought among these dimensions. Finally, the relationships are analyzed for new ideas. An example is given in Table 6.5.

6.3.2.3 The Gordon Method. In this approach the session leader is the only one who knows the actual problem. The leader stimulates the group to think out loud about some topic that is fundamentally related to the real problem. For example, if the real problem were to develop a new automobile style, the session leader might focus on "travel." The leader would first focus the discussion on aspects somewhat remote from the actual problem, then on aspects closer to it, and finally on aspects very close to the actual problem. At the end of these discussions the problem is revealed to the group and they analyze the tape recording of their discussions for possible idea "hooks." Each idea hook is then brainstormed to develop a solution to the actual problem.

The intent of the Gordon method is to avoid a premature focus or a habit pattern that would lead to trite solutions. Experience suggests that, like brainstorming, the method works best where the group is heterogeneous in backgrounds and personalities. An obvious limitation of this method is that it is highly dependent on the ability of the session leader to recognize potential idea hooks and to otherwise manage the group.

Table 6.5. Example of the forced association method.

Problem: Develop a Portable Cleanser for Travel or Picnic Applications

Step I. Elements
　　　　Cleanser; cleanliness; sanitariness; soapy; dry; portable; quick-dry

Step II. Relationships
　　　　Clean and dry; dry-cleaner; solvent cleaner; wet and dry towel

Step III. Analysis
　　　　Soap chips; carbonated soap chips; soap impregnated papers; paper that preferentially absorbs dirt; solvent impregnated paper; sandwich paper that is soapy on one side and dry on the other.

6.3.2.4 Synectics. In this approach, creative solutions to problems are generated through the three-stage process outlined in Figure 6.4. In the first stage, participants consciously reverse the order of things and "make the strange familiar," through analysis, generalization, and model-seeking. In the second stage, an attempt is made to "make the familiar strange," through personal analogy, direct analogy, symbolic analogy and fantasy analogy. The first stage of the Synectics process attempts to move the subjects to new mental domains. The second stage then builds on these new domains, using processes that are familiar and well-known to the subjects.

An often-used example of a Synectics session concerns its application to develop a new bottle closure device.[9] Stage I focused the group discussions around the concepts of "tightness" and "effectiveness of closure." The discussions generated several new thoughts about the meanings of these concepts. Stage II focused on the use of analogies with the iris of the human eye, the way that a clam shell closes and opens, and other known phenomena. A force fit exercise (Stage III) was then undertaken, in which the group was directed to focus on the use of their awareness of the human iris to devise a plastic closure device. From this exercise, the group suggested a thermos bottle with a rubber sleeve that would close as the top was twisted. One participant suggested the key analogy that spawned this idea: the device was like twisting a balloon at both ends to close down its middle.

6.3.2.5 The CNB Method. In the CNB (Collective Notebook) method, each participant receives a prepared notebook containing the problem

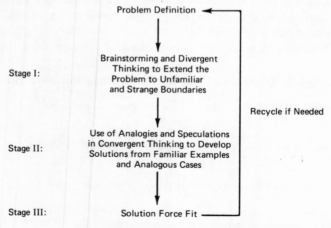

Figure 6.4. The Synectics approach.

statement in very broad terms and space to keep a diary of thoughts and ideas. At the end of a specified time period the notebooks are collected and given to a coordinator who prepares a detailed summary of all the notebooks. These summaries are then discussed by all the parties in a final creative session in which brainstorming, Synectics, etc. techniques may be used. The CNB technique enables a number of individual ideas to be developed and documented, which then benefit from a group evaluation. The format of the CNB method consists of an individual ideational period followed by a group evaluation. This format has been found to be superior to other behavioral formats for conducting creativity sessions.[7] However, the notebook coordinator must be especially skilled in organizing and summarizing the materials. The individuals must also have great trust and confidence that the coordinator will correctly represent their ideas. It is likely that much better results will be obtained where the individuals each present their own ideas in a final creative session.

6.3.3   Managing Generating Groups

Highly trained scientists and engineers tend to be their own worst enemies in creativity exercises and solution generating groups. Their training and prior successes often compel them to avoid things that seem silly, irrational or fanciful. Yet these are precisely the by-ways of the mind that can lead to innovative ideas. An avoidance of the fanciful and irrational leads to dull, boring and useless group sessions. In order to guard against this, the group must be properly constituted, structured and guided. Experiences indicate that the group should consist of at least one resident expert in the technology or topic being discussed. There should also be one persuader, one confronter, one helper and one dreamer. The resident expert supplies the depth of technological knowledge. The persuader is a friendly personality who persistently persuades the group to accept ideas and approaches on the basis of their inherent logic. The confronter is the hardnosed personality who will not let anything remain hidden under the rug. The dreamer supplies the far-out fanciful inputs. The helper maintains the group processes by periodically pausing with the group to take stock on where they are going and what they have achieved. The presence of each personality type in the group adds essential ingredients. Each offsets and complements the other. In addition to the above members, a process leader and a client should be present. These persons are not group members. They are outside helpers. The process leader is the expert on dealing with and guiding groups. The process leader monitors the group dynamics and provides periodic steerage and feedback to the group on whether or not they are being too passive, too confrontive, etc. The client is the person who will use the group's outputs. The client supplies factual knowledge to the participants and provides the criteria for judging the "goodness" of the ideas which are generated.

6.4 SUMMARY

No decision can be any better than the preparation that goes into it. The careful definition of problems, opportunities and alternatives is a critical aspect of this preparation. The exception principle, the deviation check and the management audit may be used to assist in problem definition. A pro-active posture of seeking out weaknesses and potential problems before they actually occur is the most effective approach for coping with today's rapidly changing society. A pro-active posture is absolutely necessary for the timely identification of emerging opportunities. Many environmental monitoring and technological forecasting techniques are available to help the decision maker identify opportunities.

The generation of creative solution alternatives is especially important to effective decision making. Insufficient emphasis is usually placed on generating a wide diversity of alternative solutions. The quality of the final decision can only be as good as the quality of the field of choices available. Several analytical techniques and creativity methods are available to assist the decision maker in generating alternative solutions. Training, careful selection of group members and proper group management methods are needed in order to be successful in using many of these techniques.

6.5 REFERENCES

1. Swager, W. "Perspective Trees," in *A Guide to Practical Technology Forecasting*, J. R. Bright and Milton Shoeman (eds.), Englewood Cliffs, New Jersey: Prentice-Hall, Inc., 1973.
2. Gordon, T. J. "Cross-Impact Matrices: An Illustration of their Use for Policy Analysis." *Futures*, 1, No. 6: 527–531 (1969).
3. Cetron, M. J. "Quest Status Report." *IEEE Trans. on Eng. Mgt.*, EM-14, No. 1: 51–62 (1967).
4. Souder, W. E. *Synopsis of A Series of Studies Aimed at Understanding and Encouraging Processes for the Adoption and Diffusion of Longwalls*. U.S. Department of Energy Final Report, September 7, 1978.
5. Wheelwright, S. C. and Makridakis, Spyros. *Forecasting Methods for Management*. New York: John Wiley & Sons, Inc., 1977, pp. 71–130; 143–151.
6. Forrester, Jay W. *Industrial Dynamics*. Cambridge, Massachusetts: MIT Press, 1961.
7. Souder, W. E. "Effectiveness of Nominal and Interacting Group Decision Processes for Integrating R&D and Marketing." *Management Science*, 23, No. 6: 595–605 (1977).
8. Souder, W. E. and Zeigler, R. W. "A Review of Creativity and Problem Solving Techniques." *Research Management*, 20, No. 4: 34–42 (1977).
9. Prince, G. M. *The Practice of Creativity*. New York: Harper & Row, 1970, pp. 60–78.

6.6 BIBLIOGRAPHY

Beach, L. R. and Mitchell, T. R. "A Contingency Model for The Selection of Decision Strategies." *Academy of Management Review*, July 1978, pp. 439–449.

Brown, R. V.; Kahr, A. S.; and Peterson, C. R. *Decision Analysis: An Overview*. New York: Holt, Rinehart and Winston, Inc., 1974.

Cetron, M. J. and Bartoka, Bodo (eds.). *Technology Assessment in a Dynamic Environment*. New York: Gordon and Breach, Science Publishers, Inc., 1973.

Craver, J. K. and Wharton, F. D., Jr. "Technology Assessment in Product Development." *Chemtech*, September 1975, pp. 547–551.

Lanford, H. W. "A Penetration of the Technological Forecasting Jungle." *Technological Forecasting and Social Change*, **4**, No. 2: 207–225 (1972).

MacCrimmon, K. R. and Taylor, R. N. "Decision Making and Problem Solving," in *Handbook of Organizational and Industrial Psychology*. Chicago: Rand McNally & Company, 1976, pp. 1397–1454.

Makridakis, Spyros and Wheelwright, S. C. *Interactive Forecasting*. San Francisco: Holden-Day, Inc., 1977.

Martino, Joseph. *Technological Forecasting for Decision Making*. New York: American Elsevier Publishing Co., Inc., 1972.

Mitroff, I. I. and Turoff, Murray. "Technological Forecasting and Assessment: Science and/or Mythology?" *Technological Forecasting and Social Change*, **5**, No. 1: 113–134 (1973).

Nutt, P. C. "Models for Decision Making in Organizations and Some Contextual Variables which Stipulate Optimal Use." *Academy of Management Review*, **1**, No. 2: 84–98 (1976).

Osborn, A. F. *Applied Imagination*. New York: Charles Scribner's Sons, 1963.

Prince, G. M. *The Practice of Creativity*. New York: Harper & Row, 1970.

Summers, T. and White, D. E. "Creativity and the Decision Process." *Academy of Management Review*, **1**, No. 2: 99–108 (April 1976).

The Futures Group. *A Technology Assessment of Geothermal Energy Resource Development*. NSF Final Report C-836, April 15, 1975.

Wheelwright, S. C. and Makridakis, Spyros. *Forecasting Methods for Management*. New York: John Wiley & Sons, Inc., 1977.

Young, J. W. "Some Conceptual Comments on Trust-Relevant Decision Making: A Reaction to the Bonoma and Johnson Paper," *Decision Sciences*, **10**, No. 1: 57–59 (1979).

7

Economic Evaluation of Alternatives

7.0 INTRODUCTION

The analysis and evaluation of the alternatives provides the data base and the information for making a final decision. In order to provide the decision maker with the greatest amount and the highest quality of information, the alternatives should be analyzed and evaluated with regard to their values, benefits, costs, regrets and risk characteristics. In some cases these aspects can be measured in economic or dollar terms. In other cases, only noneconomic and judgmental evaluations are possible.

This chapter focuses on economic methods for evaluating and analyzing alternatives. Present worth, return on investment and cost-benefit techniques are presented and illustrated.

7.1 ECONOMIC ANALYSIS CONCEPTS

There is an old saying that "money begets more money over time." Indeed, most of us expect that if we put aside a sum of money in a bank or savings institution, that sum will appreciate over time. These beliefs and expectations are manifestations of the *time value of money*. The idea that money has a time value is closely related to the opportunity cost idea that money can always be put to some productive use. The opportunity cost is the income lost because the money was idle, rather than productively employed.

7.1.1 Equivalence Concepts

Because money has a time value, having a dollar today may not be equivalent in worth to having a dollar a year from now. In fact, at an annual interest rate of $i\%$, the present worth of $1.00 today is equivalent to a future worth of $1.00 + ($1.00 \times i\%$). This is the equivalence concept. It has nothing to do with risk and inflation. Even in an inflationless and

100

riskless situation most investors feel that money should appreciate over time.

It is this time value of money that prohibits us from combining or comparing raw dollar values taken from different time periods. For example, suppose you are given a choice between two competing projects, A and B, both of which require the same investment and yield the same profits. But suppose project A returns its profits 2 years sooner than project B. You cannot be indifferent about the choice of A versus B. The earlier returns from project A have a time-related value which arise from your ability to use these funds productively. In short, projects A and B cannot be compared on a monetary basis until the monetary data are converted to equivalent values.

7.1.2 Equivalencing Factors

The present worth and the future worth of a lump sum of money are equivalenced as follows, where i is an interest rate:

$$\overbrace{F = P(1 + i)^n}^{caf} \tag{7.1}$$

Present Worth (P) of a Lump Sum   Future Worth (F) of a Lump Sum

$$P = F\underbrace{\left(\frac{1}{[1 + i]^n}\right)}_{pwf} \tag{7.2}$$

A present worth P is equivalenced to a future worth F at the end of n years hence by the compound amount factor or caf, which is $(1 + i)^n$. Similarly, a future worth is equivalenced to a present worth by a present worth factor or pwf (often called the discount factor, or ρ). For example, \$1,000 invested for 10 years at 6% interest per year, compounded annually, will appreciate to $F = \$1,000 (1.06)^{10} = \$1,790$. Alternatively, the equivalent present worth of \$1,790 to be received 10 years hence is $P = \$1,790/(1.06)^{10} = \$1,000$.

In the case where there is a stream of annual amounts $A_1, A_2, \ldots A_n$ invested at the start of years 1, 2, . . . n then this stream of investments will appreciate to:

$$F = A_1(1 + i)^n + A_2 (1 + i)^{n-1} + \ldots + A_n(1 + i). \tag{7.3}$$

In the special case where $A_1 = A_2 = \ldots = A_n = $ A, then Equation (7.3) reduces to:

$$F = A\left(\frac{[1 + i]^n - 1}{i}\right).\qquad(7.4)$$

Then in general:

$$\text{Series } caf$$
$$F = A\left(\frac{[1 + i]^n - 1}{i}\right)\qquad(7.5)$$

Equivalent
A Values

Future Worth (F)
of a Series
of A Values

$$A = F\left(\underbrace{\frac{i}{[1 + i]^n - 1}}_{sff}\right)\qquad(7.6)$$

The factor $(i/[1 + i]^n - 1)$ is called a sinking fund factor or *sff* because the stream of A values represents a sinking fund—a stream established or "sunk" to produce a desired equivalent F, after a prescribed time period n. (The terminology here is perhaps a bit archaic. A better name for this factor might be the commitment fund factor or the growing-fund factor.[1,2]) Equations (7.5) and (7.6) are analogous to Equations (7.1) and (7.2), respectively. Finally, by substituting $P(1 + i)^n$ for F in Equation (7.4) and rearranging we can derive Equations (7.7) and (7.8):

$$\text{crf}$$
$$A = P\left(\frac{i\,[1 + i]^n}{[1 + i]^n - 1}\right)\qquad(7.7)$$

Present Worth (P)
of a Series
of A Values .

Equivalent
A Values

$$P = A\left(\frac{[1 + i]^n - 1}{i\,[1 + i]^n}\right)\qquad(7.8)$$
$$\text{Series } pwf$$

The factor $\left(\dfrac{i[1 + i]^n}{[1 + i]^n - 1}\right)$ is called the capital recovery factor or *crf* because it gives the stream of withdrawals of capital plus interest supplied over time period n by an equivalent P, when invested at $i\%$ per year.

7.1.3   Choice of Interest Rate[1,2]

Theoretically, the appropriate interest rate to use in Equations (7.1) through (7.8) is the opportunity cost of capital rate. That is, i is the prevailing interest rate that could be earned elsewhere. However, there is no one single interest rate that is always used in Equations (7.1) through (7.8). For instance, if the decision maker is lending money, then i will be the prevailing or market rate for lending one's own money. If the decision maker is borrowing money, then i will be the prevailing or market rate for borrowing someone else's money. These rates are seldom the same, e.g., a bank will charge a borrower a higher rate than they will pay a depositor.

If a firm is financing a new investment from internally generated funds, then i may be set to the average return on current investments. The logic of this is based on the opportunity cost concept. The current investments may represent the best available alternative. And this new investment should earn at least that much. Or, i may be set at some target level above the return on current investments. This would be the case where management wishes to "discount" future earnings more heavily than current and past earnings. For example, suppose a new investment is expected to produce a stream of future earnings $A_1, A_2, \ldots$ and i is the current return on investment rate. If this new investment is more risky than the current ones, management may feel that a risk premium of k should be added to bring the target rate up to $i + k$. In essence, this target rate is the level that management feels they would have to receive in order to be induced to take the added risk of the new investment.

7.1.4   Handling the Factors

Equivalencing factors are best thought of as devices for converting given variables into desired variables. For example, given a present value P, if a series value A is desired the equivalencing factor is the *crf*. If the user recalls from Equation (7.7) that the *crf* is the A/P ratio, then label cancellation techniques can be used to set up the proper computations. As an example, suppose an individual wishes to ascertain a ten-year retirement annuity plan based on an initial investment of $84,000 at 6% interest per year. Hence, P is the given variable and A is the desired variable:

$$\begin{pmatrix} \text{Desired} \\ \text{Variable} \end{pmatrix} = \begin{pmatrix} \text{Given} \\ \text{Variable} \end{pmatrix} \times \begin{pmatrix} \text{factor} \end{pmatrix} \tag{7.9}$$

$$A \quad = \quad P \quad \times \quad (A/P). \tag{7.10}$$

Table 7.1, which gives the corresponding algebraic factors for each ratio label, shows that $A/P = [i(1 + i)^n]/[(1 + i)^n - 1]$. Table 7.2, which presents the values of the factors for selected i and n values, shows that for $i = .06$ and $n = 10$ this factor has a value of .136. Hence, continuing from Equation (7.10) we obtain:

$$A = \$84,000\left(\frac{.06\,[1 + .06]^{10}}{[1 + .06]^{10} - 1}\right)$$

$$= \$84,000(.136) = \$11,424. \tag{7.11}$$

Thus, $11,424 is the amount an individual can expect to withdraw at the end of each year for ten years from an escrow account of $84,000, and have a zero balance at the end of the tenth year.

Tabled values of all the factors listed in Table 7.1 are available for a wide range of i and n values.[1,2,3] These tables economize on the amount of calculating time and effort required in handling the factors.

Table 7.1. Equivalencing factors.

DESIRED VARIABLE	GIVEN VARIABLE	ALGEBRAIC FACTOR	RATIO LABEL	NAME	EQUATION
F	P	$(1 + i)^n$	F/P	caf	7.1
P	F	$1/(1 + i)^n$	P/F	pwf	7.2
A	F	$i/(1 + i)^n - 1$	A/F	sff	7.6
A	P	$(i[1 + i]^n)/([1 + i]^n - 1)$	A/P	crf	7.7
F	A	$([1 + i]^n - 1)/i$	F/A	series caf	7.5
P	A	$([1 + i]^n - 1)/(i[1 + i]^n)$	P/A	series pwf	7.8

Table 7.2. Illustration of tabled values.*

n	F/P	P/F	A/F	A/P	F/A	P/A
			$i = .06$			
8	1.59	.627	.101	.161	9.89	6.21
10	1.79	.558	.0760	(.136)	13.2	7.36
12	2.01	.497	.0591	.119	16.8	8.38
			$i = .08$			
8	1.86	.540	.0941	.174	10.7	5.75
10	2.16	.463	.0690	.149	14.5	(6.71)
12	2.52	(.397)	.0526	.133	18.9	(7.54)

* Circled values are used in the calculations in equations (7.11), (7.13) and (7.14).

7.2 ECONOMIC ANALYSIS MODELS

In general, an alternative will be the best choice if it "produces" an annuity stream of payments that is economically better than the next best alternative choice. If it is not better, then the decision maker incurs an opportunity cost if it is selected. The opportunity cost is the amount by which the investment is inferior. For example, if it returns $5,000 less than the alternative of putting the money in a bank, then the decision maker who selects it incurs a $5,000 opportunity cost. It is not always illogical to purposely incur opportunity costs in the short run, e.g., starting up a new business. But the decision maker who unwittingly takes such paper losses over the long term may eventually end up in very poor financial shape.

7.2.1 The PW Model

The present worth (PW) model is a very widely used economic analysis model. This model is:

$$P = A\ (P/A) + S\ (P/F) \tag{7.12}$$

where P is the present worth, A is the annual cash flow and S is a salvage value.

To illustrate this model, suppose a decision maker has two alternative choices, plan 1 and plan 2. Both plans cost the same. Plan 1 will generate an annual cash flow of $5,000 per year for ten years. Plan 2 will generate an annual cash flow of $4,000 per year for twelve years. And plan 2 will also return a lump sum of $11,000 in the twelfth year. Let us assume an interest rate of 8%. Then the present worths of the two plans are respectively:

$$P_1 = \$5,000\ (P/A)$$

$$= \$5,000 \left(\frac{[1 + .08]^{10} - 1}{.08[1 + .08]^{10}} \right)$$

$$= \$5,000\ (6.71)$$

$$= \$33,550. \tag{7.13}$$

$$P_2 = \$4,000\ (P/A) + \$11,000\ (P/F)$$

$$+ \$4,000 \left(\frac{[1 + .08]^{12} - 1}{.08[1 + .08]^{12}} \right) + \$11,000 \left(\frac{1}{[1 + .08]^{12}} \right)$$

$$= \$4,000\ (7.54) + \$11,000\ (.397)$$

$$= \$34,527. \tag{7.14}$$

Hence, plan 2 is the superior plan (though only by a small amount).

7.2.2   Return on Investment Models: IRR and NPV

The PW model is concerned with returns. Return on investment models are concerned with investments and returns.

Algebraic rearrangement of Equation (7.12) gives:

$$0 = -P + A \left(\frac{[1 + i]^n - 1}{i[1 + i]^n} \right) + S \left(\frac{1}{[1 + i]^n} \right). \tag{7.15}$$

For any given n, Equation (7.15) may be solved for i^*, the optimum value of i. This value, i^*, is the internal rate of return (IRR) of the investment P. And Equation (7.15) is the IRR model.

Now, if any $i \neq i^*$ is used in Equation (7.15) the left hand side will not be zero. In general, for any interest rate, say $\hat{i} \neq i^*$, Equation (7.15) becomes:

$$N = -P + A \left(\frac{[1 + \hat{i}]^n - 1}{i[1 + \hat{i}]_n} \right) + S \left(\frac{1}{[1 + \hat{i}]^n} \right). \tag{7.16}$$

The value N is the net present value (NPV) of the investment P. And Equation (7.16) is the NPV model.

In cases where the annual returns are not equal, then Equation (7.15) and (7.16) do not apply. Instead of Equation (7.15) the following equation applies:

$$0 = -P + F_1 \left(\frac{1}{[1 + i]} \right) + F_2 \left(\frac{1}{[1 + i]^2} \right) +$$

$$\cdots + S \left(\frac{1}{[1 + i]^n} \right), \tag{7.17}$$

where F_1, F_2, etc. are the annual returns for future years 1, 2, etc., and S is a salvage value in year n. Similarly, the following equation replaces Equation (7.16):

$$N = -P + F_1 \left(\frac{1}{1 + \hat{i}} \right) + F_2 \left(\frac{1}{[1 + \hat{i}]^2} \right) +$$

$$\cdots + S \left(\frac{1}{[1 + \hat{i}^n]} \right). \tag{7.18}$$

7.2.3   Comparison of Return on Investment Models

Table 7.3 presents cash flow data for three hypothetical investment alternatives, A, B and C. All three require the same level of investment ($100,000) and all three have the same total net cash flow. However, they differ with respect to the time distribution of these flows. Because of this, the net present values of the three alternatives differ as shown in Table 7.4. For the sake of illustration, $\hat{i}$ is set to 10% here. Equation (7.18) was used to compute these values.

Table 7.5 compares the three alternatives on the basis of four common return on investment (ROI) models. The payback period is the number of years required to recoup the investment, on a dollar cash flow basis. The ROI is the sum of the *net* dollar returns (that is, the total returns minus the investment) divided by the investment. For example, for proposal A, the % ROI is:

$$\frac{(\$25 + \$75 + \$100) - \$100}{\$100} \times 100\% = 100\%. \tag{7.19}$$

The i^* values were computed from Equation (7.17). For example, for alternative C,

$$0 = -\$100 + \frac{\$25}{(1 + i)^3} + \frac{\$75}{(1 + i)^4} + \frac{\$100}{(1 + i)^5}, \tag{7.20}$$

and solving yields $i^* = 17\%$.

Which model is best? Clearly, the % ROI criterion is not sufficient. It does not distinguish between the different time shape of the returns for alternatives A, B and C. Although the payback model is somewhat sensitive to the time lag between the investment and the returns (e.g., alternative A versus C), it is not sensitive to the time shape (e.g., alternative A versus B). Nor is it influenced by the shape or magnitude of any returns that occur beyond the recovery of the initial investment (returns greater than $100,000 in this case). The NPV model, Equation (7.16), and the IRR

Table 7.3. Data for three hypothetical projects.

	DOLLAR CASH FLOWS OF THE ALTERNATIVES $(000)			
	EOY *	A	B	C
	Investment =	$-100	$-100	$-100
	1	+25	0	0
	2	+75	+100	0
Returns	3	+100	+75	+25
	4	0	+25	+75
	5	0	0	+100
Total Net Cash Flow =		$100	$100	$100

* EOY = End of Year

Table 7.4. Net present values of the data in Table 7.3.

PRESENT VALUES OF THE ALTERNATIVES $(000) at $\hat{i}$ = 10%

	EOY	A	B	C
	Investment =	$-100	$-100	$-100
	1	+22.72	0	0
Present	2	+61.98	+82.65	0
Value	3	+75.13	+56.34	+18.78
Returns	4	0	+17.07	+51.22
	5	0	0	+62.09
Net Present Value =		$59.83	$56.06	$32.09

model, Equation (7.15), do not have any of these deficiencies. They are the theoretically correct models to apply.

The NPV and IRR models are algebraically equivalent. The difference is that the NPV model uses a given value $\hat{i}$ for i, whereas the IRR model solves for i^*, a particular value for i. If the NPV model is evaluated using the i^* value for $\hat{i}$, the NPV will be zero. For example, if the NPV computation was repeated for alternative A using $\hat{i}$ = 37%, the NPV would be zero. Why, then, do we have both models? The answer is simple. In some situations management may have specified a minimum acceptable rate of return (MARR). This could be either the firm's opportunity cost of capital or some rate which effectively serves as a cutoff rate. Where an MARR exists, the NPV can be calculated using $\hat{i}$ = MARR. If the value of the NPV is negative, the project is unacceptable.[4] For example, the NPV for alternative C will be negative for MARR = $\hat{i}$ > 17%.

The payback method, in spite of its serious inadequacies, often must be given some consideration. Let us take the extreme illustration of a cash-poor firm. An investment alternative with exponentially increasing re-

Table 7.5. Comparison of four common models.

	ALTERNATIVES		
MODELS	A	B	C
%ROI [a]	100%	100%	100%
Payback [b]	2 yrs.	2 yrs.	4 yrs.
NPV (@$\hat{i}$ = 10%), N =	$59.83	$56.06	$32.09
IRR, i^*	37%	32%	17%

Conclusion: A is preferred to B is preferred to C.

[a] %ROI = ([Σ positive cash flows − investment] ÷ investment) × 100%.
[b] Payback = number of years required to recoup the investment, in raw (undiscounted) dollar amounts.

turns that start in year eight may be rejected in favor of a more modest project whose returns begin immediately. Even though the IRR of the former project might be quite superior, the firm may be compelled to select the more modest alternative because it cannot afford to wait for the payback. Hence, in most cases either the IRR or the NPV is the primary model, with secondary consideration given to the payback period.

7.3   BENEFIT/COST METHODS

Benefit-cost or cost-benefit methods (the terms are used interchangeably) consist of a body of techniques for comparing alternatives in terms of their costs and economic benefits, relative to the achievement of specific goals and objectives. Cost-benefit methods help the decision maker decide which of several alternatives are the most profitable.

The cost-benefit approach consists of three fundamental steps. First, each alternative is assessed in terms of its life cycle costs and its benefits (see Chapter 3 for some methods and techniques). Second, a benefit/cost index or similar model is constructed to measure the relative worth per dollar cost of the alternatives. Third, this index is applied and integrated with other methods of analysis, such as sensitivity analyses or dominance checks (see Chapter 4).

7.3.1   The Benefit/Cost Index

The benefit/cost index R_j is given by

$$R_j = B_j/C_j,   \tag{7.21}$$

where B_j is the benefit and C_j is the cost of the jth alternative. When benefits and costs are measured in dollar amounts then

$$B_j = B_{jt}/[1 + i]^t   \tag{7.22}$$

and

$$C_j = C_{js}/[1 + r]^s .   \tag{7.23}$$

Here, B_{jt} and C_{js} are the dollar benefits and costs in some future time periods $t = 1, 2, . . . n$ and $s = 1, 2, . . . m$. And i and r are the appropriate interest rates for discounting benefits and costs. In most cases, the benefits will occur later in time than the costs, e.g., the costs are incurred in order to obtain the benefits. Hence, an allowance is made in this model for the two different time horizons t and s. The allowance for two different interest rates i and r permits appropriate present worth computations to be carried out. For example, the stream of future benefits can be converted to present worth benefits using the average return on investment rate i. The stream of future costs can be converted to present worth costs using the borrowing cost rate r.

Benefits may be measured in nondollar terms, e.g., through the use of Q-sorting, successive ratings or other techniques presented in Chapter 3. Then B_j becomes an index number B_j^*. Combined dollar and nondollar indexes may be constructed such as $(W_1 B_j^* + W_2 B_j)/C_j$, where W_1 and W_2 are appropriately chosen weighting factors. It is not unusual for a decision maker to have several different goals or criteria for judging the alternatives. Then a composite benefit index $\hat{B}_j = \Sigma W_i B_{ij}$ may be constructed and used. Here B_{ij} is the benefit of the jth alternative on the ith criterion, W_i is the importance weight of the ith criterion and $\hat{B}_j$ is the composite benefit of the jth alternative. Chapter 9 contains a more complete discussion of these procedures. Sometimes, disadvantages or externalities may accompany the desired outcomes. An example is the increased environmental pollution that may accompany increased industrial outputs. These aspects are usually represented as disbenefits and they are subtracted from the benefits, e.g., the benefit/cost ratio becomes $(B_j - d_j)/C_j$, where d_j is the total of the disbenefits for alternative j.

An alternative may have one or several benefit/cost ratios. If the alternative has several versions, or if it can be funded at several different levels, then there may be a corresponding different benefit for each cost level. An example is a new product whose quality may vary with the amount spent on its development. In such cases there is a functional relationship between the benefits and the costs. The form of this functional relationship may be dichotomous, stepwise or continuous. These three cases are illustrated in Figure 7.1. In the dichotomous case the funding alternatives are either zero or C_j (the cost of the item). Similarly, the benefit is either zero or B_j. In the stepwise case, there are several funding levels: the item may cost C_{j1}, C_{j2}, C_{j3}, etc. There are corresponding benefit numbers B_{j1}, B_{j2}, B_{j3}, etc. In the continuous case, $B_j = f(C_j)$, where C_j is a continuous variable. In the continuous case, a point of diminishing returns will usually be reached where continuing to put funds into the alternative does not result in any increased level of benefit. This may happen even though the goal has not been completely achieved.

If the benefits and costs are not known with certainty, or if there is some likelihood that the targeted benefits will not be achieved, then probabilistic measures may be incorporated into the benefit/cost index. For example, Equation (7.21) may be changed to $(p_j B_j)/C_j$ where p_j is the probability that benefits B_j will actually occur. In other cases the benefits may be represented as a probability distribution of the form shown in Figure 7.2. Then the benefit/cost index will be $R_j = f(B_j/C_j)$, which will be

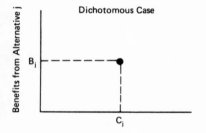

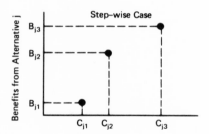

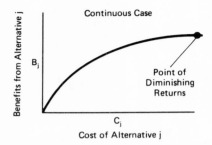

Figure 7.1. Illustration of benefit/cost functions.

a distribution shaped similar to the one in Figure 7.2. Then the likelihood $p(R_j \geq X)$ that the benefit/cost ratio will meet or exceed some targeted level X can be computed from this distribution. In particular, if there are two alternatives A and B and $p(R_A \geq X) > p(R_B \geq X)$, then alternative A is the better of the two alternatives.

7.3.2 Using the Benefit/Cost Index

The alternatives may be ranked in descending order of their benefit/cost ratios. The best alternative is the one with the largest benefit/cost index, the second best alternative is the one with the next largest benefit/cost index, etc. If the benefit/cost index is given as a distribution for each alternative, then the alternatives may be ranked in terms of parameters of this distribution. For example, the alternatives may be ranked in terms of their means, their confidence intervals, or the $p(R_j \geq X)$ values.

In general, for any j^{th} alternative that exhibits

$$R_j = B_j/C_j \leq 1.0, \tag{7.24}$$

or if

$$R_j = B_j - C_j \leq 0, \tag{7.25}$$

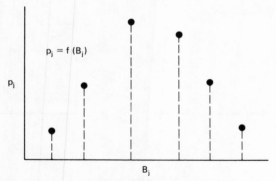

Figure 7.2. Probability function of benefits.

then that alternative should *not* be selected. Or, in the case where a distribution is being used, if

$$p(R_j \geqslant X) = 0 \tag{7.26}$$

where X is a target or a minimum level, then the jth alternative should not be chosen.

These decision rules may be modified somewhat to adjust to particular decision makers and special circumstances. For example, when the value of Equation (7.25) is negative, the alternative may nevertheless still be accepted in order to achieve some long run noneconomic goals. As another example, the decision maker may only be interested in achieving a satisfactory level of performance. Then any alternative which meets the condition $R_j \geqslant S$ is acceptable, where S is the satisfactory level.

Every decision that is based on benefit/cost computations should be carefully checked for the influence of estimation errors. Estimation errors are likely to occur in cost and benefit measurement, and their impacts on the decision should be carefully checked. The error estimation methods presented in Chapter 3 may be helpful here. Bayesian analyses can also often be used, as illustrated in Chapter 3.

In general, the application of probabilistic techniques to benefit/cost analyses is often especially enlightening. As an illustration, consider a cost-benefit study on water desalinization which was recently completed.[5] Four alternative plants were designed for a process to convert salt water to desalinized condensate. For each of these four plants, low medium and high development cost schedules were developed, representing the best judgments of the optimistic, most likely and pessimistic costs of the project. Direct primary benefits were computed in terms of the value of the expected increased agricultural outputs from new lands put into cultivation. Indirect primary benefits were added due to the expected increased

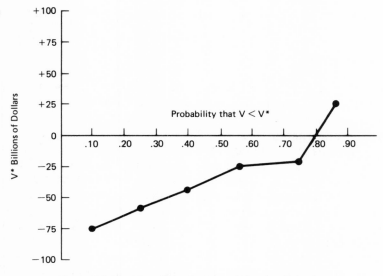

Figure 7.3. Cost-benefit analysis result for desalinization.

crops from irrigation with low-ion water, and from increased crops due to the alleviation of the risk of drought years. Secondary benefits were computed based on the estimated value of the new R&D spawned by the project and the money saved in farm subsidies that could be discontinued. The data were put into a net present dollar value criterion function $V = \Sigma([B_t - C_t]/[1 + r]^t)$, where V is the net present value of the project, B_t and C_t are the respective total benefits and costs in year t, and r is a discount rate. Six cases were used to develop a distribution, so that the data could be arrayed in terms of the probability that V would be less than some value V^*. As the results in Figure 7.3 show, the project was unattractive. There was a .80 probability that V would be less than $V^* = \$0$ and a .86 chance that V would be less than $V^* = \$25$ billion.

7.4 COST-EFFECTIVENESS METHODS

The terms cost-benefit and cost-effectiveness are sometimes used interchangeably. However, in the cost-effectiveness approach a target benefit level is given and the problem is to find the least-cost (most cost-effective) route to obtain these benefits. Thus, in a cost-benefit study both the benefits and the costs are variable and the problem is to find the optimum combination of benefits and costs. In a cost-effectiveness study, there is only one variable to be optimized: cost. Aside from this, the methodologies and approaches used are much the same in both types of analyses.

7.5 SUMMARY

This chapter has presented and illustrated several economic approaches and methods for evaluating and comparing alternatives. The analysis and comparison of decision alternatives provides the information and data on which a final decision may be based.

The difficulties encountered in applying these methods usually involve problems in data collection and specification. Much of the information is subjective and intuitive. On the one hand, there is some danger that a user will place more confidence in the numbers than they deserve. On the other hand, refining the data to exact precision is pointless if not impossible. Overall, the real value of economic analysis methods may come from the *process* of using them, even if they are not very precise. Assembling the cost data, estimates, projections and forecasts can create an awareness of the interrelatedness of the various decision elements and variables. This process can cause individuals to share opinions, viewpoints and information, and engage in problem-focused dialogues which they might not otherwise do. This may stimulate a greater awareness of the real decision problem and its alternative solutions.

7.6 REFERENCES

1. Fabrycky, W. J. and Thuesen, G. J. *Economic Decision Analysis*. Englewood Cliffs, New Jersey: Prentice-Hall, Inc., 1974, pp.41 –147; 359–382.
2. Canada, J. R. *Intermediate Economic Analysis For Management and Engineering*. Englewood Cliffs, New Jersey: Prentice-Hall, Inc., 1971, pp. 3–75; 319–352.
3. Barish, N. N. and Kaplan, Seymour. *Economic Analysis*. New York: McGraw-Hill, 1978, pp. 53–79; 182–207; 291–308.
4. If the cash flow data fluctuates widely, then multiple solutions may exist for Equation (7.15); that is, there may be more than one i^* value. For this reason, Equation (7.16) is generally the preferred model. However, both equations assume the returns are constantly reinvested at i^*. This is the "reinvestment fallacy," as described in Grant, E. L. and Ireson, W. G. *Principles of Engineering Economy*. New York: The Ronald Press Company, 1970, pp. 566–573.
5. Ben-Irion, David. "A Cost-Benefit Analysis of Sea Water Desalinization," paper presented at the First World Symposium on Energy Conservation, Rome, Italy, May 15–20, 1977.

7.7 BIBLIOGRAPHY

Barish, N. N. and Kaplan, Seymour. *Economic Analysis*. New York: McGraw-Hill, 1978.
DeNeufville, R. and Stafford, J. H. *Systems Analysis for Engineers and Managers*. New York: McGraw-Hill, 1971.

English, J. M. *Cost Effectiveness and Economic Evaluation of Engineering Systems.* New York: John Wiley & Sons, Inc., 1969.

Hatry, H. P. "Measuring the Effectiveness of Nondefense Public Programs." *Operations Research,* September-October 1970, pp. 772–784.

Reisman, Arnold. *Managerial and Engineering Economics.* Boston: Allyn & Bacon, Inc., 1971.

Stauffer, T. R.; Wyckoff, H. L.; and Palmer, R. S. "An Assessment of Economic Incentives for the Liquid Metel Fast Breeder Reactor," paper presented to the Breeder Reactor Corporation, Chicago, Illinois, March 7, 1975.

Tarquin, A. J. and Blank, L. T. *Engineering Economy.* New York: McGraw-Hill, 1976.

Thornton, V. D.; Francis, R. L.; and Lowe, T. J. "Rectangular Layout Problems with Worst-Case Distance Measures." *AIIE Transactions,* **11**, No. 1: 2–9 (1979).

8

Decision and Fault Trees

8.0 INTRODUCTION

A decision tree is a diagram that shows the decision points, the decision alternatives, the events and the outcomes. An example is shown in Figure 8.1. Diamond-shaped boxes represent decision points and circles represent points in time at which two or more events may occur. The decision alternatives and event outcomes are represented by branches in the tree. Such trees have been widely applied to equipment replacement, modernization and scale of operation decisions.[1] Decision trees are especially valuable for making the decision process more explicit, for forcing systematic analyses and for clarifying the risks and consequences of alternative actions. This chapter discusses the use of decision tree methods for analyzing decision alternatives. Multiple criteria analyses, sensitivity methods, dominance check methods and post-optimal analyses are illustrated.

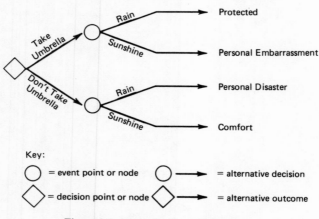

Figure 8.1. Example of a decision tree.

8.1 DECISION TREE METHODS

In order to illustrate the uses of decision trees, let us take the example in Figure 8.2. The decision problem concerns which alternative product version to develop and market. Either a low technology or a high technology grinder may be developed and marketed. The high technology grinder costs \$2M to develop (shown as C_H = \$2M in Figure 8.2) while the low technology verison only costs \$1M to develop (C_L = \$1M in Figure 8.2). However, the cheaper low technology product is more likely to encounter field failures. Engineering reliability tests indicate that the low technology product has a probability of .40 of encountering field failures (P_{LF} = .4 in Figure 8.2), while the high technology product has only a .20 probability (P_{HF} = .2). The probabilities that the high and low technology products will give fully satisfactory performances are thus, respectively, .80 and .60 (P_{HS} = .8 and P_{LS} = .6).

Because the high technology version is more efficient it will have a wider market appeal. A satisfactory performing high technology grinder is

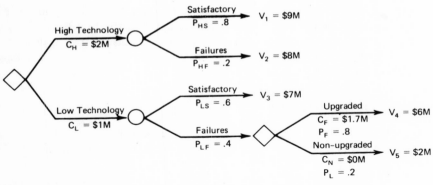

Key:

P_{HS} = probability that the high technology design will perform satisfactorily
P_{LS} = probability that the low technology design will perform satisfactorily
P_{HF} = probability that the high technology design will experience failures
P_{LF} = probability that the low technology design will experience failures
C_H = cost of the high technology design
C_L = cost of the low technology design
V_i = the market value (present worth of all future profits) of the ith outcome
C_F = cost of upgrading
C_N = cost for not upgrading
P_F = probability that upgrading can be done
P_L = probability that upgrading cannot be done

Figure 8.2. Decision tree for the grinder design problem.

thus estimated to have a market value (present worth of all future profits) of \$9M. This is shown as $V_1 = \$9M$ in Figure 8.2. This may be compared with the \$7M market value ($V_3 = \$7M$) for a satisfactory low technology product. Even if the high technology product encounters field failures, its market value ($V_2 = \$8M$) is expected to exceed the market value for a satisfactory low technology product. On the other hand, there is a .80 probability ($P_F = .8$) that the low technology product can be upgraded to satisfactory performance if it encounters field failures. But this upgraded product would have a market value that is only two-thirds as large ($V_4 = \$6M$) as the satisfactory high technology product. Furthermore, the upgrade would cost an additional \$1.7M ($C_F = \$1.7$) beyond the \$1M of original development costs. There is a small chance ($P_L = .2$) that the low technology product cannot be satisfactorily upgraded ($C_N = \$0$). If this turns out to be the case, then only a fraction of the total market ($V_5 = \$2M$) can be captured.

Thus, several questions arise in comparing the high versus low technology alternatives. Is the high technology version "worth" the extra development cost? Is the risk of failure so high with the low technology that it should not be chosen? Does the lower cost of the low technology offset its lower market value, thus making it a better choice than the high technology alternative? Is it worthwhile to upgrade the low technology product? These are the kinds of questions that a decision tree approach helps to answer. Let us now look at the various analyses that can be conducted to answer these questions.

8.1.1   Maximization Of NEV

Table 8.1 compares the high and low technology alternatives on the basis of their net expected market values (NEV). These computations are carried out according to the rules specified in Equation (3.7) of Chapter 3. The data in Table 8.1 show that the high technology grinder is the alternative with the highest net expected market value (NEV). Assuming that the maximization of NEV is the objective, then the high technology alternative should be selected.

However, this situation cannot be dispensed with this quickly. The answer is not quite so straightforward as simply selecting the alternative with the highest NEV. In the long run, the maximization of NEV is a correct economic pursuit. Yet this criterion is an average measure of goodness. Because it is an average, it may not reveal all the important things that are happening. Moreover, it is not the only important criterion to use in decision making. As we saw in Chapters 4 and 5, different

Table 8.1. Comparison of alternatives based on net expected value (NEV).

High Technology Alternative
$$NEV_H = (.8 \times \$9M + .2 \times \$8M) - \$2M = \$6.8M$$
Low Technology Alternative
$$NEV_L = (.6 \times \$7M + .4 [.8 \times \$6M + .2 \times \$2M]) - \$2.7M = \$3.58M$$
Conclusion: The High Technology Alternative is Better.

objectives may be pursued, depending on the decision settings. Let us now look at some other important decision criteria.

8.1.2 Return Per Dollar

The first two lines of Table 8.2 compare the high and low technology alternatives on the basis of their expected market values per dollar spent to obtain this reward. In the low technology calculation in the second line of Table 8.2, it is assumed that no attempt is made to upgrade the low technology if failures occur. Curiously, this non-upgraded low technology alternative gives the highest return per dollar spent! How can this be?

The answer is that this is an excellent illustration of what happens with averages like the NEV. As the data in the third line of Table 8.2 show, the upgrade is in fact the least productive use of the available funds. It is this incremental upgrade expenditure, with its low productivity, that depresses the result in the last line of Table 8.2. Note how the calculations in the third line of Table 8.2 are contained within the calculations in the last line of Table 8.2.

Thus, from an economic standpoint the upgrade is an inferior investment relative to the other alternatives. Of course, it may be that there are no better alternative uses for the $1.7M that the upgrade would cost. That is, the return per dollar for all the other available alternative applications of $1.7M may be less than 3.06 (Table 8.2). In that case, the upgrade may look more attractive. Even so, management would be wise to reconsider all the available alternatives, and to even consider holding onto the $1.7M in anticipation that better opportunities will arise. The difference between the return per dollar for non-upgraded and upgraded technologies is striking.

Thus, when the return per dollar cost (or the productivity) of the investment is considered, the non-upgraded low technology design is the best alternative. The high technology design is a close second.

Table 8.2. Return per dollar comparisons.

High Technology =
$\qquad$ (.8 × \$9M + .2 × \$8M)/\$2M = \$8.8M/\$2M = 4.4
Nonupgraded Low Technology =
$\qquad$ (.6 × \$7M + .4 × \$2M)/\$1M = \$5.0/\$1M = 5.0
Upgrade, by Itself =
$\qquad$ (.8 × \$6M + .2 × \$2M)/\$1.7M = \$5.2M/\$1.7M = 3.06
Upgraded Low Technology =
$\qquad$ (.6 × \$7M + .4 [.8 × \$6M + .2 × \$2M])/\$2.7M = \$6.28M/\$2.7M = 2.33

8.1.3 Regrets Analysis

There are several good reasons why a manager might decide to go ahead with the upgrade even though it is not economical. As one example, if the low technology version is chosen and if failures are encountered then the reputation of the company may be at stake. The manager may literally feel he cannot afford the risk of damage to the company's reputation. It may not be possible to predict the extent of this damage; e.g., this is decision making under a state of uncertainty. The damage could include much more than just the warranty costs on the grinder. The future loss of the company's markets may be at stake if this one experience causes customers to completely lose faith in the company. It may be extremely difficult to estimate the extent of this effect on the company's future. Long hours of debate may occur among the firm's executives without developing any exact damage estimates or resolving the issue of whether or not the upgrade should be carried out.

However, it is clear that the potential long term harm or "regrets" to the company could be much greater than the \$4M market value difference between upgrading and not upgrading that is shown in Figure 8.2 (compare V_5 vs. V_4). Thus, from the standpoint of a regrets analysis, if the low technology design is chosen the firm may want to keep \$1.7M in reserve against the contingency that the upgrade will be needed. Later in this chapter, a fault tree model is presented and illustrated for carrying out a more detailed regrets analysis in cases like this.

8.1.4 Opportunity Losses

Whichever alternative is chosen, only two outcomes are possible: satisfactory field performance or field failures. Suppose a satisfactory outcome occurs, and suppose the low technology alternative had been chosen and not upgraded. Then the market value would be \$9M − \$7M = \$2M less than if the high technology alternative had been chosen. However, \$2M −

$1M = $1M less funds would have been spent to develop and market the product. Thus, a *net opportunity loss* of $2M − $1M = $1M will occur under this set of circumstances. Table 8.3 presents the opportunity loss results for other circumstances. The analyses in Table 8.3 follow the methodology presented in Chapter 3 for computing the minimum opportunity loss strategy (see Equation [3.8]), and the strategies model in Chapter 4.

These analyses show that the high technology alternative is not only the minimum loss strategy, it is the *no-loss* strategy. If the high technology alternative is *not* selected, then the opportunity loss may range from small ($1M) to medium ($2.7M) to large ($5M). The size of the loss will depend on whether or not the low technology is upgraded, and whether or not a satisfactory performance is achieved. The net opportunity loss data in Table 8.3 show that the high technology alternative protects the decision maker from a substantial ($5M) opportunity loss in the event that failures occur. But it does not greatly increase ($1M) the rewards for satisfactory performance. However, the results show that in all cases the low technology alternative has at least some opportunity losses. The high technology alternative has no opportunity losses connected with it, under any of the circumstances.

The above calculations have followed the decision making strategies model (see Table 4.2 of Chapter 4). It is also useful to examine the *expected net opportunity losses* connected with the high and low technology alternatives. A comparison of these two alternatives shows that the low technology alternative has expected opportunity losses, under either the satisfactory or failures outcomes. These results are presented in Table 8.4. The calculations are carried out according to the rules specified in Chapter 3 for opportunity losses. The results in Table 8.4 confirm the results in Table 8.3. The low technology alternative carries some regret or opportunity loss under all outcomes.

Why do we need both of the analyses in Tables 8.3 and 8.4? The answer is that Table 8.3 shows the extremes. Table 8.3 is an *ex post* analysis. It

Table 8.3. Net opportunity loss (NOL) comparisons.

OUTCOME	NET OPPORTUNITY LOSS (NOL) FOR THE LOW TECHNOLOGY ALTERNATIVES		
	MARKET VALUES	COSTS	NOL
Satisfactory, Without Upgrade	($9M − $7M)	− ($2M − $1M)	= $1M
Failures, Without Upgrade	($8M − $2M)	− ($2M − $1M)	= $5M
Failures, With Upgrade	($8M − $6M)	− ($2M − $2.7M)	= $2.7M

Table 8.4. Expected net opportunity loss comparisons.

OUTCOME	EXPECTED NET OPPORTUNITY LOSS (ENOL) FOR THE LOW TECHNOLOGY				
	EXPECTED MARKET VALUES		COSTS		(ENOL)
Satisfactory	($7.2M – $4.2M)	–	($2M – $1M)	=	$2M
Failures	($1.6M – $2.08M *)	–	($2M – $2.7M)	=	$0.22M

* Calculated as follows: (.4)([.8]$6M + [.2]$2M) = $2.08.

shows the results under the assumptions that either satisfactory or failure performances have occurred, and under the assumptions that upgrading either was or was not done. This analysis provides an opportunity to see what the best strategy *would have been* is this or that had happened. Table 8.4 is an *ex ante* analysis. It shows what is *expected to happen,* on the average. On the average, Figure 8.2 shows that the high technology alternative is expected to perform satisfactorily 80 times out of 100 (that is, P_{HS} = .8), etc. Table 8.4 combines all these data from Figure 8.2 into an "on the average" picture. The two analyses in Table 8.3 and Table 8.4 provide a check on each other.

8.1.5 Post-Optimal Analyses

If much time transpires while the decision is contemplated then the probabilities may be subject to change, as a result of changing circumstances during this time lapse. Or as more information is acquired during the analysis, revisions in the probabilities may be appropriate. Bayes' theorem gives the correct computations for revising these probabilities (see Equation [3.10] of Chapter 3).

No decision is complete unless sensitivity analyses have been carried out. In a sensitivity analysis, a check is made to see if the decision is sensitive to changes in the base data. The influence of estimation errors, optimistic versus pessimistic assumptions or differences in perceptions can thus be tested. To illustrate, let us assume the data in Figure 8.2 represent the "best case." Then suppose that the "worst case" is V_1 = $8M, V_2 = $7M, P_{HS} = .6, V_3 = $6M, V_4 = $5M, V_5 = $0M and all the other data are the same as in Figure 8.2. Repeating the calculations in Table 8.1 with these "worst case" data gives:

$$NEV_H = (.6 \times \$8M + .4 \times \$7M) - \$2M = \$5.6M, \qquad (8.1)$$

$$NEV_L = (.6 \times \$6M + .4[.8 \times \$5M + .2 \times \$0M]) - \$2.7M = \$2.5M. \quad (8.2)$$

The high technology alternative is superior, just as it was in the "best case" (Table 8.1). Hence, the NEV decision is *insensitive* to a change from the best to the worst case.

It is always useful to check to see if one alternative is *globally dominant* over the other. A globally dominant alternative is the dominant choice for all values of the variables and parameters of the problem. If one alternative is not globally dominant over another, then the two will cross over or meet at some values of the variables. This is the indifference point, as discussed in Chapter 4. For the decision tree in Figure 8.2, the indifference point is given by $NEV_H = NEV_L$ or:

$$P_{HS}V_1 + P_{HF}V_2 - C_H = P_{LS}V_3 + P_{LF}(P_FV_4 + P_LV_5) - (C_L + C_F). \quad (8.3)$$

Substituting the appropriate values into Equation (8.3) from Figure 8.2 and using the relationships $P_{HF} = 1 - P_{HS}$ and $P_{LF} = 1 - P_{LS}$, an equation in two unknowns results:

$$9P_{HS} + 8(1 - P_{HS}) - 2 = 7P_{LS} + 5.2\,(1 - P_{LS}) - 2.7. \quad (8.4)$$

This equation reduces to

$$P_{HS} = 1.8\,P_{LS} - 3.5, \quad (8.5)$$

which has no solution. Hence, the two alternatives are never equivalent for any values of P_{HS} and P_{LS}. Thus, the high technology alternative is *globally dominant* for all probability of success values.

Checks for dominance and indifference points can be especially helpful. The location of the indifference point is an important datum for a decision maker. If the indifference point is not within the likely range of the parameters then there will be a globally dominant alternative. All the decision maker needs to do is find that dominant alternative. However, if the equivalence point does happen to fall within the likely range of the parameters, then the decision maker must consider several options. These options are: carefully recheck the data and attempt to sharpen the numbers; work out a contingency plan that will cushion the effects of selecting the "wrong" alternative; diversify by selecting some parts of both alternatives; build flexibility into one of the alternatives and select it. More is said about these problems of implementing a final decision in Chapters 14 and 15.

8.1.6   Influence of Noneconomic Considerations

The above analyses lead to the conclusion that the high technology alternative is the better choice. The decision tree suggested areas to examine, evoked several analyses and assisted in presenting an improved picture of the alternatives and their outcomes. Although the maximization of NEV is the correct economic criterion, it is always wise to examine several other criteria (as illustrated above) to see if the optimum NEV alternative remains optimal with respect to these criteria. When it is not, then the decision maker should carefully reexamine the objectives and goals to be sure that these subsidiary criteria are viable. More is said in Chapter 14 about making a final decision under these circumstances. But, basically, when this occurs the decision maker must chose between the goals and decide which are more important.

In the end, the decision maker may purposely select an alternative that is not the "best" economic choice. For instance, the low technology alternative may be selected because of limited development funds. However, the above analysis shows that it is important to look beyond one's budget. The decision maker who failed to look beyond a $1M budget would not have discovered the global superiority of the high technology alternative. On the other hand, there may be good reasons for selecting the low technology alternative, e.g., minimizing costs in the event of failure, a lack of organizational support for radical new technologies, the manager's track record with high technologies, etc. Whatever the motivation for selecting an uneconomic alternative, the above types of analyses are meaningful in showing the decision maker how far away these choices are from the optimal economic decision. The size of this difference may influence the final decision.

8.1.7   Using Decision Trees

Like most decision aids, decision trees do not provide final answers or decisions. However, they do provide a useful framework for analysis. They help the decision maker structure problems, they guide in assembling relevant decision data, they provide a format for analyzing that data and they encourage a systematic approach. When combined with other methods such as sensitivity analyses, Bayesian statistical analyses and dominance checks, decision tree methods can be valuable decision aids.

In actual practice the process of developing and drawing up a decision tree may be one of "fits and starts." Typically, a tree diagram emerges only after a large amount of groping. The final tree may not emerge until the post-optimal analysis has been completed and one or more new branches or alternatives have been discovered. The use of group meetings and interdisciplinary teams is often necessary in order to collect the data. The NI (nominal-interacting) process may be especially helpful here (see Chapter 5). Different departments may normally have various bits of the total data needed to run a tree analysis, so that the assistance of several persons may have to be solicited (see Chapter 5). For instance, marketing departments may be in the best position to supply the market values, engineering in the best position to supply the cost estimates, etc. The probabilities may best be solicited by consensus or by averaging individual estimates across several concerned individuals (see Chapters 3 and 5). The use of group meetings to examine the tree and its data are often a productive way to stimulate creative discussions and questions. Those present may be encouraged to ask questions and make suggestions which they would not otherwise make.

In many cases it is important to quickly get some initial estimates and develop a first set of results from the tree so the decision maker can begin to see the totality of the system that is being built up. Experience shows that this helps the decision maker define the problem, and it promotes a more serious second round solicitation of data. In many cases, the process and discipline of working through a tree, even with scanty data, is quite valuable to a decision maker.[2, 3, 4]

There is the ever-present problem of what level of detail to use in describing a tree. Much of the utility of a tree lies in its abstractness, because real problems often defy a complete description in which all aspects are shown. In general, the tree should be developed in sufficient detail that it includes the major considerations, yet is not cumbersome to use. This is a rather imprecise rule, but it is about the only one that can be given. The tree should cover the entire period of the important decisions to be made. But it should not attempt to go beyond the time horizon within which the decision maker feels comfortable and is able to supply data.

8.2 STOCHASTIC TREES [5]

Stochastic trees are useful where there are many branches and probabilities. Figure 8.3 illustrates how, in a stochastic tree, a probability distribution may be constructed to replace the finite probabilities at a node. Instead of an expected value or a single NEV number, a stochastic tree provides a probability-value distribution for each outcome branch. For example, the $p(V_i \leq x)$ data in Figure 8.3 show the distribution of market values if path ab is followed. These results show that there is slightly more than a 50-50 chance (.504) that the market value will be equal

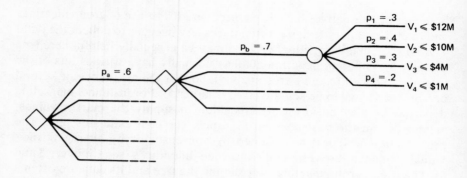

	Cumulative Distribution	x	Probability-Value Distribution: $p(V_i \leq x)$
$p_a \times p_b \times p_1 \leq .126$	.504	\$12M	.504
$p_a \times p_b \times p_2 \leq .168$	.378	\$10M	.378
$p_a \times p_b \times p_3 \leq .126$	.210	\$4M	.210
$p_a \times p_b \times p_4 \leq .084$	.084	\$1M	.084

Figure 8.3. Illustration of a stochastic tree.

to or below \$12M. However, it is not likely (.210) to be equal to or less than \$4M. Or, to put it positively, there is a .790 probability (1.00 − .210) that the market value will exceed \$4M. This result may be compared with other paths and the best one may be chosen on the basis of the distributions. For example, suppose another path *cd* had a distribution indicating that its market value would be equal to or below \$10M with a probability of .95, equal to or below \$8M with a probability of .60, and equal to or below \$2M with a probability of .55. Clearly, path *ab* is the better decision path to select.

An all-stochastic network consists of probability distributions at each node. Then, to obtain the final probability-value distribution for each outcome branch, joint probability distributions must be computed. These are computed in much the same way that point probabilities are compounded, following the rules presented in Chapter 3. Figure 8.4 illustrates the mechanics of computing a joint probability distribution. Computerized techniques are often used to relieve the tedium of all these calculations.

The real advantage of stochastic trees is that point probabilities need not be solicited at all. Rather, all that is needed is for the decision maker to specify the general shape of the probability distribution at each node.

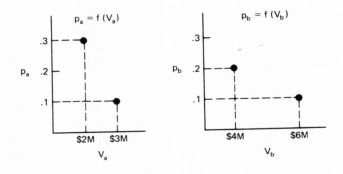

Figure 8.4. Illustration of joint distribution computations.

Then, using computerized methods, a distribution can be simulated. In cases where the probabilities are totally unknown, a random distribution may be assumed and the outcomes may be simulated using Monte Carlo methods.[5]

8.3 FAULT TREES [3, 5]

A fault tree is a kind of decision tree that focuses on the consequences and regrets of *not* selecting particular activities. This focus can often produce a very different picture from the usual decision tree approach, which focuses on the benefits from selecting particular activities. As an illustration, consider a new product that permits a company to just maintain its market share in a highly competitive market. Having the new product will not increase the current flow of revenues into the firm. But *not* having the product will substantially lessen current and future revenues. In this case, it may be said that the regrets from not having the product far outweigh the benefits from having it.

8.3.1 Developing the Fault Tree

To develop a fault tree, first list all the potential problems that could arise if a "do-nothing" policy is taken. In a "do-nothing" policy, no actions are taken to ward off the occurrence of the potential problems, and no solutions to the problems are implemented. Then, for each potential problem indicate the potential causes that could contribute to its existence. For each cause, develop a list of alternative actions or solutions which could be undertaken to eliminate that cause. Assemble these factors in a tree that depicts a chain of problems, causes and solutions. Start with solutions on the right, and work towards potential causes on the left, and terminate the tree in potential problem nodes on the far left. Once the tree is diagrammed, various parameters and data may be solicited and estimated. Estimate the regret R_r for each rth problem under a "do-nothing" policy. Estimate the cost D_j of each jth potential solution or alternative. Estimate the following probabilities:

$P_r = p(H_r)$; the probability that the rth problem will occur under a "do-nothing" assumption, where H_r denotes the rth problem;

$p_{ir} = p(C_i \mid H_r)$; the conditional probability that the rth problem will be caused by each of the ith causes, where C_i denotes the ith cause;

$q_{ij} = p(S_j \mid C_i)$; the conditional probability that the jth solution will *not* eliminate the ith cause, where S_j denotes the jth solution.

The compound probabilities for each branch of the tree are computed as follows:

$$p(H_r \mid S_j) = P_r \times p_{ir} \times q_{ij} \qquad (8.6)$$

Equation (8.6) gives the probability that the rth problem will *not* be solved by the jth solution if the jth solution is implemented. Then the expected regret for n problems under a "do-nothing" solution is given by:

$$\text{Expected Regret Under Do-Nothing} = \sum_{r=1}^{n} P_r R_r. \qquad (8.7)$$

The expected regret for any problem H_k under a decision to implement the jth solution is given by:

$$\text{Expected Regret Under } S_j = p(H_k \mid S_j) \times R_k + \sum_{r=k+1}^{n} P_r R_r, \qquad (8.8)$$

where problem H_k is influenced by the jth solution and where r = k + 1, . . . n problems are *not* influenced by the jth solution. These calculations all follow the probability concepts presented in Chapter 3.

8.3.2   An Illustration

Figure 8.5 presents an example of a fault tree for a new product which a manufacturer was anticipating introducing to the marketplace. Engineering calculations indicated that two kinds of product failures could occur with this product. These failures could be caused by metal fatigue (cause C_1), by boundary wear (cause C_2) or by weld-fatigue (Cause C_3). The marketing department personnel indicated that these product failures could result in a large ($500M) loss in market share and /or excessive ($100M) warranty costs. The R&D personnel indicated that there were three potential solutions to these problems. One was a laboratory study (S_1) at a cost of $1,000,000, which is D_1. Another was an analytical study (S_2) at a cost of $500,000, which is D_2. Finally, there was a stress analysis study (S_3) at a cost of $750,000, which is D_3. It should be noted that there may be many behavioral problems in soliciting such data in addition to the technical problems of estimating the probabilities, regrets and costs. For example, the engineering personnel may be psychologically unable to find fault with their work and therefore unable to foresee the list of potential causes. Similarly, the marketing personnel may grossly understate or overstate the amount of the regrets, some of the parties may be unwilling to face the "facts," the data may not be believed by some of the parties, etc. Some of these obstacles may be circumvented by soliciting the data in a nominal-interacting format, by consensus, or with the aid of the other methods discussed in Chapter 3.

The decision problem depicted in Figure 8.5 concerned whether or not additional development monies should be spent on the product before

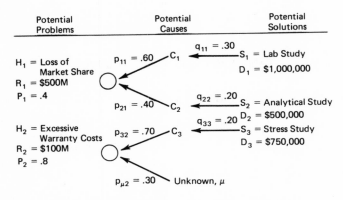

Figure 8.5. Illustration of a fault tree.

marketing it. In the one extreme, the decision could be to spend no more additional development monies. This would mean that the firm would take the risk of incurring the potential problems H_1 and H_2 depicted in Figure 8.5. In the other extreme, all three potential solutions S_1 plus S_2 plus S_3 could be implemented, at a total development cost of $2,250,000. In between these two extremes are several alternative combinations of solutions S_1, S_2 and S_3. Which alternative is best?

8.3.3   Regret-Cost Trade-Offs

Table 8.5 presents the eight alternatives, their costs and the corresponding expected regrets if the alternative is implemented. The expected regrets are computed from Equations (8.7) and (8.8). For example, for the "do-nothing" alternative, Equation (8.7) becomes $(.4)\$500M + (.8)\$100M = \$280M$. If solution S_1 (alternative number 4 in Table 8.5) is implemented, Equation (8.8) becomes $(P_1)(p_{11})(q_{11})R_1 + (P_1)(p_{21})R_1 + (P_2)R_2 = (.4)(.6)(.3)\$500M + (.4)(.4)\$500M + (.8)\$100M = \$196M$.

In order to better visualize which alternatives are superior, let us examine Figure 8.6, which is a plot of the data in Table 8.5. Note that alternatives number 3 and 7 are inferior and should never be chosen. This conclusion is not obvious from the tree diagram in Figure 8.5. But as Figure 8.6 shows, a lower regret can be achieved for less money in both cases. Alternative 2 is superior to alternative 3, and alternative 6 is superior to alternative 7. Thus, we can eliminate alternatives 3 and 7 from further consideration.

The question of the optimal level of expenditure for the project is not completely obvious from these analyses. The determination of how much

Table 8.5. Decision alternatives.

ALTERNATIVE NUMBER	ALTERNATIVE	COST	EXPECTED REGRET
1	Do Nothing	$ 0	$280.0M
2	Do S_2	500,000	216.0M
3	Do S_3	750,000	235.2M
4	Do S_1	1,000,000	196.0M
5	Do $S_2 + S_3$	1,250,000	171.2M
6	Do $S_1 + S_2$	1,500,000	132.0M
7	Do $S_1 + S_3$	1,750,000	151.2M
8	Do $S_1 + S_2 + S_3$	2,250,000	87.2M

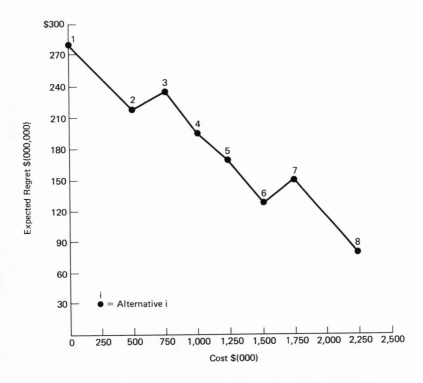

Figure 8.6. Expected regret vs. cost.

to spend should be based on a comparison of the reductions in the expected regret per dollar expended to achieve these reductions. Table 8.6 compares the alternatives on this basis. In Table 8.6, ΔR_j is the difference between the expected regret for the "do-nothing" alternative and the expected regret for the jth alternative. The variable D_j is the total expenditure level or cost of the jth alternative. The ratio $\Delta R_j/D_j$ is the reduction in expected regrets per dollar expended on alternative j. As Table 8.6 shows, alternative 2 gives the largest regret reduction per dollar expended. Alternative 6 gives the next largest regret reduction per dollar expended. The remaining three alternatives all give about the same results; alternative 5 is slightly better than alternative 8, which is better than alternative 4. Thus, this analysis shows that alternatives 4 and 5 are inferior and should never be chosen, for the same reasons that alternatives 3 and 7 were found to be inferior. Hence, this analysis shows that only alternatives 1, 2 and 6 are economically viable.

The above analyses are only economically correct if funds are available

Table 8.6. Incremental regret reduction per expenditure.

ALTERNATIVE NUMBER $j =$	TOTAL EXPENDITURE LEVEL *, D_j	EXPECTED REGRET	REDUCTION IN EXPECTED REGRET, ΔR_j	$\dfrac{\Delta R_j}{D_j}$
1	\$ 0	\$280.0M	—	—
2	500,000	216.0M	\$64.0M	128.0
4	1,000,000	196.0M	84.0M	84.0
5	1,250,000	171.2M	108.8M	87.0
6	1,500,000	132.0M	148.0M	98.6
8	2,250,000	87.2M	192.8M	85.7

* D_j = the cost of the jth alternative, which is a solution or a combination of solutions.

and if there are no better alternatives at each stage of the analysis. For instance, suppose that only \$1,350,000 is available, and suppose there is a competing project that exhibits a $\Delta R_j/D_j$ ratio of .950 for D_j = \$850,000. Then the optimum economic allocation of the available budget would be to select alternative 2 here (spend \$500,000) and allocate the remaining \$850,000 to the other competing project.

The final choice of a best alternative may depend on the decision maker's willingness to assume the risk of the potential problems, the desire to protect the firm's reputation for high quality products, the legal implications of a possible product failure, the available funds, the other projects competing for these available funds, and other noneconomic factors. In general, the process of developing a fault tree analysis will usually generate a great deal of interdepartmental communication and it will focus attention on a rational approach. These experiences may increase the decision maker's awareness of the risks and trade-offs available, and help all the parties arrive at an acceptable solution. For example, in the fault tree situation discussed here, none of the solutions (S_1, S_2, etc.) were implemented. Rather, it was decided to introduce the new product on a limited trial basis, under contractual arrangements with selected customers. However, it was the fault tree exercise that crystallized this alternative and pointed towards its implementation.

8.4 SUMMARY

This chapter has reviewed and illustrated decision tree methods for analyzing and evaluating alternatives. Applications were discussed which illustrated economic analysis methods, as well as some of the decision theory and probabilistic methods presented in Chapter 3 and Chapter 4. In particular, expected value, opportunity loss and regret-cost trade-off analyses were illustrated. A post-optimal analysis was carried out to show how sensitivity analyses and dominance checks could be used to make the analyses more effective. Stochastic trees and fault trees were illustrated to show how they can increase the depth of understanding of a decision problem.

Although significant improvements in decision behaviors may thus result from the use of these methods, there are some hazards inherent in their implementation. It seems redundant but nevertheless necessary to repeat that one does not simply go into an organization with a preconceived model and implement it. A useful model must be as individualistic as the organization it serves. Even if a general model is available that is relevant to a particular organization, it has to be fine tuned. Aside from this, there are significant organization behavior aspects which must be considered in the implementation of an organizationally relevant model. Considerations of trust, openness, participation, sense of ownership and organization change are relevant to the process of inducing the adoption of a suitable model. To some individuals in the organization it may seem intuitively obvious that it is good to have many alternatives and their consequences systematically displayed. But to others in the organization this may be viewed as providing self-exposure to external criticism. These issues must be resolved as a prerequisite to successful implementation. Overall, a major consideration is the balance between the cost of getting believable data for the model and the benefits derived from it. The data must be believable. The process must not be looked upon as "just another exercise." Achieving this is largely a matter of building good cooperative relationships, and constructing suitable and useful models.[4] More is said about these aspects in Chapter 15.

8.5 REFERENCES

1. Canada, J. R. *Intermediate Economic Analysis for Management and Engineering.* Englewood Cliffs, New Jersey: Prentice-Hall, Inc., 1971, pp. 319–352.
2. Whitehouse, G. E. "Using Decision Flow Networks." *Industrial Engineering,* July 1974, pp. 18–25.
3. Souder, W. E. "A Fault Tree Model for Measuring Risk and Budgeting R&D Programs." Technology Management Studies Group, University of Pittsburgh, Pittsburgh, Pennsylvania, February 10, 1976.
4. Souder, W. E.; Maher, P. M.; Shumway, C. R.; Baker, N. R.; and Rubenstein, A. H. "Methodology for Increasing the Adoption of R&D Project Selection Models." *R&D Management,* 4, No. 2: 75–83 (1974).
5. Canada, J. R. *op. cit.,* pp. 335–352.

8.6 BIBLIOGRAPHY

Bussey, L. E. *The Economic Analysis of Industrial Projects*. Englewood Cliffs, New Jersey: Prentice-Hall, Inc., 1978.

Canada, J. R. *Intermediate Economic Analysis for Management and Engineering*. Englewood Cliffs, New Jersey: Prentice-Hall, Inc., 1971, pp. 319–352.

Hespos, R. F. and Strassman, P. A. "Stochastic Decision Trees for the Analysis of Investment Decisions." *Management Science*, 11, No. 10: 157–174 (1965).

Raiffa, Howard. *Decision Analysis*. New York: Addison-Wesley Publishing Co., Inc., 1970.

Stumpf, S. A., Zand, D. E., and Freedman, R. D. "Designing Groups for Judgmental Decisions." *The Academy of Management Review*, 4, No. 4: 589–600 (1979).

Part IV
Planning and Budgeting

Planning and budgeting are at the heart of the decision making function. Deciding what to do and how much to spend are fundamental decision making problems. These tasks are difficult because there is a lack of well-developed prescriptive theories and rules which a manager can routinely apply to all situations. However, there are some sound practices and systematic approaches. Modern managers must avail themselves of these if they want to be successful in coping with the modern-day challenges discussed in Chapter 1 of this book. The two chapters in this part of the book discuss some systematic approaches to planning and budgeting. Chapter 9 discusses some of the most useful systematic approaches for screening and selecting new ideas and projects. Chapter 10 discusses some modern-day principles and methods for systematic budgetary planning.

9

Project Screening, Evaluation and Selection

9.0 INTRODUCTION

Research, development and engineering projects have become increasingly more complex and costly over the past few years. Today's projects often entail large organizational commitments that can turn into significant opportunity costs if a wrong choice is made. Thus, it is important to select only the very best projects. Inferior projects should be identified and screened out early in the decision process. This chapter presents several methods and techniques that a decision maker can use to help distinguish superior projects and project proposals from inferior ones.

9.1 PROJECT SELECTION

9.1.1 The Meaning of "Project Selection"

The term "project selection" has many different connotations.[1] In its narrowest sense, project selection means determining which *one best* project to work on. In its broadest sense, project selection may be viewed as a sequential portfolio determination process. In this broader view, the decision maker wishes to determine the *best allocation* of the *available funds* among the alternative projects. Each project can be funded at several different levels, with each level yielding a different contribution to the individual or organizational goals. Insufficient resources are available to fund all the projects at their highest levels. Thus, the decision maker wishes to determine how much to spend on which alternative project, so as to obtain the largest total return possible with the available funds. Let us suppose that such a portfolio decision has been made, and it is now one year later. The portfolio decision may now be repeated for the set of projects available for funding. This set includes projects which were not completed during the past year, plus any new ideas that came in during the year. These new ideas may be better than the old unfinished projects. If this is the case, then the old unfinished projects may be terminated and replaced with the new ideas. Thus, a sequential decision making process may unfold over time, with the portfolio decision being repeated at the end of each year (or some other suitable time interval).

9.1.2 Project Selection Processes

Figure 9.1 depicts the range of project selection activities which may occur. New project proposals may arrive from a variety of sources. The employees may submit ideas for new projects, customers may suggest ideas, etc. A new project idea may be either temporarily backlogged or put through a screening model. A screening model provides useful preliminary information for distinguishing candidate projects on the basis of a few prominent criteria. It provides a kind of quick and inexpensive first-level sorting out of the candidates. The results from the screening model

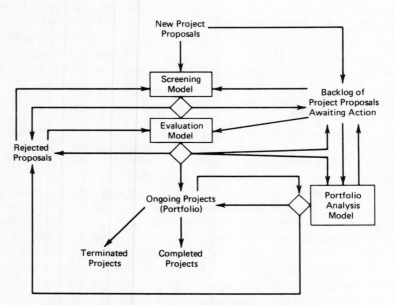

Figure 9.1. Illustration of a project selection decision process.

may indicate that the project proposal is so poor that it should be rejected. Or the results may indicate that the project is acceptable, but work on it should be delayed. Hence it may be backlogged. Or the results may indicate that a more in-depth analysis is warranted.

To obtain an in-depth analysis, the project may be put through an evaluation model. An evaluation model provides a rigorous and comprehensive analysis of the project and its characteristics. As with the screening model, the evaluation model may indicate that the project should be either rejected or backlogged. Or it may indicate that this idea is so good it should be immediately funded and put into the current portfolio. Or it may indicate that this idea should be competitively evaluated against the ongoing projects in a portfolio analysis model.

A portfolio analysis model is the most sophisticated of the three types of models, and it is usually the most expensive and the most time-consuming model to use. It determines the best way to allocate the available resources (or budget) among all the alternative projects. The result may be that the new project is so good that one or more old projects are terminated and the new project replaces them. Or the old projects may be temporarily backlogged in favor of the new project. Or the new project may be backlogged, or even rejected. Backlogged projects will normally be retrieved at some later point in time. But rejected projects will not. However, new information or changed circumstances may suddenly make a previously rejected project more attractive, or may cause a previously backlogged project to be rejected. Therefore, it can happen that a rejected proposal is retrieved at a later date and a backlogged project is not.

Thus, project selection consists of three distinct kinds of decision making: screening, evaluation and portfolio analysis. As we move from screening to portfolio analysis, more factors are considered and the procedures become more complex. A variety of outcomes may occur as a result of each kind of decision, as illustrated in Figure 9.1. As time passes, these three types of decisions may be repeated many times in response to changing information states, changes in the available resources and funds, changes in project achievements or the arrival of new project proposals.

9.2 SCREENING MODELS

Screening models economize on the total evaluation efforts by eliminating the most undesirable proposals from further consideration. Screening models are quick and easy to use and they operate with very little data. Four types of screening models are available: profile models, checklists, scoring models and frontier models.

9.2.1   Profile Models

An example of a profile model is shown in Table 9.1. Note that the ratings are qualitative in nature. No numerical assessments are made. Rather, the project proposals are compared on the basis of a subjective evaluation of their attributes. These evaluations could be done by one individual or by group consensus. Alternatively, the profiles developed by several informed individuals could be compared. Q-sorting or some of the other value assessment methods presented in Chapter 3 could be used to obtain the ratings.

Profile models are simple and easy to use. They display the project characteristics and ratings in such a way that they are easily communicated and readily visualized. For instance, in Table 9.1 it is apparent at a glance that project X is superior to project Y on all the criteria but one. It is also clear that project X is a generally high performer, while project Y is a generally low-performer. Maintainability is the only criterion where project Y is superior to project X. On the other hand, a profile model does not tell us anything about the trade-offs among the criteria. For example, the profile model in Table 9.1 does not tell us if the high performances of Project X on reliability, cost-effectiveness and durability compensate for its medium performances on maintainability and safety. The fact that it is left up to the decision maker to evaluate this trade-off suggests that profile models are best used as screening devices or as stimulants to further inquiry and dialogue.

Table 9.1. Example of a profile model.

CRITERIA OR REQUIREMENTS	EXTENT TO WHICH PROJECTS X AND Y MEET THE CRITERIA		
	HIGH	MEDIUM	LOW
Reliability	X		Y
Maintainability	Y	X	
Safety		X	Y
Cost-Effectiveness	X	Y	
Durability	X		Y

X = project X's score
Y = project Y's score

Profile models are useful where there is a minimum amount of information available, or where the projects are incompletely understood.[2] For instance, profile models may be the most sophisticated methods that can be used for evaluating and comparing exploratory research projects. However, because the evaluations are totally subjective, the rating scale points must be carefully defined. "High," "medium" and other ratings must mean the same to all the evaluators.

9.2.2   Checklists

Table 9.2 shows an example of a checklist. This type of model assumes that the decision maker can distinguish between several finite levels of the criteria or requirements. Each candidate proposal or project is then subjectively evalutated by the decison maker and assigned a criterion score on each requirement. The criterion score is ascertained from a predesignated scoring scale that translates subjective evaluations into numerical scores. A total score is obtained for each project by summing its criterion scores. In general, for a checklist model

$$T_j = \sum_i s_{ij}, \qquad\qquad (9.1)$$

where T_j is the total score for the jth project and s_{ij} is the score for project j on the ith requirement or criterion.

Checklist models improve on profile models by providing both a graphic profile of checkmarks and an overall total score for each candidate project. An analysis of target achievements and a comparison of several candidate projects is facilitated by the total scores. For instance, a total score of +2 or greater may be specified as a cut-off point for acceptable proposals. Projects could be priority classified by specifying total score ranges, e.g., $T_j > +3$ is a high priority project, $+1 \leqslant T_j \leqslant +3$ is a medium priority project, etc. On the other hand, the criterion scores may not properly reflect the trade-offs in the requirements. Then a simple summation of the criterion scores is inaccurate. For instance, projects X and Z in Table 9.2 have the same total score of +5. Yet, it is hard to accept project Z and project X as equals on the basis of the profiles. These two projects would only be equal when above-average ratings on cost-effectiveness and durability compensate for a below-average rating on safety. If the decision maker wants to compare candidates on the basis of their total scores it is better to use a scoring model. A scoring model explicitly takes these kinds of trade-offs into account.

Table 9.2. Example of a checklist.

CRITERIA OR REQUIREMENTS	TOTAL SCORE	CRITERION SCORES [a]				
		-2	-1	0	+1	+2
Project X	+5					
Reliability						✔
Maintainability					✔	
Safety			✔			
Cost-Effectiveness						✔
Durability					✔	
Project Y	-2					
Reliability		✔				
Maintainability						✔
Safety			✔			
Cost-Effectiveness				✔		
Durability			✔			
Project Z	+5					
Reliability						✔
Maintainability						✔
Safety			✔			
Cost-Effectiveness					✔	
Durability					✔	

[a] *Scoring Scale:*
+2 = Best possible performance.
+1 = Above average performance.
 0 = Average performance.
-1 = Below average performance.
-2 = Worst possible performance.

9.2.3 Scoring Models

It is a short step from checklist models to scoring models. In a scoring model, each of $j = 1, \ldots n$ candidate projects are scored on each of $i = 1, \ldots m$ performance requirements or criteria. The criterion scores for each project are then combined with their respective criterion importance weights w_i to achieve a total score T_j for each project. Projects may then be ranked according to their T_j values. For example, a simple additive scoring model would be

$$T_j = \sum_i w_i s_{ij} \tag{9.2}$$

where s_{ij} is the score for project j on the ith criterion, and w_i is the criterion weight. This model is illustrated in Table 9.3.

The influence of the weights becomes apparent if one compares the

Table 9.3. Example of an additive scoring model.

CRITERION, i	CRITERION WEIGHT, w_i ×	CRITERION SCORE,* s_{ij} =	WEIGHTED SCORE
Project X:			
Reliability	4	5	20
Maintainability	2	3	6
Safety	3	3	9
Cost-Effectiveness	5	5	25
Durability	1	4	4
		$T_1 =$	64
Project Y:			
Reliability	4	1	4
Maintainability	2	5	10
Safety	3	2	6
Cost-Effectiveness	5	3	15
Durability	1	2	2
		$T_2 =$	37
Project Z:			
Reliability	4	5	20
Maintainability	2	5	10
Safety	3	2	6
Cost-Effectiveness	5	4	20
Durability	1	4	4
		$T_3 =$	60

* Scale: 5 = Excellent, . . . , Poor = 1.

results for the Weighted Scores in Table 9.3 with the results for the Total Scores in Table 9.2. The Criterion Scores in Table 9.3 contain the same information as the Criterion Scores in Table 9.2. The difference is simply a scale transformation; each Criterion Score in Table 9.3 is +3 larger than its counterpart in Table 9.2. The Weighted Scores in Table 9.3 show that projects X and Z do indeed differ. The checklist model (Table 9.2) did not show any difference between the Total Scores for these two projects. Scoring models are more accurate because they take the trade-offs between the criteria into account, as defined by the criterion weights.

In constructing a scoring model, the criteria or performance dimensions should be selected so that they represent independent and mutually exclusive dimensions. In practice, this ideal is not always possible; criteria will almost always overlap or be interdependent to some degree. The criteria weights should reflect the relative importance of the criteria, and they may be ascertained by using the value methods presented in Chapter 3. In most cases, the weights will be ranks or ordinal level measurements. That is, they are orders of magnitude only. If this is the case then the T_j scores are also ranks or ordinal level numbers, and the discriminatory power of the model is restricted. For example, if the T_j's in Table 9.3 are ordinal level numbers, then it can only be said that project X is better than project Z which is better than project Y. But if $w_1 = 4$ and $w_2 = 2$ means that criterion 1 is twice as important as criterion 2, and so forth, then the magnitudes of the differences between T_1, T_2 and T_3 in Table 9.3 are significant. In that case, from Table 9.3, project X is 85% perfect, project Y is 49% perfect and project Z is 80% perfect, where the perfect score T_{max} is given by

$$T_{max} = \sum_i 5\,w_i = 75. \tag{9.3}$$

Note that a score of zero (or a zero weight) must not be used, since this would zero-out that criterion in the final analyses.

The scales for deriving the s_{ij} scores should always reflect actual performance dimensions. To insure that this is the case, the scoring scale can be empirically derived from historical data on prior projects. To illustrate these procedures, let us define a scoring scale for cost. Let us assume that a plot of the actual costs of twenty-one projects carried out over the past few years has been developed, as shown in Figure 9.2. This actual distribution can be used to generate a cost performance scoring scale by first

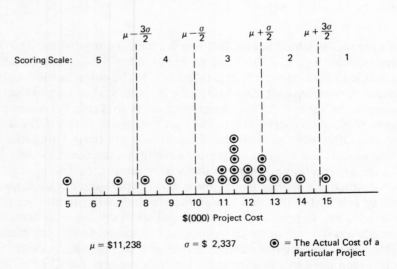

Figure 9.2. Performance distribution with imposed scoring scale.

dividing it into a number of cost score-categories and then assigning appropriate scale values to each score-category. Statistical procedures may be used to divide the distribution into an appropriate number of score-categories. As illustrated in Figure 9.2, the mean (μ) and standard deviation (σ) of the distribution are computed and the $\mu \pm \dfrac{\sigma}{2}$, and $\mu \pm \dfrac{3\sigma}{2}$ points are then located in order to divide the distribution into five performance categories. Any number of score-categories may be used. However, five categories are often reasonable.[3, 4] The appropriate scale values "1," "2," etc. are assigned to the five categories in inverse order of the dollar cost values, so that the larger the score the lower the cost. To use the model depicted in Figure 9.2, the decision maker simply finds a historical project in the distribution that is most like the new one being rated and assigns that score to it. For instance, the new project would be scored "4" on cost if it is most like the historical project that cost \$9,000 in Figure 9.2.

The form of a scoring model can usually be varied to suit the objectives of most decision makers and most situations. The criteria and weights can be varied to reflect different goals and preferences. In some cases, the multiplicative model form,

$$T_j = (w_1 s_{1j})(w_2 s_{2j})(w_3 s_{3j}) \ldots (w_n s_{nj}), \qquad (9.4)$$

may be more appropriate than the additive form shown in Equation (9.2) above. In general, scoring models are natural to construct and use. They permit the decision maker to examine the performance of different projects on several criteria as a basis for decision making. They provide a moderately quick analysis of the relevant decision aspects, without a great sacrifice in accuracy. The use of scores in place of the actual data (as in Figure 9.2) may in fact absorb some of the random errors that are inherent in the actual data. For instance, errors often abound in cost measurement, and scores may provide just as much real discrimination as the actual error-laden numbers.

9.2.4   Frontier Models [5, 6]

Figure 9.3 illustrates the outputs from a frontier model for seven different projects. The projects are plotted in such a way as to show their relative risks and returns. "Risk" expresses the project's chances of failure. This may be measured as $1-p$ where p is the project's probability of success. Or it may be measured in terms of the likelihood that the project will *not* achieve some desired level of output, profit, etc. "Return" expresses the project's anticipated profits, sales or some other measure of value which the decision maker wishes to use. The efficient frontier in Figure 9.3 tracks the path of the most efficient return/risk ratios. For example, project 5 (denoted as X_5 in Figure 9.3) is more return/risk efficient than project 2 (denoted as X_2). Project 5 has the same return as project 2, but it has a lower risk level. Similarly, project 3 is more return/risk efficient than project 6 because of its higher return at the same risk level as project 6. The maximum desired risk and the minimum desired return levels established by the organization are also depicted in Figure 9.3. Acceptable projects must fall in the region formed by these boundaries. Thus, Figure 9.3 shows that a decision maker should accept projects 3, 5 and 7 and reject the others.

Frontier models are often very useful for examining return/risk tradeoffs within the organizational objectives. For instance, Figure 9.3 shows that the high risk and high return project 4 is ruled out by its high risk

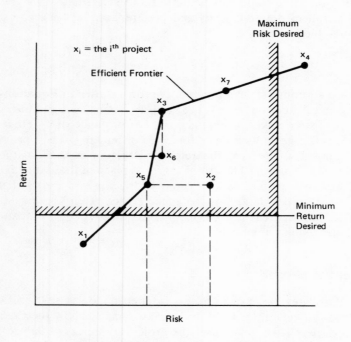

Figure 9.3. Illustration of a frontier model.

level. Yet its incremental return/risk ratio is the same as the acceptable projects 3 and 7. (All of these projects lie on the same line.) Thus, the decision maker may want to make an exception and retain project 4 for further study and analyses.

Frontier models may be used to indicate the need for greater diversification in idea generation and project proposals. For example, Figure 9.3 shows that the acceptable projects are primarily of the medium to high-risk variety. Whether or not the portfolio ought to be more diversified must be resolved on the basis of the organization's goals and objectives. The frontier model can only point out trends and situations for further analysis.

9.2.5   Using Screening Models

Screening models are very useful for weeding out those projects which are the least desirable. Since screening models are quick and inexpensive to use, they can economize on the total evaluation efforts by reducing the number of projects to be further evaluated. Because they require a relatively small amount of input data, they can be used where the projects are not well understood or where there is a minimum of data available on them. However, screening models do not provide much depth of information. And they usually are not sensitive to many of the finer distinctions between the projects. Rather, screening models are like a coarse sieve that provides a partial separation but permits some undesirables to pass through. Thus, screening models can be very useful for some applications. But the decision maker should not expect them to provide a comprehensive or complete analysis.

9.3   EVALUATION MODELS

Evaluation models require a greater volume and depth of input data than screening models. But in return, they provide a more comprehensive and accurate analysis. These models permit the candidate projects to be rated, ranked and assigned priorities on the basis of several characteristics. There are four types of evaluation models: economic index models, decision theory models, risk analysis models and value-contribution models. Let us now examine each of these model types.

9.3.1   Economic Index Models

An index model is simply a ratio between two variables, and the index is their quotient. Changing the values of the variables changes the value of their quotient, or the index. An example of a commonly used index model is the return on investment (ROI) index model

$$ROI \text{ Index} = \sum_i (R_i/[1 + r]^i)/\sum_i (I_i/[1 + r]^i) \tag{9.5}$$

where R_i is the net dollar returns expected from the project in the ith year, I_i is the investment expected to be made in the ith year, and r is an interest rate. The numerator of Equation (9.5) is the present worth of all future revenues generated by the project, and the denominator is the present worth cost of all future investments.

Some other examples of index models are shown in Table 9.4. Ansoff's model uses both dollar values and index numbers as input data. The index numbers T and B are judgments that may be arrived at with the aid of the value assessment methods described in Chapter 3. Olsen's index is a variation on Ansoff's index that uses dollar input data. Viller's index is a kind of return on investment model, discounted by the compound likelihood of the project's success. Disman's index looks at the expected earnings over and above the cost to complete the project.[4]

Table 9.4. Examples of index models.

Ansoff's Index

$$\text{Project Figure of Merit} = \frac{rdp(T + B)E}{\text{Total Investment}}$$

Olsen's Index

$$\text{Project Value Index} = \frac{rdpSPn}{\text{Project Cost}}$$

Viller's Index

$$\text{Project Index} = rdp \left(\frac{E - R}{\text{Total Investment}}\right)$$

Disman's Index

$$\text{Project Return} = rp(E - R)$$

Key: r = the probability of research success, d = the probability of development success, p = the probability of market success, T and B are respective indexes of technical and business merit, E = the present worth of all future earnings from the project, S = annual sales volume in units, P = unit profit, n = number of years of product life, R = present worth cost of research and development activities to complete the project.

The single-number index or score that is produced by an index model can be used to rate and rank candidate projects. An example of the use of an index model is shown in Table 9.5. The index model shown there is:

$$V = \frac{P \times R}{C}, \qquad (9.6)$$

where V is the index. Four projects are evaluated using this model, and their relative rankings on the basis of the index V are shown in the last column of Table 9.5. Two projects, project 4 and project 5, are tied for first place in the rankings. These hypothetical results point up some of the weaknesses of index models. One such weakness is the implicit trade-offs that often occur. For example, in computing the V index, project 5's lower cost compensates for its lower probability of success. This is why project 5 is as good as project 4 on the V index. However, any decision maker who wishes to avoid high risks would never rank project 5 as high as project 4. Note that project 5 has a risk of failure of $1 - P_5 = 1 - .4 = .6$. In fact, instead of ranking it first, the risk-averse decision maker might eliminate project 5 from any consideration at all. Thus, the index model in Table 9.5 may be inappropriate for some decision makers. It could lead them to make completely wrong decisions relative to their objectives. This example shows that all index models should be carefully examined for their internal trade-offs. Unless the trade-offs are representative of those the decision maker would actually be willing to make, the model is inappropriate.

Another weakness of many index models is the insensitivity of the index to changes in some of the parameters. As an illustration, let us examine what happens to the V index as one goes from project 4 to project 1 in Table 9.5. The return increases by 50% (from \$80,000 to \$120,000).

Table 9.5. Example of the use of an index model.

	RETURN (R)	COST (C)	PROBABILITY OF SUCCESS (P)	$V = \dfrac{P \times R}{C}$	RANKING
Project 4	\$ 80,000	\$2,000	.7	28	1st ⎫ tie
Project 5	70,000	1,000	.4	28	1st ⎭
Project 1	120,000	2,000	.2	12	2nd
Project 3	10,000	1,000	.7	7	3rd
Project 2	10,000	1,000	.3	3	4th

The risk goes from $1 - P_4 = .3$ to $1 - P_1 = .8$, for a 167% increase. Yet the V index falls by only 57%: from $V_4 = 28$ to $V_1 = 12$. Thus, these analyses show that this index model is relatively insensitive to risks. In fact, it is a biased model; it is biased toward obscuring risks.

Still another weakness of index models lies in their inability to consider multiple objectives. Because of this, an index model may be inadequate. For example, suppose that the decision maker also wishes to diversify the portfolio, in addition to achieving high V values. Then, the decision maker might accept project 3 (Table 9.5) because it is a relatively inexpensive way (low cost project) to get a high probability project. Having some high probability projects in the portfolio may be important. This may be especially true if the high-cost and high-risk project 1 is included in the portfolio. Yet the index model ranked project 3 next to last, because it could not incorporate this other objective for diversification into its analyses. It was inadequate to handle this objective.

Of course, no index model can include everything. Index models are appealing because of their simplicity and ease of use. That is, they are attractive because they do not include everything. But the decision maker should be wary; index models can be deceivingly appealing. Before placing great faith in the outputs from an index model, the decision maker should make sure that the model is unbiased and appropriate.

9.3.2   Decision Theory Models

Decision theory models are based on the economics and strategies approaches to statistical decision making (see Chapter 4). These models are based on the idea that a rational decision maker will only adopt those policies which maximize the expected value of the outcomes.

An illustration of a decision theory model is shown in Table 9.6 for two candidate projects. A payoff matrix is constructed by arraying the data for the candidates under the assumptions that mother nature is either adverse or benign. The relative worth numbers in the payoff matrix in Table 9.6 are anticipated profits. Other kinds of worth numbers can also be used, i.e., present worths, index numbers from an index model, etc. In the simplest case, the probabilities of mother nature being adverse, $p(A)$, and benign, $p(B)$, can be estimated. Then the respective expected worths W_1 and W_2 of project 1 and project 2 can be computed as follows:

$$W_1 = \$100,000,000\, p(A) + \$300,000,000\, p(B) \tag{9.7}$$

$$W_2 = \$50,000,000\, p(A) + \$500,000,000\, p(B). \tag{9.8}$$

Table 9.6. Illustration of a decision theory model.

PAYOFF MATRIX OF
RELATIVE WORTHS ($000,000)

MOTHER NATURE IS:

	ADVERSE (A)	BENIGN (B)
Project 1	100	300
Project 2	50	500

The project with the larger expected worth would be the preferred candidate.

In more complex situations, $p(A)$ and $p(B)$ are unknown. This is the case of decision making under uncertainty, which was discussed in Chapter 4. Then, following the procedures detailed in Chapter 4, the indifference point may be computed by solving Equations (9.7) and (9.8), with the aid of the equation $p(A) + p(B) = 1.0$. The solution yields an indifference point of $p(A) = .80$ and $p(B) = .20$. Thus, the decision maker will be indifferent between projects 1 and 2 when the probability of mother nature being benign is .20. Hence, if the decision maker believes that mother nature will be benign more than twenty percent of the time, then project 2 will give the larger expected worth, and it is the better alternative choice. Otherwise, project 1 is the better choice. If the decision maker misjudges these likelihoods, then an opportunity loss may result. For instance, if project 1 is selected, and mother nature turns out to be benign, then an opportunity loss of $200,000,000 is incurred because choosing project 2 would have resulted in precisely that much more profit. Similarly, if project 2 is selected and mother nature turns out to be adverse, then an opportunity loss of $50,000 results because choosing project 1 would have yielded exactly that much more. In short, project 2 is a bullish strategy with the potential for extreme rewards. Project 1 is a more moderate strategy.

Decision theory models may help to clarify the characteristics and to define the implications of the available decision strategies. Decision theory models may thus be particularly useful for interdepartmental decision making, where natural differences in the risk-taking propensities of the departments may get in the way of consensus. Typically, one department may be a risk-averter (i.e., they select project 1) while the other is a risk-taker (i.e., they select project 2). Decision theory models may be used to help clarify and display these differences in such a way that the parties are more able to work out an acceptable joint decision.

9.3.3 Risk Analysis Models

A risk analysis model provides a complete picture of the distribution of outcomes for each alternative project. An illustration of a risk analysis approach to the comparison of two candidate projects is shown in Figure 9.4. Project 1 has a most likely lifetime profit of $100,000,000, and project 2 has a most likely lifetime profit of $150,000,000. However, there is only a .4 probability that project 2 will in fact achieve the $150,000,000 level, while there is a .8 probability that project 1 will achieve the $100,000,000 level. Project 2 provides an opportunity to achieve a larger profit than project 1. But it also carries some downside risk relative to project 1. In fact, there is a .3 probability that project 2 will yield lower profits than project 1, as shown in Figure 9.4. Given these data, a risk-averter would be inclined to select project 1. Project 1 has a high chance of achieving a moderate profit, with very little chance of anything less or greater. A gambler would be more inclined to select project 2, which has a small chance at a larger profit. Thus, the risk analysis approach makes the risk-averter and gambler strategies more visible, thereby permitting a decision maker to consciously select decisions consistent with one of these chosen strategies.

A picture like Figure 9.4 is usually not especially difficult to construct from a relatively small amount of data. In most cases, three points are all that are needed. For example, the performance distribution shown for

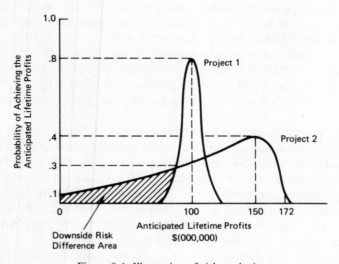

Figure 9.4. Illustration of risk analysis.

project 2 in Figure 9.4 can be estimated from the most likely, optimistic and pessimistic data points. The optimistic and pessimistic points are the upper and lower deciles of the distribution, and the most likely point is its mode. For project 2, the pessimistic point is the coordinate ($0, .1), the optimistic point is the coordinate ($172,000,000, .1) and the mode is the coordinate ($150,000,000, .4). Other common methods for developing performance distributions for risk analysis include curve fitting techniques, Monte Carlo simulation methods and modeling techniques.[7]

9.3.4   Value-Contribution Models

Value-contribution models are a combination of several methods. An example of a value-contribution (V-C) model is given in Table 9.7. Value-contribution models permit the decision maker to examine the degree of contribution which a project makes to the organization's hierarchy of goals. Thus, to develop a V-C model, one must first list the goals. Several of the techniques described in Chapter 3 may be used for this. In most cases, the goals may be listed as a nested hierarchy. For instance, as shown in Table 9.7, there are two supergoals: short range and long range. Within each of these two supergoals, there are several subgoals. Within the short range supergoal, the organization desires to achieve new product dominance, a profitability target and to reduce their present environmental impacts. Within the long range supergoal, the organization desires to maintain their technological state-of-art and market share.

The second step in developing a V-C model is value-weighing the goals. The techniques presented in Chapter 3 and in the ''Scoring Models'' section of this chapter may be used for this. In the model illustrated in Table 9.7, the long range and short range supergoals are respectively value-weighted as $V = 60$ and $V = 40$. Note that these values must sum to 100. That is, the value-weights are determined by allocating a total of 100 points among the supergoals according to their relative importance. In Table 9.7, the value-weights indicate that the short range supergoal is one and one-half times as important as the long range supergoal. Within each supergoal, the total points are similarly spread among the subgoals, in such a way as to indicate their relative importance. The complete set of value-weights thus indicates the ''perfect'' level of value contribution which a project could make. For instance, a perfect project would score 30 on ''Achieve New Product Dominance.'' Thus, a project with a perfect contribution to all the goals would have a total value-contribution score of 100 points.

The actual scaling and scoring of the candidate projects within a V-C model can be done individually or by consensus. Scoring scales can be

Table 9.7. Value-contribution model.*

| | PROJECT COSTS ($000) | SHORT RANGE ORGANIZATIONAL GOALS (V = 60) | | | LONG RANGE ORGANIZATIONAL GOALS (V = 40) | | TOTAL VALUE-CONTRIBUTION SCORE |
		ACHIEVE NEW PRODUCT DOMINANCE (V = 30)	ACHIEVE THE PROFITABILITY TARGET (V = 20)	REDUCE ENVIRONMENTAL IMPACTS (V = 10)	MAINTAIN THE TECHNOLOGICAL STATE-OF-ART (V = 25)	MAINTAIN MARKET SHARE (V = 15)	
				Scores			
Project A	$100	30	20	5	15	5	75
Project B	200	15	10	10	20	10	65
Project C	150	25	10	5	15	10	65

Normalized Value-Contribution:
Project A: $75 \div \$100,000 = \$75.0 \times 10^{-5}$
Project B: $65 \div \$200,000 = \$32.5 \times 10^{-5}$
Project C: $65 \div \$150,000 = \$43.3 \times 10^{-5}$

Rankings:
Project A: First
Project C: Second
Project B: Third

* V = the goal value-weight.

constructed using some of the value assessment methods described in Chapter 3, or by using some of the scoring model techniques discussed in this chapter. The successive ratings method (see Chapter 3) is ideally suited to use for scoring the candidate projects on each subgoal within a V-C model. To use the successive ratings method, the decision maker would first score all the projects with respect to the highest value-weighted subgoal. Then the projects would be scored with respect to the next highest value-weighted subgoal, etc.

An application of a V-C model is illustrated in Table 9.7 for three candidate projects. Project A is short-range oriented, project B is more long-range oriented and project C is about evenly oriented to both the long and the short range. Project A has perfect scores on the new product dominance and profitability subgoals. It has less than perfect scores on the other goals. But because project A is more oriented toward the short range, it contributes more toward these higher-valued subgoals. Thus, it has the highest overall total value-contribution (last column of Table 9.7). Since the total costs of the projects vary, the total value-contribution scores must be normalized by dividing them by their respective project costs. These resulting normalized value-contribution scores may then be used to rank the candidates, as shown in the lower half of Table 9.7.

V-C models permit the decision maker to think in terms of the goals of the candidate projects, and the levels of goal achievements. For example, an examination of Table 9.7 shows that none of the three candidate projects are expected to achieve a perfect contribution to the short range supergoal. Project A is 5 points less than perfect on environmental impacts, and the other projects have even greater deficiencies. Thus, no one of the available candidates can be employed to completely achieve the desired short range targets. The shortfall is even greater for the long range supergoal. Here, the best project (project B) is a total of 10 points short of the 40-point perfect contribution score for the long range supergoal.

V-C models may also be useful when the decision maker is trying to assemble a balanced portfolio of several projects. For instance, the results in Table 9.7 show that projects A and B together provide the maximum contributions to the short range subgoals, and they jointly make major contributions to the long range subgoals. If a third project can be added which achieves the maximum contributions to the long range subgoals, then a well-balanced portfolio has been achieved.

9.3.5 Using Evaluation Models

Evaluation models are useful when the decision maker feels a need to have a more detailed and in-depth analysis than screening models can provide. Evaluation models permit the decision maker to make much finer discriminations between the candidate projects. On the other hand, evaluation models generally require a much greater volume and detail of data than screening models. Some evaluation models require finite numbers for life cycle sales volumes, probabilities of success and other parameters that may be very difficult to estimate.

In spite of the difficulties in applying them, evaluation models clearly have a place. There are times when it is difficult to make a decision without the kind of data and information that go into an evaluation model. Thus, by using the model as a guideline, the decision maker will be urged to more carefully search out and analyze the proper information. In many cases, using an evaluation model with only approximate data and rough estimates can be revealing and helpful to the decision maker.

9.4   PORTFOLIO MODELS

9.4.1   The Portfolio Problem

Table 9.8 illustrates the use of a portfolio model. The objective is to determine the best allocation of the available funds among the three alternative candidate projects. Projects A, B and C each have four alternative funding levels: $0, $100,000, $200,000, and $300,000. The expected profits from the projects vary with these funding levels, as shown in Table 9.8. The higher funding levels result in improved products, which yield higher expected profits.

Several alternative allocations of the available $300,000 are possible. For instance, the funds can all be allocated to project C, for an expected profit return of $350M. In this case, the other two projects would be zeroed-out—no money would be spent on them. The available funds could also be spread evenly across the three projects. This would yield an expected profit return of $100 M + $120 M + $10 M = $230 M. This is inferior to the above alternative of funding only project C at its upper limit. Continued searching will show that the optimum allocation is to fund project A at its $100,000 level, project B at its $200,000 level, and to zero-out project C. This portfolio yields the largest possible total expected profits, as shown in Table 9.8. There is no other allocation of the available funds that will achieve a higher total expected profit.

It should be clear from this illustration that there are occasions when it may be more fruitful to purposely fund some projects at their lowest levels (project A) or to completely reject some projects (project C), in order to marshal funds for more productive uses (project B). However, the $100,000 level is *not* the most productive way to use funds *on project A*. The expected profit yield per dollar expended, or the productivity per

Table 9.8. Illustration of a portfolio model.

ALTERNATIVE FUNDING LEVELS FOR EACH PROJECT	AVAILABLE FUNDS = $300,000 EXPECTED PROFITS ($M)		
	PROJECT A	PROJECT B	PROJECT C
$ 0	$ 0	$ 0	$ 0
100,000	100	120	10
200,000	250	285	215
300,000	310	335	350

Optimum Portfolio		Expected Profits
Project A	$100,000	$100M
Project B	200,000	285M
	$300,000	$385M

dollar spent, is *highest* for project A at the $200,000 funding level. From Table 9.8, for project A at the $100,000 level the productivity is $100M/$100,000 = 1.00×10^3; at the $200,000 level it is $250M/$200,000 = 1.250×10^3; and at the $300,000 level, $310M/$300,000 = 1.033×10^3. The $100,000 funding level is thus the *least* productive use of funds on project A. How, then, can the portfolio shown at the bottom of Table 9.8 be optimal? The answer is easy to see if one examines the productivities of the funding levels on the other projects. Table 9.9 presents the productivity data for all three projects. The $200,000 level of project B is the most productive of the twelve alternative project-funding level combinations. Once this alternative is selected, then $100,000 is left over. The most productive use for this remaining $100,000 is project A. (Note that project B, which actually has a higher productivity than project A at the $100,000 level, has already been funded at $200,000 and cannot be selected again.) The reader should note in particular how this example has shown that, under a budget constraint, the *overall optimum* decision may not be the sum of the *individual project optimum decisions*. It is only when the budget (or the available funds) reach $700,000 that each project would be funded at its individual optimum decision point, or its most productive level. With a $700,000 budget, the optimum portfolio would be to spend $200,000 each on projects A and B, and $300,000 on project C. These are the most productive individual project funding levels.

The simple problem shown in Table 9.8 can be readily solved by exhaustively enumerating and tabulating all the productivities (Table 9.9), and then working back through the table to find the best allocation. But when there are many candidate projects or alternative funding levels, computerized search methods and mathematical programming models become necessary. These models have the advantage that various con-

Table 9.9. Expected profits ÷ funding levels, or productivities.

FUNDING LEVELS	PRODUCTIVITY $\times 10^3$		
	PROJECT A	PROJECT B	PROJECT C
$ 0	0	0	0
100,000	1.000 **	1.200	0.100
200,000	1.250	1.425 *	1.075
300,000	1.033	1.117	1.167

* Largest productivity value.
** Next largest productivity value, when $100,000 remains to be spent.

straints may be included to insure that the portfolio is balanced for risk, or that exploratory research projects will not be disadvantaged in competing with other projects.

9.4.2   Using Portfolio Models

Many portfolio models have been developed to handle a wide variety of decision problems.[4, 8, 9] Though these models were developed to find the one best portfolio in a particular situation, this is not the most productive way to use them.[10, 11] Rather, portfolio models are best used to help the decision maker discover new solution alternatives, to examine the rationale for funding some projects, or to answer "what if" questions about various alternatives.[12, 13] In this way, a portfolio model can be used as a management decision laboratory, to test various alternatives and discover others.

9.5   GROUP AND ORGANIZATIONAL MODELS

9.5.1   Need for Structured Group Processes

Project selection decisions that are performed in organizational and group settings are often deeply influenced by many human emotions, desires and departmental loyalties. Many different parties normally become involved in the project selection decision making process, either as suppliers of decision data and information, as champions of projects, as influencers or as decision makers. Unless a spirit of trust and openness is felt by these parties, it is not likely that essential information will be completely and freely exchanged. Each involved party must come to appreciate the needs of others, and the larger missions of the organization vis-à-vis their own wants. In order to achieve a total organizational consensus and commitment to a final decision, those involved must fully comprehend the nature of the proposed projects. This means that they must have a depth of factual knowledge. It also means that the parties must have a complete awareness of their own feelings, since much of the decision data are highly personal. Many decision settings fail because the participants' feelings are not crystallized and they have not fully exchanged their feelings. Thus, there is a need for a structured process that bridges these behavioral gaps, which are peculiar to organizational and group decision making settings.

These aspects were discussed in Chapter 5, where a nominal-interacting (NI) decision making process was described as a potential solution to these needs. When used in combination with the Q-sort (QS) method presented in Chapter 3, the NI process appears to be a very effective approach to group and organizational project selection decision making.

9.5.2   The QS-NI Decision Process

The QS-NI process begins with a nominal period in which each individual in the group silently and anonymously Q-sorts the candidate projects. These results are then tabulated and displayed to the entire group. Table 9.10 presents an illustration of such a tally chart, which is discussed below. The tally chart focuses on the group consensus process and the agreement-disagreement statistics, without revealing who voted for what.

The group is then given an interacting period in which they discuss the results in the tally chart. During this period, they may share and exchange data and rationales, they may challenge each other, etc. To help guide the group in their accomodation patterns, group process measures are taken and periodically fed back to the group. These measures generally indicate whether the group is becoming more or less cohesive, and what they can do to improve their team potency. It is left up to the group to decide whether or not to take these potency-improving actions.[1, 14, 15]

This NI sequence of an individual or nominal period followed by a group discussion or interacting period can be repeated for several rounds. Experience shows that two to three rounds are needed to stimulate complete information exchange, but more than four rounds dissipates the subjects, as discussed in Chapter 5. The nominal periods permit the individuals to reconcile their individual thoughts. The interacting periods provide a forum for the individuals to adopt from each other, refine opinions and work toward consensus.

Table 9.10 presents an illustration of the tally charts for a twenty-person group engaged in a QS-NI process with seven projects. The arrows trace the changes in the individual Q-sorts from the first to the second nominal period. Note that the degree of consensus actually declined during this part of the exercise for project G. In this case, the discussion revealed a

Table 9.10. Illustration of results from the QS-NI process.

	Projects		A	B	C	D	E	F	G
Categories	Very High Priority		⦿//	/		⦿////	// ⦿//	⦿///	↗
	High Priority		⦿卌	卌↗↗	卌 ⦿//	⦿/// ⦿///	⦿///	/ ⦿//	⦿/// // 卌 ///
	Intermediate Priority		// ////	⦿卌 ⦿////	卌 卌	⦿///	卌	⦿卌 ⦿/	// ⦿/// ⦿//
	Low Priority		⦿卌	⦿//	⦿///	⦿//	⦿////	⦿//	
	Very Low Priority		⦿//	⦿///		////	⦿////	⦿// /	
1st Round	K.S. Test[a]	D =	.10	.15	.25	.10	.05	.15	.40
		p =	>.20	>.20	<.15	>.20	>.20	>.20	<.05
	Consensus?[b]		No	No	T	No	No	No	T
2nd Round	K.S. Test[a]	D =	.40	.60	.40	.65	.40	.35	.25
		p =	<.05	<.01	<.05	<.01	<.05	<.05	<.15
	Consensus?[b]		Yes	Yes	Yes	Yes	Yes	Yes	No

[a] Kolmogorov-Smirnov one-sample test of significance. The null hypothesis is that the cumulative observed distribution of votes (for that project) is not different from the cumulative rectangular distribution 4, 8, 12, 16, 20. "D" is the largest absolute difference between the observed and rectangular distributions for any category, divided by N. See: Siegel, Sidney. *Nonparametric Statistics*. New York: McGraw-Hill, 1965, pp. 47–52.

[b] Group consensus for a single category exists where it contains 50% more votes than any other category and $p \leq .10$ in the K. S. test ($p \leq .10$ can exist for bimodally distributed votes). "T" indicates a tendency for consensus, in that two adjacent categories contain $\geq 2/3$ of the votes.

heretofore hidden lack of information and a fundamental lack of comprehension of this project by some of the subjects. This proposal was returned to the submitter for additional work and subsequent resubmittal. A consensus was reached on this resubmitted project at the end of another round of the QS-NI process. The other projects rapidly converged to strong consensus, as shown in Table 9.10. The reader should note the high incidence of "block voting" or coalition voting among these data. That is, small clusters of three to five persons are voting alike and changing their votes in a like manner. This is a common phenomenon in QS-NI exercises. The QS-NI process usually reveals a great deal about group interaction patterns and interpersonal power play strategies. Coalitions and advocate and adversary positions are usually made very visible by the QS-NI process.[14, 15]

9.6 SUMMARY

The selection of the best projects is a very important decision problem for modern managers. Today's projects entail very large commitments which have the potential to become enormous regrets if an inferior project is selected. A large number of techniques and models have been developed to aid managers in project screening, evaluation and selection decision making. As Table 9.11 shows, the choice of one type of method over another will depend on the nature of the projects being assessed and the decision problem at hand.

Checklists, profile models and scoring models are appropriate for exploratory projects because these models require a minimum of data. In the case of applied projects, the evaluation data will usually be relatively less subjective and more plentiful. Thus, frontier models, index models, decision theory models and risk analysis models are appropriate. For development projects, the amount and quality of the evaluation data available on each project may be sufficient for the use of value-contribution and sophisticated computerized portfolio models. As Table 9.11 shows, the nature of the decision problem may also govern the choice of models used. Some of the models are appropriate for screening decisions, where only "ballpark" accept/reject decisions are needed. Other models that are more discriminatory are appropriate for decisions which assign priorities. If resource allocations or budgetary decisions are involved, then value-contribution or portfolio models should be considered. Portfolio models are especially recommended if the projects involve multiple funding levels and trade-offs. In organizational and group settings, a QS-NI process may be useful. This process has been found to be very helpful in reaching consensus decisions, achieving organizational commitments and building lasting teamwork relationships.

Table 9.11 Guide to applying project selection models.

	RELEVANT TYPE OF MODEL OR PROCESS									
	CHECKLISTS	PROFILES	SCORING	FRONTIER	INDEX	DECISION THEORY	RISK ANALYSIS	VALUE-CONTRIBUTION	PORTFOLIO	QS-NI
Type of Projects:										
Exploratory	X	X	X							X
Applied				X	X	X	X			X
Development						X	X	X	X	X
Type of Decision Problem:										
Screening	X	X	X	X	X	X				X
Assigning Priorities					X	X	X	X	X	X
Resource Allocation								X	X	X

9.7 REFERENCES

1. Souder, W. E. "Field Studies With a Q-Sort/Nominal Group Process for Selecting R&D Projects." *Research Policy*, **5**, No. 4: 172–188 (1975).
2. Souder, W. E. "A System for Using R&D Project Evaluation Methods." *Research Management*, **21**, No. 5: 29–37 (1978).
3. Moore, J. R. and Baker, N. R. "An Analytical Approach to Scoring Model Design: Application to Research and Development Project Selection." *IEEE Trans. on Eng. Mgt.*, **EM-16**, No. 3: 90–98 (1969).
4. Souder, W. E. "Project Selection, Planning and Control," in *Handbook of Operations Research: Models and Applications*, J. J. Moder and S. E. Elmaghraby (eds.), New York: VanNostrand Reinhold Company, 1978, pp. 301–344.
5. Markowitz, H. *Portfolio Selection*. New York: John Wiley & Sons, Inc., 1960.
6. Sharpe, W. F. "A Simplified Model for Portfolio Analysis." *Management Science*, **9**, No. 1: 277–293 (1963).
7. Hertz, D. B. "Risk Analysis in Capital Investment." *Harvard Business Review*, **42**, No. 1: 95–106 (1964).
8. Rosen, E. M. and Souder, W. E. "A Method for Allocating R&D Expenditures." *IEEE Transactions on Engineering Management*, **EM-12**, No. 4: 87–93 (1965).
9. Dean, B. V. *Project Evaluation: Methods and Procedures*. New York: American Management Association, 1970.
10. Souder, W. E. "Analytical Effectiveness of Mathematical Programming Models for Project Selection." *Management Science*, **19**, No. 8: 907–923 (1973).
11. Souder, W. E. "Utility and Perceived Acceptability of R&D Project Selection Models." *Management Science*, **19**, No. 12: 1384–1394 (1973).
12. Souder, W. E. "Selecting and Staffing R&D Projects Via Op Research." *Chemical Engineering Progress*, **63**, No. 11: 27–37 (1967).
13. Bobis, A. H.; Cooke, T. F.; and Paden, J. H. "A Funds Allocation Method to Improve the Odds for Research Success." *Research Management*, **14**, No. 2: 34–39 (1971).
14. Souder, W. E. "Effectiveness of Nominal and Interacting Group Decision Processes for Integrating R&D and Marketing." *Management Science*, **23**, No. 6: 595–605 (1977).
15. Souder, W. E. "Achieving Organizational Consensus With Respect to R&D Project Selection Criteria." *Management Science*, **21**, No. 6: 669–691 (1975).

9.8 BIBLIOGRAPHY

Augood, Derek "A Review of R&D Evaluation Methods." *IEEE Transactions on Engineering Management*, **EM-20**, No. 4: 114–120 (1973).
Clarke, T. C. "Decision Making in Technologically Based Organizations: A Literature Survey of Present Practice." *IEEE Transactions on Engineering Management*, **EM-21**, No. 1: 9–23 (1974).
Gear, A. E.; Lockett, A. G.; and Pearson, A. W. "Analysis of Some Portfolio Selection Models for R&D." *IEEE Transactions on Engineering Management*, **EM-18**, No. 2: 66–76 (1971).
Merrifield, Bruce. "Industrial Project Selection and Management." *Industrial Marketing Management*, **7**, No. 5: 324–331 (1978).
Murdick, R. G. and Karger, D. W. "The Shoestring Approach to Rating New Products." *Machine Design*, January 25, 1973, pp. 86–89.
Souder, W. E. "A Comparative Analysis of Risky Investment Planning Algorithms." *AIIE Transactions*, **4**, No. 1: 56–62 (1972).

10

Program Planning and Budgeting

10.0 INTRODUCTION

The program plan specifies the program goals and the means to achieve them. For example, the program plan for the development of a new product would specify the nature of the work to be carried out, the assignment of the various responsibilities, the time phasing of the work, the performance targets to be met by the new product, the milestones and the deadlines. The program budget is the monetized version of this plan. The program budget specifies the cost of achieving the desired targets and goals. Program budgets permit managers to plan the future amount and timing of money needs. They help in coordinating activities, and in controlling and monitoring achievements.

An effective planning and budgeting system can reduce inefficiencies through the careful scrutiny and analysis of achievements, costs and program allocations. Plans and budgets provide a highly communicable measure of expected contributions and achievements, thus permitting managers to fix responsibilities within the organization. Plans and budgets are also powerful influences on human behavior. They can be motivating or demotivating, depending on how they are established and used.

This chapter presents several methods and techniques for planning and budgeting projects and programs. Each approach is discussed and its application is illustrated within an organizational setting.

10.1 PROGRAM PLANNING PRINCIPLES

There are four basic principles that should be adhered to in designing any planning system. These four are: the commitment horizon principle, the principle of flexibility, the principle of navigational change and the principle of the most limiting factor.

10.1.1   The Commitment Horizon Principle

There is always a minimum future period of time during which one must be patient and remain committed in order to see the plans fulfilled. Once a plan is specified, one must stay committed to this strategy over some minimum horizon. Otherwise there is no chance that the plan can be achieved.

Like all the principles discussed here, the commitment horizon principle requires great judgment in its application. Clearly, staying too long can prove to be financially embarrassing, as anyone who invests in the stock market can testify. But if the plans are sound and the information and premises on which they are based are correct, then management must stay with the plans in order to achieve the goals.

The commitment principle tells us to carefully examine the feasibility of the plan before it is implemented. If the commitment horizon is longer than management can normally be expected to be patient, or if the horizon requires more time and resources than may be available, then the plan is not feasible. The ability of the organization to follow through is vital. When there is any doubt about the ability of the organization to accept the commitment horizon, then the plan should be seriously questioned and suitably modified. It is usually better to forego an opportunity or abandon a seemingly good alternative before the plan is implemented, than it is to have to terminate it later because the commitment has become too large a burden. The regrets and opportunity costs of having to terminate an effort once it has begun can be quite large.

10.1.2   The Principle of Flexibility

This principle says that any plan should have an element of flexibility within it. It should be able to bend and accommodate to changing environments and circumstances.

There are two ways that flexibility can be designed into the plan. One way is through a diversification strategy. An example is the funding of two or more alternatives in parallel as a way of increasing the chances of achieving the objective. This is sometimes done where it is difficult to predict which alternative will succeed, or where each alternative by itself may have a low probability of success. Another way is through contingency planning. In the contingency planning approach, funds are made ready for alternative plans which can be put into effect quickly, contingent upon various events.

Flexibility always has a cost. Diversification and contingency planning approaches are an added cost in time and effort. Through a comparison of the relative costs and benefits, the decision maker must decide whether or not such added costs are worthwhile.

10.1.3 The Principle of Navigational Change

According to this principle, it is better to make many small corrective changes, spread over a horizon, than it is to make one radical change at one point in time. In reality it is almost always necessary to take corrective steerages from time to time in response to unexpected events. Any plan that cannot adapt in this way will soon be out of date.

This principle is related to the principle of flexibility. However, the ideas behind these two principles are somewhat different. A flexible plan can accommodate many changes in the environment. This is a built-in quality of the plan. Navigational change refers to the managerial process of making small changes in response to ever-shifting forces. Even the most flexible plan may have to be constantly fine-tuned through periodic navigational changes.

10.1.4 The Principle of the Most Limiting Factor

In every situation there will normally be only one factor that is critical to the success of the plan. This is the factor that should receive the greatest attention in the planning process.

As an example, in introducing a new consumer product there is one factor that will normally determine its success. That factor is customer acceptance. Financing, production, engineering and other traditional business functions are of course highly important. But they are not usually the most limiting factors. Customer acceptance is paramount. Without it, the product will surely fail. This does not mean that the other factors are unimportant. They are highly important for complete success. But their absence will not necessarily kill the product. A lack of customer acceptance certainly will.

Once the limiting factor is ascertained, it should receive the bulk of attention within the planning process. Contingency plans and other ways around the limiting factor must be sought before the plan is launched. Any plan that does not contain effective ways to overcome the limiting factor is not a very worthwhile plan.

10.1.5 Using the Principles

Taken collectively, the four principles represent a set of design specifications for an effective program planning system. The system should be flexible enough to be useful in an environment where many unexpected events may occur. It should be possible to make small navigational changes in the plans and budgets with ease. At the same time, the system should provide for a sufficient amount of funding and a sufficient time commitment to see the plans through. There is nothing more damaging, to both the programs and the personnel, than an on-again/off-again program that vacillates due to a lack of commitment. Finally, the system should highlight and focus on the most limiting factor. The system should aid in planning for and effecting actions with this factor in mind.

The four principles are only general guidelines. Their implementation requires astute judgment in their balanced use. For example, an over-emphasis on the commitment principle rules out the flexibility and navigational change principles. Alternatively, a too-flexible budget may result in very little commitment to a decisive program.

10.2   DESIGN AND IMPLEMENTATION GUIDELINES

There are four fundamental questions to be answered in designing a planning system. These four questions are: How long should the planning horizon be? How rigid should the system be? What levels of the organization should be involved? How can the motivation to engage in planning be instilled?

10.2.1   Length of the Horizon

The length of the planning and budgeting horizon is often naturally delimited by several factors. The anticipated life of the project or the product places a natural limit on the length of the planning horizon. The organization's conventional accounting practices also establish a natural boundary. For example, most businesses account for their operations on an annual basis and they spend capital on a five-year basis. The length of the planning and budgeting horizon may also be limited by the amount of data available. As one looks further into the future, the uncertainty of the premises and the inaccuracy in the data may make the results almost useless. Thus, the choice of a horizon may be influenced by many factors. A judgment decision is required about all of these in establishing a horizon that is both useful and feasible.

10.2.2   Degree of Rigidity

All plans must have some rigidity. One of the purposes of a plan is to focus behaviors and align responsibilities. Thus, the plan must be somewhat resistant to modification. However, it is also clear that the plan must be flexible enough to adapt to changing premises (flexibility principle) and shifting trends in the environment (principle of navigational change). The practice of tying plans to annual periods with intermediate semiannual and quarterly review points provides a compromise between rigidity and flexibility. It also promotes the acceptability of planning. The users come to expect that these points will provide them with opportunities to make revisions and alterations, so that they are not rigidly locked in over a long time horizon.

10.2.3   Levels of Organizational Involvement

All levels of the organization must be involved in the planning process. Otherwise the plan cannot be an articulated system which coordinates and harmonizes all individual and departmental behaviors. The planning process cannot simply be delegated to a staff group which closets itself once a year and mysteriously emerges with a full blown plan. Rather, planning is a continuous process that involves all departments and levels of the organization. The overall process is very dynamic. The long range plans and projections must be tied to and coordinated with the short range plans. At each annual point, the short-range and long-range plans may be modified to bring them more into line with each other, to take changing conditions into account, etc. As time passes, the long-range plans eventually become the short-range plans under this scheme. Thus, there is a gradual movement towards increasing levels of detail in the plans, as they become more short-range with the passage of time.

Though all plans must be approved at the higher levels of the organization, many lower-level decisions and activities must precede these approvals. Detailed information must be assembled on the alternatives and detailed cost estimates must be made. It is natural that many parties within the organization will be involved in this process. As discussed in Chapter 5, because of the usual diffuseness of information and splinteredness of responsibilities within most organizations, several departments may be involved. A lengthy information collection and documentation process may take place before the program goes to upper management. And a long approval chain may occur before the plan is finalized. This process may involve several recycles back to the lower levels of the organization for more information or analyses. Though this process may seem to be a lengthy, time consuming and inefficient process, it is essential for implementation that all parties be involved throughout. Each party must be able to say that they have been heard from, and that they have been adequately represented in the process.

10.2.4   Instilling the Motivation to Plan

Careful planning and budgeting do not seem to be prevalent human behavior patterns. The establishment of a planning and budgeting mentality often requires a major cultural change.

There are three essential ingredients in developing a planning culture. The first ingredient is participation. All parties must be participatively involved in the design and implementation of the systems. A "hands-on" approach should be taken throughout. Many mistakes and false starts will occur. But it is only through the personal involvement and daily use of planning methods that individuals come to appreciate and adopt them.

The second ingredient is top management involvement. Top management must support the effort by showing the lower levels how careful planning can help the overall organization achieve its objectives, and how this reflects on the individual's own goals. Time and resources must be provided and an attitude of fatherly patience must be maintained by top management. Early mistakes must be overlooked with an eye toward "doing it better" the next time. The early years will be difficult ones in which the usefulness of planning is severely questioned, the payoffs are seriously doubted and there are many pressures to abandon the effort.

The third ingredient is positive reinforcement. During the early years, rewards should be given for simply engaging in the planning process— regardless of the quality of the plans which result. Any focus on accuracy may induce the planner to set readily attainable goals. Note that the rewards should not be monetary in nature. Monetary rewards may not have lasting effects, and may even be seen by the recipients as cheapening the process. Nonmonetary rewards that elevate one's peer status, that make individual contributions visible to others, or that increase the individual's sense of group involvement are normally much more effective. Thus, award dinners, dinners to "launch the plan," study committees and task force assignments can often serve as both rewards for the individual and the means to establish the planning culture.

10.3   TYPES OF BUDGETS

There are basically two kinds of budgets that managers must use. One is the cash budget. The other is the capital budget.

10.3.1   The Cash Budget

Table 10.1 is an illustration of a cash budget for a small operating department. The beginning of month (BOM) cash balance is carried over from

Table 10.1. Example of a cash budget.

						CASH BUDGET FOR DEPARTMENT A							YEAR TOTALS
	JANUARY	FEBRUARY	MARCH	APRIL	MAY	JUNE	JULY	AUGUST	SEPTEMBER	OCTOBER	NOVEMBER	DECEMBER	
BOM Cash	+$20,000	+$12,000	+$12,500	+$3,000	+$ 500	+$2,500	-$ 1,750	-$11,350	-$ 950	+$ 850	+$3,150	+$ 150	$20,000 *
Direct Costs													
Payroll [a]	3,000	3,000	3,000	3,000	3,000	3,000	2,500	2,500	2,500	2,000	3,000	2,000	$32,500
Supplies [b]	1,000	500	500	1,000	500	500	500	500	500	500	0	0	6,500
Travel	0	0	0	500	0	0	500	1,000	0	0	0	0	2,000
Salaries [c]	2,000	2,000	2,000	2,000	2,000	2,000	2,500	2,500	2,500	2,500	2,500	2,500	27,000
Inventories [d]	1,000	1,000	1,000	500	0	500	1,500	1,000	500	500	500	0	8,000
Totals	$ 7,000	$ 6,500	$ 6,500	$7,000	$ 5,500	$6,000	$ 7,500	$ 7,500	$ 6,000	$ 5,500	$6,500	$4,500	$76,000
Indirect Costs													
Rentals [e]	1,000	1,000	1,000	1,000	1,000	1,000	1,000	1,000	1,000	1,000	1,000	1,000	12,000
Heat	1,000	1,000	1,000	500	500	250	100	100	200	200	500	1,000	6,350
Light	1,000	1,000	1,000	1,000	1,000	1,000	1,000	1,000	1,000	1,000	1,000	1,000	12,000
Totals	$ 3,000	$ 3,000	$ 3,000	$2,500	$ 2,500	$2,250	$ 2,100	$ 2,100	$ 2,200	$ 2,200	$2,500	$3,000	$30,350
Transfers	+$ 2,000	+$10,000	$ 0	+$7,000	+$10,000	+$4,000	$ 0	+$20,000	+$10,000	+$10,000	+$6,000	+$9,000	$88,000
EOM Cash	+$12,000	+$12,500	+$ 3,000	+$ 500	+$ 2,500	-$1,750	-$11,350	-$ 950	+$ 850	+ 3,150	+$ 150	+$1,650	$ 1,650 **

[a] Wages of hourly employees.
[b] Expendable office supplies.
[c] Administrative and supervisory employees.
[d] Raw material purchases.
[e] Equipment.
* Beginning balance at start of year.
** Ending balance at end of year.

the end of month (EOM) cash balance for the previous month. The EOM cash balance is computed by deducting the direct and indirect costs from the BOM cash balance and adding or subtracting the "transfers." Positive transfers in Table 10.1 are the net payments to department A from other departments for work that department A did for them. Negative transfers are the net payments that department A must make to other departments for the use of equipment and space or for work that department A contracted out.

It is essential that the cash budget be developed on a monthly basis. There are many month-to-month swings in the cash balances that will not show up in an annual or quarterly analysis. This is illustrated in the data for June, July and August in Table 10.1. Severe cash shortages occur in these months. The cash budget plan shows that the manager cannot meet all the payroll, salary and other bills during June, July and August. This is the case, even though the plan shows a positive cash balance for the year as a whole.

This illustration shows the value of detailed month-to-month planning and budgeting. Severe shortages are highlighted and recognized before they occur. Several actions can now be taken to avoid the imminent cash problems in June, July and August. One method is to request more funds from upper management. Another method is to stretch out the payments for supplies and raw materials. The payroll and salaries accounts must be met, but trade payables can automatically be stretched out. However, this is an expensive form of borrowing. As an illustration, suppose the purchaser can take a 10% discount if bills are paid within 10 days of delivery. Referring to Table 10.1, such trade discounts amount to a total of 10% × ($8,000 + $6,500) = $1,450 for the year. This is a sizeable amount of funds. It is equivalent to the cost of about two to three months of supplies. Furthermore, stretching out these trade accounts is only a temporary solution. The bills must eventually be paid, usually within 30 to 45 days time. Stretching out payables may help the manager get over a minor temporary problem in one month, but the account must usually be paid in the subsequent month. This may come on top of that month's bills, so that postponing payments may only create larger problems in some subsequent month. In general, the adequacy of the EOM cash balances can be tested by several rules of thumb. Many firms and departments attempt to keep about two to four months' cash on hand at all times. This protects them against a sudden unexpected surge in their cash needs. For other firms or departments in more or less stable businesses a smaller or larger EOM balance may need to be maintained.

The budget in Table 10.1 shows that department A expects to encounter large swings in its cash position if the plan which lies behind this budget is implemented. Aside from the severe cash shortages during June, July and August, the budget shows several periods of large cash surpluses. From a financial management perspective, carrying such large balances is not economical because these funds are nonproductive. An examination of Table 10.1 shows that the transfers are the major contributor to these wide oscillations in the cash position. It might be better for upper management to provide more operating funds for the department, thereby reducing their dependency on the transfer payments. Alternatively, perhaps an improved manpower plan, or a better workload schedule, or an improved accounting charge-out plan is needed that smooths out the transfers and spreads them over several months.

10.3.2 Capital Budgets

Table 10.2 is an illustration of a capital budget for four projects, over a three-year horizon. Many detailed worksheets and calculations may be

Table 10.2. Illustration of a capital budget.

YEARS AND QUARTERS	INVESTMENTS REQUIRED $(000)				
	PROJECT A	PROJECT B	PROJECT C	PROJECT D	TOTALS
1979					
1st	$1,000	$ 0	$100	$ 0	$1,100
2nd	1,000	500	100	100	1,700
3rd	500	500	100	200	1,300
4th	300	750	100	0	1,150
Totals	$2,800	$1,750	$400	$300	$5,250
1980					
1st	200	1,000	100	200	1,500
2nd	200	1,000	100	0	1,300
3rd	0	800	0	0	800
4th	0	200	0	300	500
Totals	$400	$3,000	$200	$500	$4,100
1981					
1st	0	100	0	0	100
2nd	0	0	0	200	200
3rd	200	0	0	0	200
4th	200	0	0	0	200
Totals	$400	$100	$ 0	$200	$700
Project Totals	$3,600	$4,850	$600	$1,000	$10,050

used in arriving at the budget in Table 10.2. A summary worksheet is illustrated in Table 10.3.

A capital budget like the one in Table 10.2 provides upper management with a great deal of decision data. Table 10.2 shows that over the three-year horizon from 1979 to 1981 the firm will have to find a total of $10,050,000 for capital investment. Most of these funds are needed in 1979, and most of the 1979 funds are for project A. Project B is the largest user of funds. Most of the funds for project B are needed in 1980. Thus, it is fortunate that the need for funds is staggered in this way, and the two large projects do not occur in the same year. It is also fortunate that the four projects generally have different funding profiles. Thus, even though they exist within the same time frame, the projects do not all require heavy funding at the same point in time. Project A has a "front-end load" funding pattern and project B has a "mid-load" funding pattern. Project D shows a relatively level funding pattern. Thus, in the event that the total need for capital exceeds the available funds, management may consider the possibilities of shifting the project funding patterns. For example, it may be possible to shift project A from a front-end to a mid-load pattern, to delay the start of some projects, etc.

The capital budget is the starting point for financial management planning with regard to the sources of the needed funds. Will the funds come from inside or outside the firm? If internal funds are to be used, will this cause a sufficient drain on dividends that investors may lose interest in the stock? If external financing is sought, which source will be used? Will the company borrow the money or sell stock? If the company decides to borrow, will it issue bonds or try to get a bank or institutional loan? These are some of the policy questions for the top managers and the financial officers of the company. If sufficient funds are not available from a single

Table 10.3. Illustration of worksheet.

SUMMARY WORKSHEET FOR PROJECT A FOR 1979
$(000)

	1ST QTR	2ND QTR	3RD QTR	4TH QTR	TOTALS
Piping	$ 100	$ 100	$ 0	$ 0	$ 200
Mill Equipment	800	400	0	0	1,200
Casings	0	100	200	0	300
Fittings	100	0	0	0	100
Other Equipment	0	200	0	0	200
Other Capital	0	200	300	300	800
Project Totals	$1,000	$1,000	$500	$300	$2,800

source, e.g., selling bonds, then several sources may be combined. For example, the firm may devise a combined package of internal funds, stocks, bonds and bank borrowings. If insufficient funds are still not available with these combinations, then some projects may have to be eliminated.

Obtaining investment capital often requires long lead times. Therefore, capital budgets and capital forecasts usually are projected well into the future. Typically, ten-year, five-year and three-year capital projections are made and revised annually. This gives the corporate financial officer the details and lead times required to plan the amount and sources of funds needed.

10.3.3 Steps in Making Cash and Capital Budgets

There are four basic steps to be performed in making up budgets. The first step is data collection and solicitation. There is almost never enough data nor sufficiently accurate data to satisfy the desires of the budgeteer. Nevertheless, even the most conjectural budget is usually an improvement over no budget at all.

The second step is setting the planning premises. This involves making assumptions, or deciding to commit to various action-plans about levels of outputs and operations. Generally, the greater the output levels, the greater will be the needs for cash and/or capital. On the other hand, the higher output levels will also generally bring higher levels of revenues into the firm as the products are sold. But these revenues will usually lag the cash and capital needs by several months, so the start-up cash and capital levels will be the same with or without higher revenues. Simply put, it takes money (cash and capital) to make money (generate revenues).

The third step is making projections and extrapolations. These projections may be based on historical costs that have been converted to present values, using the methods discussed in Chapter 7. Anticipated future operating conditions and any new factors that were not historically present can be taken into account in making the projections.

The fourth step is developing the actions program and the follow-up controls. In this step, the organizational loci of responsibility for various parts of the budget are specified and the control systems are set up. In most organizations, cost centers will be set up and various costs will be collected and monitored within those centers. For example, the purchasing department may be charged with materials costs, the production department may be charged with all production and inventory costs, etc. The control systems will include methods for determining when the actual expenditures have exceeded the budgeted numbers by a significant amount, and what action should be taken to bring things back "into control." Control methods involve the use of variance accounts, in which the difference between actual and budgeted expenditures are tallied for those line items which management considers critical. Rules are proposed such as the following: "If the variance in the salary account exceeds 10% of the salary budget, a control action review is called for." The control action review involves a meeting with upper management to review the causes of the variance and to develop a solution which will bring salaries back in line with the plans. One of the conclusions of such a review, of course, may be that the original plan was unrealistic and a revised plan must be made. This illustrates the "management by exception" approach, discussed in Chapter 6. Upper management only becomes involved when the work is "out of control" or "out of variance." Chapter 15 presents a detailed example of these ideas on an actual project.

10.4   SYSTEMS BUDGETING METHODS

Systems budgeting approaches take the viewpoint that planning specifies the end objectives or outputs, and budgeting specifies the inputs to achieve these outputs. In the systems budgeting approach the end objectives are defined first. Then the best programs are developed to achieve these objectives. Finally, budgets are developed that actuate these programs.

There are many different kinds of systems budgeting methods. The two most widely known methods are the Planning-Programming-Budgeting System (PPBS) and the Zero-Base-Budgeting System (ZBBS).

10.4.1   The PPBS Method

PPBS (Planning-Programming-Budgeting System) is a way of thinking about goals and objectives and relating them to planned activities. There are two aspects to PPBS: the program structure and the objectives. The program structure consists of program categories and the finite program elements or activities within these categories. The PPBS methodology is quite simple: select, group and fund programs in such a way as to make the largest impacts on the objectives.

There are three steps in the PPBS methodology. First, obtain a list of goals or objectives for the organization. This can be done with the aid of the NI process discussed in Chapter 5 or by using some of the value assessment methods presented in Chapter 3. Second, assemble the programs and relate them to the goals in a relevance mapping or tree. Third,

Table 10.4. Example of a PPBS plan.

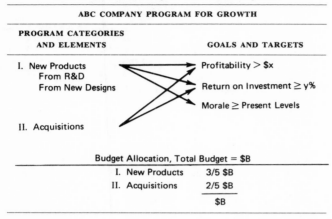

ABC COMPANY PROGRAM FOR GROWTH

PROGRAM CATEGORIES
AND ELEMENTS

GOALS AND TARGETS

I. New Products
   From R&D
   From New Designs

Profitability $> \$x$

Return on Investment $\geq y\%$

Morale $\geq$ Present Levels

II. Acquisitions

Budget Allocation, Total Budget = $B	
I. New Products	3/5 $B
II. Acquisitions	2/5 $B
	$B

design the budget on the basis of the relevance tree. An example is shown in Table 10.4. There are two program categories: new products and acquisitions. These categories represent the two basic means for achieving the company growth goals. The goals are specified in terms of three dimensions: profitability, return on investment and morale. Targets are specified for each goal. Profitability is required to exceed x, the return on investment is required to be greater than or equal to $y\%$, and the program must not decrease morale (morale must be greater than or equal to the present levels).

The relevance mapping in Table 10.4 indicates that the new products program is expected to achieve all three of the goals, while the acquisitions program is expected to achieve only two of the goals. If both programs are deemed worthy and nonoverlapping, then the relevance analysis implies they should respectively receive 3/5 and 2/5 of the total available budget of B. If a choice must be made between the two programs, then the new products program should be selected over the acquisitions program.

10.4.2   Extensions of the PPBS Model

The PPBS approach provides many opportunities to apply various kinds of scoring methods and cost-benefit analyses of the types discussed in Chapter 7 and Chapter 9. Table 10.5 presents an illustration of a PPBS benefits analysis, based on the data shown in Table 10.4. The impact of each ith program on each jth goal is specified as the value V_{ij}. These values

Table 10.5. Example of benefit analysis with PPBS.

	IMPACTS			IMPORTANCE
PROGRAMS	VALUE *	TO	GOALS	WEIGHTS
P_1 = New Products	V_{11} = 10	G_1	G_1 = Profitability	w_1 = 2
	V_{12} = 10	G_2	G_2 = Return on	w_2 = 3
	V_{13} = 4	G_3	Investment	
P_2 = Acquisitions	V_{21} = 10	G_1	G_3 = Morale	w_3 = 1
	V_{22} = 10	G_2		

Benefit Score S_i, where $S_i = \sum_{j} (V_{ij} w_j)$

P_1 = New Products	$S_1 = (10 \times 2) + (10 \times 3) + (4 \times 1) = 54$
P_2 = Acquisitions	$S_2 = (10 \times 2) + (10 \times 3) = 50$

Decision: New Products is preferred to Acquisitions

* On a value scale from 1 (least) to 10 (most).

may be solicited using the value assessment techniques discussed in Chapter 3. The relative importance of each goal is specified by the importance weight w_j. The value assessment methods discussed in Chapter 3 and the NI process discussed in Chapter 5 may be used to develop these weightings. A scoring model can be used to compute a benefit score for each alternative program, as discussed in Chapter 9. The benefit scores in Table 10.5 suggest that the new products program is preferred over the acquisitions program, since it yields a higher S_i score.

It should be noted that this example could be taken one step further, and a benefit/cost analysis could be carried out, as discussed in Chapter 7. If each S_i is divided by its respective program cost, the resulting benefit/cost ratios may be compared. Then the best program is the one with the highest ratio.

10.4.3   Experiences with PPBS

PPBS has been more widely used in government and nonprofit organizations than it has in private sector firms. The classification of programs into categories and elements seems to be more appropriate for government and nonprofit organizations. However, many firms have used it quite successfully. They have found that it aids in structuring their plans and budgets and assures that all their projects match up with the organizational goals.

PPBS is a highly flexible technique that can be used in many different ways to meet various needs. It provides a sound basis on which to build and apply cost-benefit methods and other systems analysis procedures. The PPBS concepts provide a sound structure for a rational budget development and program analysis. The PPBS logic assures that any proposed program that cannot be justified on the basis of its contribution to the organizational goals will not be funded. And the PPBS approach assures that the budget will be allocated to each program in proportion to its expected contributions.

PPBS has often been criticized because it requires subjective inputs and conjectural data. However, this is really not a criticism of PPBS. Rather, it is a criticism of all planning and budgeting processes. All planning and budgeting methods require the decision maker to deal with subjective data. The alternative to coping with subjective inputs is to perform no planning and budgeting at all. This is certainly a worse alternative. In reality, decision makers must make decisions. And these decisions must necessarily be made on the basis of much conjectural data. Systems techniques like PPBS can guide the decision maker in handling that data by providing a systematic structure. PPBS has also been criticized because it takes considerable time to carry out a PPBS exercise and it generates a vast amount of paper. This criticism is more an indictment of the way it has been used than a criticism of the method itself. Any tool can be applied in a rigid and bureaucratic fashion. The PPBS ideas are sufficiently basic and flexible that they can be used quite loosely. The user is free to select only those parts of the PPBS method that are most relevant and useful for particular applications.

10.4.4 The ZBBS Method

The Zero-Based-Budgeting System (ZBBS) is a technique for relating action plans to dollar plans. This is done in such a way that upper management can evaluate the action plans and determine the appropriate funding allocation for each plan. ZBBS is basically a way of assembling and reporting planned activities to top management for budgetary decision making. The budget is built up from the smallest activity, based on the assumption that anything could be zeroed-out. The ZBBS approach begins with zero activities and zero benefits. The budget is then built up by first selecting the most cost-effective activity, then the second most cost-effective activity, then the third most cost-effective activity, etc. until the available budget is exhausted.

There are five steps in a ZBBS exercise, as outlined in Figure 10.1. First, the organizational goals and objectives are defined and management makes sure that all the parties understand them. Second, the alternative

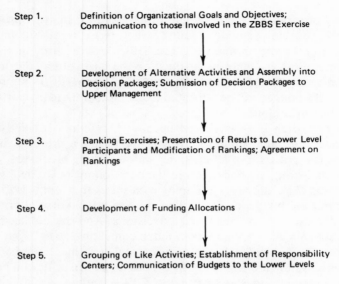

Step 1.   Definition of Organizational Goals and Objectives;
          Communication to those Involved in the ZBBS Exercise

Step 2.   Development of Alternative Activities and Assembly into
          Decision Packages; Submission of Decision Packages to
          Upper Management

Step 3.   Ranking Exercises; Presentation of Results to Lower Level
          Participants and Modification of Rankings; Agreement on
          Rankings

Step 4.   Development of Funding Allocations

Step 5.   Grouping of Like Activities; Establishment of Responsibility
          Centers; Communication of Budgets to the Lower Levels

Figure 10.1. Basic steps in a ZBBS exercise.

activities are proposed and assembled into decision packages which are submitted to upper management. Third, upper management ranks the alternatives and presents these results to the lower-level participants who originally developed them. The agreement of the lower-level participants is sought. The rankings may be modified on the basis of new information that comes to light during these presentations and discussions, on the basis of negotiations, etc. Fourth, upper management develops the funding allocations among the activities, based on the consensus rankings. Fifth, activities are grouped together, responsibility centers are established and the budgets are communicated to the lower levels of the organization.

10.4.5 Developing the Decision Package

A decision package is a list of alternative activities that relate to a particular organizational goal, with cost estimates for each activity. Each decision package includes statements about the purpose of the alternative activities, the consequences of not doing each activity, and its costs and benefits. A sufficient level of documentation is achieved when each activity can be evaluated and ranked, and when management can decide whether or not to fund it.

Note that in the ZBBS methodology the consequence of *not* funding each activity is specified. This is a rather interesting approach. The idea here is to ascertain the *criticality* of each activity. This can yield a very different perspective of the activity than would be gained from simply looking at the positive benefits derived from it. For example, the benefits derived from introducing a new product into the marketplace may not be very great in terms of the new revenues and new market shares that are captured. But if the new product is not introduced then the firm could fall completely behind its competition. Thus, looking at the regrets from *not* funding this new product program gives quite a different picture of its criticality.

The alternative activities which are presented in a decision package should include different ways to perform each activity and the corre-

Table 10.6. Illustration of a ZBBS decision package.

Project X Decision Package

Project X Goals:
    Provide a new type K product
    Meet customer needs for a high-performance pump
    Design a pump assembly whose performance-cost is less than product Y

Benefits:
    Increase in market share by 100% within 3 years of introduction
    Increase profits on type K products by 6%

Alternatives and Their Relative Benefits:
  1. Improve existing products
      No increase in market share
      Increase in profits on type K products by 1%
  2. Modify friction ratio
      No increase in market share
      Meet 5% of customer needs
      Increase profits by ½%

Consequences of Not Funding:
    Complete loss of market for type K products within six years
    Decrease in company profits by 1% in two years, and 7% in six years

Budgets Needed:

	1st qtr	2nd qtr	3rd qtr	4th qtr	Total
Project X =	$500,000	$700,000	$200,000	$50,000	$1,450,000
Alternative 1 =	$200,000	$200,000	$100,000	0	$ 500,000
Alternative 2 =	$ 50,000	$ 50,000	$ 25,000	0	$ 125,000

sponding levels of effort required. A minimum and a best level of effort should be specified, along with the relative contributions to the objectives for each level. Any alternatives that have been examined and discarded in making up the decision package should also be listed. An example of a completed decision package is shown in Table 10.6.

10.4.6   Ranking the Alternatives

The rankings are conducted on the basis of the information contained in the decision packages (e.g., see Table 10.6). Various procedures may be used to carry out the rankings, as illustrated in Chapters 3 and 5. Activities which have high regrets if they are not funded may be Q-sorted into a separate "must-do" category which will be funded. Activities which have few regrets if they are not funded can be sorted into a "do if money is left over category." These activities can then be further Q-sorted or ranked against each other. Rankings can be solicited from several parties or levels of the organization and compared. Then, consensus rankings can be developed by the application of the NI method discussed in Chapter 5, or the Delphi method presented in Chapter 6. If there are many different activities, they may first be sorted into categories and ranked within each category. Then, upper management can importance-weight the categories. Following this, all the ranks can be converted to importance-weighted rankings or scores using a scoring model approach (see Chapter 9). All the activities can then be compared on their weighted scores. This "nesting" procedure is especially useful in hierarchical organizations or departmentalized organization structures.[1,2] The ranked activities can then be arrayed from highest to lowest rank.

10.4.7   Funding and Budget Allocation

The ranked alternatives are funded from the top to the bottom of the list. The total contribution toward the objectives is ascertained by cumulating the individual contributions. If this contribution is deemed to be too low, then a larger budget may be indicated. If it is decided that the total contribution will not fall off greatly with some reduction in the budget then the total budget may be reduced.

Once a suitable program is determined, the activities are assembled into like units or organizational entities. The organizational responsibilities are determined for each activity and the activities are then formally assigned to each responsibility center.

10.4.8 Experiences with ZBBS

ZBBS has been widely used in government and industry with mixed results. Basically, top management likes the level of detail provided. But the lower levels do not like the amount of effort needed to supply these details. The amount of detail required and the paperwork volume sometimes creates a defensive reaction in those who must supply it.

10.5 GEMPA CHARTS [3]

10.5.1 Example of a GEMPA Chart

A Goals-Ends-Means-Programs Analysis (GEMPA) chart classifies programs into categories in such a way that they are viewed as means to specific ends or achievements. These ends are then related to the established organizational goals. Figure 10.2 presents an example of a completed GEMPA chart for a major research activity within a federal government agency.

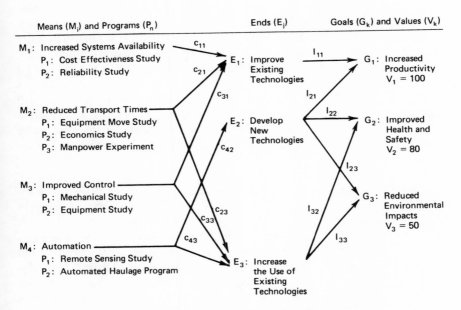

Figure 10.2. Example of a GEMPA chart.

10.5.2   Relevance and Contributions-Impacts Analyses

Using the successive ratings technique described in Chapter 3, the agency's goals were respectively value assessed as $V_1 = 100$, $V_2 = 80$ and $V_3 = 50$, as shown in Figure 10.2. The relevance of each means-ends chain to the achievement of each goal is specified by the arrows. For example, automation (M_4) is relevant to the goals of improved health and safety (G_2) and reduced environmental impacts (G_3), through its contribution to increasing the use of existing technologies (E_3). Automation is also relevant to all three goals through its contribution to the development of new technologies (E_2). Thus it is clear from this simple relevance mapping that the automation programs are highly relevant.

Once the relevance mapping is completed, a contributions-impacts analysis can be carried out. To do this, the individual contribution that each program makes to each end is described in writing. These contribution statements are then examined and discussed with other knowledgeable individuals within the organization. A contribution number c_{ij} is developed for the overall contribution which this mean is predicted to have on the associated end. This is a number on a scale from 0.0 to 1.0, where 1.0 represents the maximum contribution. To develop this number, a statement of the maximum contribution, in terms of effects and events, must be written so as to define the 1.0 point on the scale. The contribution number can then be developed in individual or group sessions, using the value assessment and group methods described in Chapters 3 and 5. Finally, the cost and relative contribution of each program are estimated and all the results are summarized in a contribution chart. Such a chart is illustrated in Table 10.7. The contribution number may be less than 1.0 because all the problems cannot be eliminated with the available technologies, or because the state-of-art is inadequate or because more information is required before any other meaningful programs can be devised.

The contribution charts for all the means leading to every end are consulted and studied. The ends statements and descriptions are then carefully studied in relation to the contribution charts. Then an impacts statement is written for each selected end relative to each goal that it impacts. This statement is discussed with and approved by the authors of the contribution charts. A total impacts number I_{jk} is developed for each end-goal combination. This number, on a scale from 0.0 to 1.0, is developed in the same way as the contribution number c_{ij}. Note that each goal is stated in quantitative terms, e.g., increase productivity from a yearly average of x tons to y tons per day. Thus, the I_{jk} number reflects the

Table 10.7. Illustration of a GEMPA contribution chart.

Total Contribution of M_4 to E_2 = .85
Total Cost of M_4 = $4,350,000

M_4 Programs:	Program Contribution, c_{ij}
P_1: Remote Sensing *Contribution* = defines major variables and relates them in a simulation model that predicts actual performance *Cost:* $850,000	.35
P_2: Automated Haulage Study *Contribution* = tests major theories and concepts in a field setting to disclose bottlenecks and inefficiencies *Cost:* $3,500,000	.50
	.85

relative amount of this difference achieved by E_j. For example, if I_{21} = .40, this means that it is expected that E_2 will impact G_1 by increasing the productivity by $.40(y-x)$ tons per day. It should be noted that the c_{ij} and I_{jk} numbers may have to be carefully normalized and standardized in those cases where a mean is relevant to several ends, and where an end is relevant to several goals.[3,4]

The worth W_j of each end may be computed from:

$$W_j = \sum_k I_{jk} V_k.$$

$$(10.1)$$

The total cost TC_j of the means leading to E_j is taken as the cost of achieving worth W_j. Thus, the benefit-cost ratio B_j for the jth end E_j is given by

$$B_j = W_j/TC_j.$$

$$(10.2)$$

The cost-effectiveness of any program package may be measured by the W_j values, the c_{ij} numbers and the program costs. For example, referring to Table 10.7, the value of program P_2 within mean M_4 is .50 W_j/.85. If P_2 is canceled, then B_j will become $(.35\ W_j/.85)/(TC_j - \$3,500,000)$. Thus, an incremental benefit-cost analysis can be made of every alternative mean and program. The relationship between benefits and costs is quantified in such a way that the effects of dropping out one or more programs or one or more means can be measured, in terms of the ultimate benefits and costs.

10.5.3   Uses of GEMPA Charts

The GEMPA approach provides important information to the program planner in designing the most cost-effective program packages and means. Using the worth numbers, impact values, contribution numbers and the program costs, the benefit and cost effects of various changes and configurations in program packages and means can be measured. By experimenting with various configurations, the program planner is able to arrive at the one configuration which gives the highest ultimate benefits for the least total cost.

A wealth of important information is contained in a completed GEMPA chart that may be highly valuable to the top level decision maker. All of the decision alternatives are arrayed, and the benefit and cost impacts of these alternatives are visible. Sufficient information is available to assist the decision maker in determining whether or not to accept the plan or ask for changes. On the other hand, GEMPA charts are very tedious to construct. A detailed benefit-cost analysis may involve many man-hours of time in data collection, group discussions and the resolution of issues. The contribution and impact numbers may be conjectural and their use in the benefit-cost calculations may involve many tenuous assumptions. However, the GEMPA approach need not be taken to such extreme detail. Even a simple relevance tree analysis like the one in Figure 10.2 can be quite helpful. A GEMPA chart that shows the alternative programs and how they interrelate with the organizational goals can be especially revealing and useful to a decision maker. The process of drawing up a GEMPA chart can improve the comprehensions of the programs and goals and provide a better climate for decision making. The communication benefits from GEMPA charts can be substantial if the organization is complex or hierarchical, or if there are many different programs and goals. GEMPA charts are thus likely to be more useful in large hierarchical organizations, where the general structure of the chart may parallel the structure of the organization.

10.6   FUNDING MODELS

A funding model is an integrated budgeting model. It can specify which alternatives to work on and how much to spend on each of them.

Table 10.8. Algorithm for the zero-one funding model.

STEP	ACTION OR DECISION
1	Rank the decision alternatives in decreasing order of their value. Alternatives with the same ranking (ties) may be listed in any order.
2	Select the highest-ranked alternative. If ties exist, select the highest ranked alternative with the lowest cost. Remove this selected alternative from the list of candidates and place it in the set of funded alternatives.
3	Subtract the cost of this selected alternative from the available funds. If the available funds are inadequate for this selected alternative, then replace it in the candidate list and select the next best alternative that can be funded with the available funds.
4	Iterate (continue performing) steps 2 and 3 until the available funds or the budget is exhausted. If funds remain after funding all the alternatives, or if the remaining alternatives each cost more than the available funds, then these funds are simply left over.

10.6.1 Zero-one Funding Models [4, 5, 6]

The simplest type of funding model is the so-called "zero-one" model. In this type of model, each alternative is either not selected and funded (the "zero" case), or it is selected and funded at a particular cost level (the "one" case). We may define a very simple zero-one funding model as follows. Let B be the available funds, let C_i be the cost of the ith alternative and let R_i be the contribution which the ith alternative makes to the organizational goals. The objective is to spend the available funds in such a way that the contribution to the goals is maximized per dollar expended. To achieve this, compute the value V_i of each project,

$$V_i = R_i/C_i, \tag{10.3}$$

and follow the algorithm in Table 10.8. This algorithm insures that the available funds will not be exceeded that is, it insures that $\Sigma C_i \leq B$.

10.6.2 An Example

To illustrate this model, let us take the data in Table 10.9 for five alternatives. The problem is to use the available budget of $6,000,000 so as to achieve the $120M sales target that has been set for department A. Each alternative is a different program or means toward the sales target. Alternative 1 is an advertising campaign, alternative 2 is a sales training pro-

Table 10.9. Five alternatives for achieving the $120M sales target for department A.

BUDGET, B = $6,000,000

ALTERNATIVES, i =	EXPECTED CONTRIBUTION, R_i	COST, C_i	$V_i = \dfrac{R_i}{C_i}$
1	$30M	$2,500,000	12
2	3M	1,000,000	3
3	10M	500,000	20
4	40M	2,000,000	20
5	28M	1,000,000	28

gram, alternative 3 is a new product introduction program, alternative 4 is an engineering development activity and alternative 5 is a present product improvement and product redesign effort. These alternatives may be used individually or in any combination.

Table 10.10 shows the results from step 4 of the algorithm at each iteration. The best alternative, the one with the largest V_i number is selected first. This is alternative 5. Then the next best alternative is selected, and so forth, until the budget is exhausted. The indicators in the last two columns of Table 10.10 track the changes in the decision variables at each iteration. The "Increase in ΣV_i" column of Table 10.10 shows the incremental change in the total value of the portfolio for each incremental expenditure. The last column of Table 10.10 tracks the average change in total contribution per total expenditure level. Collectively, these two columns show the effects of selecting the best alternative first. The results in Table 10.10 show that the $120M sales target cannot be met with the available $6,000,000 budget. Increasing the budget to $7,000,000 and funding all five of the alternatives in Table 10.9 would raise the total contribution, ΣR_i, to $111M. This is still short of the $120M target. The five alternatives are simply not sufficient to achieve the desired target.

It may be that the $120M target is simply too high for department A. Moreover, the budget may also be too large. In fact, if the five alternatives shown in Table 10.9 are the only ones available, then the wisdom of spending much more than $3,500,000 (iteration 3, Table 10.10) should be questioned. Beyond this point, the incremental value per dollar expended falls off rapidly, as shown by the data in the "Increase in ΣV_i" column of Table 10.10. One must wonder if the $2,500,000 expended at iteration 4 in Table 10.10 can be used more productively elsewhere. Thus, it appears that $78M is a much more viable target for department A than the $120M goal that has been set. In short, the budget may have been set *too large*. A $3,500,000 budget may be more reasonable.

Table 10.10. Results from the algorithm.

ITERATION NUMBER	PORTFOLIO	ΣC_i	ΣR_i	ΣV_i	INDICATORS INCREASE IN ΣV_i	$\dfrac{\Sigma R_i}{\Sigma C_i}$
1	Alternative 5	$1,000,000	$28M	28	28	28.0
2	Alternative 5 +Alternative 3	$1,500,000	$38M	48	20	25.3
3	Alternative 5 +Alternative 3 +Alternative 4	$3,500,000	$78M	68	20	22.3
4	Alternative 5 +Alternative 3 +Alternative 4 +Alternative 1	$6,000,000	$108M	80	12	18.0

Budget is exhausted

The more common situation, of course, is the case where a department feels their budget has been set too low. Table 10.11 illustrates a case where the total budget has, indeed, been set so low that it adversely constrains the department's contributions. The difference between the purchasing power of this $2,500,000 budget and a $3,500,000 budget can be seen by comparing the data in Tables 10.10 and 10.11. For the additional $1,000,000 difference between the $2,500,000 budget in Table 10.11 and a $3,500,000 budget in Table 10.10, there is, an additional increase in ΣR_i from $41M to $78M. That is, the incremental value-contribution rate is ($78M − $41M)/$1,000,000 = 37. This is higher than the rate (the V_i number) for any of the alternatives in Table 10.9. How can this be? The answer is that the $2,500,000 budget is a *very* uneconomical one. From Table 10.11 we can see that the economically questionable alternative 2 (see Table 10.9) was funded at the last iteration. Why? Because there was no other alternative use for the $1,000,000 which remained at iteration 3, the algorithm brought alternative 2 into the portolio. If the total budget had been $3,500,000 the algorithm would *not* have selected alternative 2. Rather, it would have selected the economically superior alternative 4. This is precisely what happened in Table 10.10. Thus, it is the suboptimal $2,500,000 budget that severely constrains the results in Table 10.11.

Table 10.11. Results under a budget limit of $2,500,000.

ITERATION NUMBER	PORTFOLIO	ΣC_i	ΣR_i	INDICATORS INCREASE IN ΣV_i	$\dfrac{\Sigma R_i}{\Sigma C_i}$
1	Alternative 5	$1,000,000	$28M	28	28
2	Alternative 5 Alternative 3	$1,500,000	$38M	20	25.3
3	Alternative 5 Alternative 3 Alternative 2	$2,500,000	$41M	3	16.4

Budget is exhausted

10.6.3   General Form Funding Models

In the general form funding model, each decision alternative has several alternative funding levels. Recall that in the zero-one case, either $0 or C_i could be allocated to the ith alternative. In the general form model, either $0, C_{i1}, \$C_{i2}, \$C_{i3}, \ldots \$C_{in}$ may be allocated to the ith alternative. Thus, the objective is to find the best level of expenditure for each alternative that is selected, in addition to selecting the best alternative(s). This is a complex analytical problem, and much more complex algorithms than the one in Table 10.8 are required to solve such problems. Sophisticated mathematical programming methods are normally used to solve these types of problems.[5,6] More is said about this in Chapter 14.

10.6.4   Uses of Funding Models

Funding models can assist in the arduous and clerically burdensome task of making up budgets. They are especially useful where there are many alternative combinations of programs and projects or activities. In large organizations, budgets and targets are sometimes arbitrarily set. Like the above example for department A, the targets and budgets may not be completely consistent and appropriate. A funding model can be used to suggest more appropriate goals and budgets, and to insure that the alternatives are funded at levels that are consistent with their contributions to the organizational goals.

10.7 SUMMARY

The effectiveness of program planning can be improved by devoting proper attention to the commitment horizon, the flexibility and navigational change principles, and the most limiting factor concept. By involving all levels of the organization in participation in the planning exercises, by using some simple motivational methods, and by carefully paying attention to basic human needs, a planning culture can be instituted. Modern cash budgeting and capital budgeting techniques, PPBS and ZBBS methods, GEMPA charts and other systems concepts can thus come to be a natural part of the daily decision making processes within any organization.

These techniques and processes provide the basis for the application of funding models. Such models can significantly aid in reducing the arduous clerical chores in budget development. They can also increase the capability of the decision maker to develop budgets that are neither too small nor too large, and to insure that these budgets are consistent with the organizational goals and performance targets.

10.8 REFERENCES

1. Easton, Allan. *Complex Managerial Decisions Involving Multiple Objectives*. New York: John Wiley & Sons, Inc., 1973, pp. 70–123; 168–217.
2. Fishburn, P. C. *Decision And Value Theory*. New York: John Wiley & Sons, Inc., 1964, pp. 77–130.
3. Souder, Wm. E. "Goals, Ends, Means, Programs (GEMPA) Charting—A New Approach to Program Planning and Analysis." Technology Management Studies Group, University of Pittsburgh, Pittsburgh, Pennsylvania, June 5, 1977.
4. Churchman, C. W.; Ackoff, R. L.; and Arnoff, E. L. *Introduction to Operations Research*. New York: John Wiley & Sons, Inc., 1957, pp. 136–154.
5. Mangasarian, O. L., "Nonlinear Programming," in the *Handbook of Operations Research: Foundations and Fundamentals*, Vol. 1, J. J. Moder and S. E. Elmaghraby (eds.), New York: Van Nostrand Reinhold Company, 1978, pp. 245–262.
6. Souder, Wm. E. "Analytical Effectiveness of Mathematical Programming Models for Project Selection." *Management Science*, **19**, No. 8: 907–923 (1973).

10.9 BIBLIOGRAPHY

Bussey, L. E. *The Economic Analysis of Industrial Projects*. Englewood Cliffs, New Jersey: Prentice-Hall, Inc., 1978.
Drucker, P. F. *Management: Tasks, Responsibilities, Practices*. New York: Harper & Row, 1974.
Johnson, R. A.; Kast, F. E.; and Rosenzweig, J. E. *The Theory and Management of Systems*. New York: McGraw-Hill, 1967.

King, W. R. and Cleland, D. I. *Strategic Planning and Policy.* New York: Van Nostrand Reinhold Company, 1978.

Moder, J. J. and Elmaghraby, S. E. (eds.), *Handbook of Operations Research: Models and Applications,* Vol. 2. New York: Van Nostrand Reinhold Company, 1978.

Pyhrr, P. A. *Zero-Base Budgeting.* New York: John Wiley & Sons, Inc., 1973.

Robbins, S. P. *The Administrative Process.* Englewood Cliffs, New Jersey: Prentice-Hall, Inc., 1978.

Senju, Shizo and Toyoda, Yoshiaki. "An Approach to Linear Programming with 0–1 Variables." *Management Science,* **15,** No. 4: B-196 to 207 (1968).

Souder, W. E. "A System for Using R&D Project Evaluation Models in Organizations." *Research Management,* **21,** No. 5: 29–37 (1978).

Souder, W. E. "Budgeting R&D." *Business Horizons,* **13,** No. 3: 31–38 (1970).

Sutherland, J. W. *Administrative Decision-Making.* New York: Van Nostrand Reinhold Company, 1977.

Wheelwright, S. C. and Makridakis, Spyros. *Forecasting Methods for Management.* New York: John Wiley & Sons, Inc., 1973.

Wommack, W. W. "The Board's Most Important Function." *Harvard Business Review,* **57,** No. 5: 48–50 (1979).

Part V
Scheduling

Planning, scheduling and budgeting are all part of the decision making function. Theoretically, planning, budgeting and scheduling are activities that logically follow in sequence. In actual practice, these events seldom rigidly follow each other in such a neat sequential pattern. The decision making function could be made much more efficient if all these activities could be performed in some integrated fashion. But today's state-of-art in decision making methods is not yet at the point where this is possible. However, modern techniques and methods are available to increase the effectiveness of scheduling decision making within the overall decision process. The two chapters in this part of the book present and discuss these modern methods. Chapter 11 presents the most useful methods for sequencing individual jobs and groups of jobs. Chapter 12 presents the most effective methods for scheduling projects. Collectively, these two chapters summarize the state-of-art in scheduling methods.

11

Job Scheduling and Sequencing

11.0 INTRODUCTION

Scheduling and sequencing determine how the various jobs within the plan will be carried out. If there are many alternative schedules, finding the best one can be a difficult analytical problem. In addition, the choice of a best job sequence may be constrained by time limitations, delay penalties, target dates, physical layouts, manpower availabilities or budgetary considerations. It is not uncommon for a manager to have to fit the jobs into time spans and target dates that have been imposed by others. This chapter presents the most useful approaches for solving these commonly encountered job scheduling problems.

11.1 STATIC SINGLE-STATION PROBLEMS [1,2]

In the static case, all the jobs are on hand waiting to be processed. This is in contrast to the dynamic case, where new jobs may arrive and preempt the ongoing jobs.

As an example of the static case, suppose the six jobs listed in Table 11.1 are awaiting processing at a single machine or station. Let us further

Table 11.1. Static single-station problem data.

JOBS	JOB DURATIONS (DAYS)	TARGET COMPLETION DATES (DAYS)
A	11	40
B	7	22
C	6	9
D	3	16
E	8	13
F	21	35

assume the jobs are technically independent, e.g., there are 6! = 720 different alternative sequences of these six jobs. The choice of the best schedule will depend on the decision maker's objectives. Let us now look at the optimum schedules for some typical objectives.

11.1.1 Minimizing the Number of Late Jobs: Late-Job Schedules

If the decision maker wishes to minimize the *number* of late jobs, the algorithm presented in Table 11.2 will give the optimal solution. Applying this algorithm results in the computations shown in Table 11.3.

The job sequence C-D-B-A-E-F is the optimum "late-job" schedule. Two jobs (E and F) are late and the other four jobs are early. There is no better schedule, in terms of the number of late jobs. Given these results the decision maker may wish to renegotiate or reestablish the target dates for Jobs E and F.

11.1.2 Least Amount of Tardiness: Due-Date Schedules

The late-job algorithm in Table 11.2 can result in excessive negative job variances or tardiness for some jobs, as was the case for jobs E and F in Table 11.3. The "due-date" schedule is used when the objective is to minimize the maximum job tardiness. To obtain the due-date schedule, simply sequence the jobs in increasing order of their target or due dates. For example, the due-date schedule for the above six jobs is C-E-D-B-F-A, as shown in Table 11.4. There are five late jobs, as shown by the variances. Jobs E and D are each completed one day late, job B is two days late, job F is ten days late and job A is sixteen days late. These variances may seem excessive, but every other schedule that can be

Table 11.2. N-Jobs/one-station algorithm to minimize the number of late jobs.

STEP	DECISION OR ACTION
1	Sequence the jobs to be processed in increasing order of their target dates. If two or more jobs have equal target dates, then either may follow the other.
2	Obtain the completion dates (cumulative job durations) up to the point of the first late job.
3	Reject the late job. Repeat steps 2 and 3 until all those jobs which are not late have been scheduled.
4	Place the late jobs at the end of the schedule determined from step 3. Sequence these late jobs in increasing order of their durations.
5	Compute the job variances (target date minus completion date) for each job.
6	Note the number of late jobs, as indicated by negative variances.

Table 11.3. Example of late-job schedule computations.

(All times are in days)

		C	E	D	B	F	A
Step 1	Job Sequence	C	E	D	B	F	A
	Target Dates	9	13	16	22	35	40
Step 2 and Step 3	Job Durations	6	8	3	7	21	11
	Completion Dates	6+0=6	6+8=14	6+3=9	9+7=16	16+21=37	16+11=27

Reject E Data and Continue

Reject F Data and Continue

Step 4	Optimum Job Sequence	C	D	B	A	E	F
	Target Dates	9	16	22	40	13	35
	Completion Dates	6	9	16	27	35	56
Step 5	Variances	+3	+7	+6	+13	-22	-21
Step 6	Number of Late Jobs	= 2 jobs (Jobs E and F)					

Table 11.4. Example of due-date schedule computations.

(All times are in days)

Optimum Job Sequence	=	C	–	E	–	D	–	B	–	F	–	A
Target Dates	=	9		13		16		22		35		40
Job Durations	=	6		8		3		7		21		11
Completion Dates	=	6		14		17		24		45		56
Variances	=	+3		−1		−1		−2		−10		−16
Maximum Job Tardiness	=	16 days (Job A)										

generated from the data in Table 11.1 will have at least one job that is sixteen or more days late. The due-date schedule is, therefore, a very useful diagnostic tool which should be applied as part of a preliminary analysis of any scheduling problem. For example, if the best one can do is to have at least one job that is sixteen days late, then this ought to be known as soon as possible.

11.1.3   Minimum Net Late Time: Late-Time Schedules

There are some cases where it is desirable to schedule the jobs so that the total amount of tardiness in the late jobs is offset by the total amount of "earliness" from jobs completed ahead of their targets. For instance, this would be the case where there is an incentive plan that respectively rewards and penalizes early and late job completions. The net late time, or the algebraic sum of job earliness and tardiness, is minimized by the "late-time" schedule. To obtain the late-time schedule, simply sequence the jobs in increasing order of their durations. As shown in Table 11.5, the late-time schedule for the above six jobs is D-C-B-E-A-F. The job variances in Table 11.5 show that job D is completed thirteen days early, job B is six days early and job A is five days early. Jobs E and F are completed eleven and twenty-one days late, respectively. Job C is on time (zero variance). The total earliness of twenty-four days from the three early jobs does not quite offset the total tardiness of thirty-two days from the two late jobs. However, there is no other schedule that will yield a net late time of less than eight days with these data.

It should be noted that there can be more than one schedule with the same net late time. That is, there may be alternate optima. These alternate schedules may differ in terms of the individual job variances and job sequences. Thus one of the alternates may be more attractive than another for reasons other than the net late time. Unfortunately there is no very efficient way to find all these alternate optima.[2] The decision maker

Table 11.5. Example of late-time schedule computations.

(All times are in days)

Optimum Job Sequence =	D	– C	– B	– E	– A	– F
Target Dates =	16	9	22	13	40	35
Completion Dates =	3	9	16	24	35	56
Variances = +13		0	+6	–11	+5	–21
Net Late Time = 24 – 32 = –8 days						

may simply have to hunt for them by examining several other job orderings within the sequence.

11.1.4   Minimum Waiting Time

If the decision maker wishes to minimize the total amount of waiting time
in the system, the late-time schedule gives the optimal solution.[2] This is
because waiting time is a constant function of net late time. The waiting-
time computations for the above six jobs are shown in Table 11.6. Note
how the late-time schedule makes the growth in the waiting times visible.
Any levels which may be considered intolerable by management can easily be perceived as they build up.

For some purposes and in some industries the optimum schedule is
taken as the one that minimizes the difference between the sum of the
completion times and the total waiting time.[2] It can be shown that this is a
variant of the late-time algorithm. Thus, if the objective is to minimize this
difference, the late-time algorithm will determine the optimal solution.

11.1.5   Minimum Average Job Flowtime

The flowtime for a job is defined as the time from the point at which it is
ready for processing until it is completed. If the manager wishes to
minimize the average job flowtime in the system, the late-time schedule

Table 11.6. Example of minimum waiting time schedule computations.

(All times are in days)

Job Sequence	= D	– C	– B	– E	– A	– F
Job Durations	= 3	6	7	8	11	21
Job Waiting Times	= 0	3	9	16	24	35
Total Waiting Time	= Σ job waiting times = 87 days					

will also give the optimal answer to this problem. This is because flowtime is a constant function of net late-time. For example, from the optimum late-time schedule D-C-B-E-A-F in Table 11.5, the total system flowtime is the sum of the completion times (or dates) = 3 + 9 + 16 + 24 + 35 + 56 = 143 days. The average job flowtime is 23.8 days. By comparison, the total system flowtime and the average job flowtime for the late-job schedule in Table 11.3 are respectively 149 days and 24.8 days.

11.1.6   Importance-Weighting

It is not unusual for the jobs to vary in their relative importance. One job may be more critical than the others because its outputs will be used in another important contract, one job may be more important in terms of the dollars involved, etc. Any of the above schedules may be used under such circumstances. However, the job durations must first be importance-weighted. One importance-weighting scheme is to divide each job duration by the respective job importance weight. In this scheme, the importance-weighted duration I_i of the ith job is given by:

$$I_i = D_i/R_i, \tag{11.1}$$

where D_i is the duration of the ith job and R_i is its importance rank.

As an illustration, reference to Table 11.1 shows that for the six jobs, $D_A = 11, D_B = 7, D_C = 6$, etc. Suppose that job F is four times as important as any of the other jobs, which are all equally important. Then $R_A = R_B = R_C = R_D = R_E = 1$ and $R_F = 4$. And $I_A = 11, I_B = 7, I_C = 6, I_D = 3, I_E = 8$ and $I_F = 21/4 = 5.25$. Then the late-time schedule is D-F-C-B-E-A based on these I_i data.

11.1.7   Time-Weighting and Priority-Constraining

As Table 11.5 shows, late-time schedules tend to result in large positive and negative variances among the individual jobs. Even though these variances may cancel each other out in a large population of jobs, it is poor management practice to plan for jobs to miss their target dates by wide margins. Because such planning leaves little room for error, it can leave a decision maker feeling very uncomfortable.

Sometimes a target-date weighted late-time schedule can smooth out the individual job variances. One such target-date weighting scheme would be

$$T_i = r_i D_i, \tag{11.2}$$

where D_i is the unweighted duration of the ith job, r_i is its target date ranking and T_i is the target-date weighted duration. For example, using the above six jobs, the target date rank of job C is 1 or $r_C = 1$. The target date rank of job E is 2 or $r_E = 2$. Similarly, $r_D = 3$, $r_B = 4$, $r_F = 5$ and $r_A = 6$. Then from Equation (11.2), $T_A = 66$, $T_B = 28$, $T_C = 6$, $T_D = 9$, $T_E = 16$ and $T_F = 105$. This is only one of many weighting schemes that could be used. This scheme weights the jobs on the basis of their relative absolute target dates. In general, the appropriate weighting system is the one which reflects the decision maker's criteria. The late-time schedule based on these T_i data is shown in Table 11.7. Note that the order of the sequence C-D-E-B-A-F is ascertained from the T_i values. But the target dates, completion dates and other statistics in Table 11.7 are all based on the D_i values. In comparison with the results in Table 11.5, the weighted schedule smooths out the variances of the first five jobs. However, job F still has a large tardiness (negative variance) in Table 11.7.

One way to reduce this large tardiness in job F is to priority-constrain the system in such a way that F is forced to be processed earlier. As an example, suppose job F is constrained to zero tardiness. To do this, note from Table 11.1 that there are 14 days of slack between job F's duration and its target date. By examining the durations of the other jobs in Table 11.1 it can be seen that some jobs could be completed ahead of job F, within this 14 days of slack time, and still not make job F late. Suppose jobs C and E precede F. The total durations of these two jobs is $6 + 8 = 14$ days. Hence, if the sequence C-E-F-D-B-A is used the variances will be: C = +3, E = −1, F = 0, D = −22, B = −23 and A = −16. A little thought will show that this is precisely the due-date schedule (Table 11.4) with job F constrained to zero tardiness. This schedule has a maximum job tardiness of 23 days (job B). There is no other schedule with job F constrained to zero tardiness that will give a lower maximum job tardiness. It is of interest to compare these results to the results for the unconstrained due-date schedule in Table 11.4, which minimizes the maximum job tardiness. The unconstrained due-date schedule has a maximum tardiness

Table 11.7. Example of target-date weighted late-time schedule computations.

Optimum Job Sequence	=	C	−	D	−	E	−	B	−	A	−	F
Target Dates	=	9		16		13		22		40		35
Completion Dates	=	6		9		17		24		35		56
Variances	=	+3		+7		−4		−2		+5		−21
Net Late Time	=	+15 − 27 = −12 days										

of 16 days (job A). The difference of eight days in maximum job tardiness between the two schedules C-E-D-B-F-A and C-E-F-D-B-A is the penalty for constraining F to finish on time.

11.1.8   Satisfying Multiple Criteria and Constraints

As the above examples have shown, it is usually not possible to have the best of all worlds in a single schedule. There will seldom be a single schedule in which the number of late jobs, tardiness, net late time, average flowtime and total waiting time are all minimized. However, it is often possible to retain some satisfactory characteristics while improving others by developing hybrid schedules. This approach starts with the due-date schedule and adjusts it by interchanging adjacent jobs so as to make it more like the late-time schedule. These changes create hybrid schedules that have the combined characteristics of both the late-time and due-date schedules. For example, the sequence C-E-F-D-B-A is the due-date schedule with job F constrained to zero tardiness, as discussed above. If jobs E and D are interchanged in this schedule, the sequence shown in Table 11.8 results. This is a hybrid schedule with some of the characteristics of both the due-date and late-time schedules. It has some slack (positive variances) to take care of the eventuality that jobs C, D or F may actually run over their anticipated durations. The maximum job tardiness (25 days) is not far above the 23 day minimum that can be achieved with the F-constrained due-date schedule (C-E-F-D-B-A). The net late time is 49 days, the average job flowtime is 30.7 days and there are three late jobs (E, B and A). By comparison, the F-constrained due-date schedule (C-E-F-D-B-A) has a net late time of 59 days, an average job flowtime of 32.3 days and there are four late jobs. Thus, the hybrid schedule in Table 11.8 is better than the C-E-F-D-B-A sequence in some respects, and worse in others. Depending on the decision maker's objectives, the hybrid schedule in Table 11.8 may or may not be an improvement over the C-E-F-D-B-A schedule. If it is not, then other adjacent interchanges can

Table 11.8. Example of interchange of adjacent jobs, starting from the due-date schedule with job F constrained at zero tardiness.

Job Sequence	= C	− D	− F	− E	− B	− A
Target Dates	= 9	16	35	13	22	40
Completion Dates	= 6	9	30	38	45	56
Variances	= +3	+7	+5	−25	−23	−16

Table 11.9. Slack-time algorithm for improving net late time while minimizing maximum job tardiness.

STEP	DECISION OR ACTION
1	Start with the optimum due-date schedule.
2	For each job in the due-date schedule, compute the job slack S_i, where $S_i = (\Sigma d_i) - t_i$ for $i = 1, 2, \ldots n$ jobs. Here, t_i is the target date of job i, and d_i is the duration of job i. Circle all S_i values that are less than or equal to the magnitude of the maximum tardiness value.
3	From the circled values, select the one corresponding to the job with the longest duration, d_i. Place a subscript on the circled value which denotes that job is to be sequenced in position n of the n-job sequence. Of course, if only one S_i value is circled, then that job is selected as the nth position job.
4	Remove the job selected in step 3, and recompute Σd_i for the remaining jobs.
5	Repeat steps 2, 3 and 4 above until all the jobs have been examined, successively denoting each selected job as belonging in the n-1, n-2, etc. position.
6	Sequence the jobs according to the position denoted by the subscripts.
7	Compare the improvements over the original due-date schedule.

Table 11.10. Example of an application of the algorithm in Table 11.9.

			C	E	D	B	F	A
Step 1	Job Sequence, i	=	C	E	D	B	F	A
	Target Dates, t_i	=	9	13	16	22	35	40
	Job Durations, d_i	=	6	8	3	7	21	11
Steps 2 and 3	$\Sigma d_i = 56; S_i$	=	47	43	40	34	21	$(16)_6$
Steps 4 and 5	$\Sigma d_i = 45; S_i$	=	36	32	29	23	$(10)_5$	—
	$\Sigma d_i = 24; S_i$	=	(15)	$(11)_4$	(8)	(2)	—	—
	$\Sigma d_i = 16; S_i$	=	(7)	—	(0)	$(-6)_3$	—	—
	$\Sigma d_i = 9; S_i$	=	$(0)_2$	—	(-7)	—	—	—
Step 6	Optimum Job Sequence	=	D	C	B	E	F	A
	Target Dates	=	16	9	22	13	35	40
	Completion Dates	=	3	9	16	24	45	56
Step 7	Variances	=	+13	0	+6	-11	-10	-16
	Net Late Time	=	+19 - 37 = -18 days					
	Average Job Flowtime	=	25.5 days					

Table 11.11. Precedence-constrained algorithm for minimizing maximum job tardiness in the presence of desired job precedences.

STEP	DECISION OR ACTION
1	For each job, list out the desired successor jobs.
2	List the job(s) that are available for the nth position in the n-job sequence. The available jobs are those with no successors. (If all of the jobs have one or more successors, the problem is infeasible.)
3	Select, from the available jobs, the job with the latest due date. If there are ties, either may be selected. (Alternate optima are indicated when there are ties.) Sequence this job last in the schedule, and remove it from the available job set.
4	Define the available jobs for the n-1 position. The available jobs for the n-1 position will be those left over from the set available for the nth position, plus any that are desired predecessors to the job selected to fill the nth position. These predecessors can be deduced from the original desired successor job list.
5	Repeat steps 3 and 4 for the n-2, n-3, n-4 positions, etc., until the entire sequence of n jobs has been scheduled.
6	List the optimum schedule.

Table 11.12. Example of an application of the algorithm presented in Table 11.11.

	JOB	JOB DURATIONS (DAYS)	TARGET DATES (DAYS)	DESIRED SUCCESSOR JOBS
	A	11	40	D, B, F
	B	7	22	None
Step 1.	C	6	9	A, D, B, F
	D	3	16	None
	E	8	13	D, B, F
	F	21	35	None

Steps 2. and 3. The available jobs for $n = 6$ are B or D or F; the selected job = F
Steps 4. and 5. The available jobs for $n - 1 = 5$ are B or D; the selected job = B
Step 5. The available job for $n - 2 = 4$ is D (this is the only choice here)
Step 5. The available jobs for $n - 3 = 3$ are E or A; the selected job = A
Step 5. The available jobs for $n - 4 = 2$ are E or C; the selected job = E
Step 5. The available job for $n - 5 = 1$ is C (this is the only choice here)

Step 6.	Optimum Job						
	Sequence	= C	— E	— A	— D	— B	— F
	Target Dates	= 9	13	40	16	22	35
	Completion Dates	= 6	14	25	28	35	56
	Variances	= +3	−1	+15	−12	−13	−21

be made to generate other hybrid schedules that may be satisfactory compromises.

Occasions often arise in which the decision maker wishes to develop a schedule with a low flowtime or waiting time or net late time, while also minimizing the maximum job tardiness. The slack-time algorithm in Table 11.9 will often provide an answer to this type of problem.[3,4] Note that this algorithm begins by first optimizing on the primary criterion (tardiness), and it then seeks an improvement on the secondary criterion. An application of the algorithm is shown in Table 11.10, starting with the due-date schedule from Table 11.4. The algorithm results in a schedule D-C-B-E-F-A shown in step 6 of Table 11.10. This schedule improves on the 27-day net late time and the 27-day average job flowtime of the due-date schedule in Table 11.4. And it maintains the tardiness of 16 days.

It is not unusual for a manager to have to work within some job precedences which are imposed by other departments, by the nature of the work, etc. For example, it may be that job C must precede job E because its outputs are an essential input to job E. At the same time, the manager may want to minimize tardiness. The algorithm in Table 11.11 can usually provide a good solution to this problem.[3,4] An application is shown in Table 11.12 (using the data from Table 11.1 and some assumed precedences). The resulting schedule C-E-A-D-B-F shown in step 6 in Table 11.12 has four late jobs and a maximum job tardiness of 21 days. By comparison, the unconstrained due-date schedule (C-E-D-B-F-A in Table 11.4) had a maximum job tardiness of 16 days, with five late jobs.

In many cases, the decision maker may desire to minimize late-time in the presence of precedence constraints. The basic algorithm in Table 11.11 also applies to this case. However, instead of selecting the job with the latest due date in step 3, the job with the longest duration is selected. Thus, the algorithm for minimizing either tardiness or late-time in the presence of precedence constraints is the same, except that in the former the focus is on due-dates and in the latter the focus is on job durations.

11.1.9   Manpower-Time Trade-Offs

Table 11.13 presents three alternative manpower-time plans for performing six jobs. The "normal" job durations are the same as the ones in Table 11.1 at the first of this chapter. The "expedited" job durations are the case where additional manpower is applied. The "extended" job durations are the case where manpower is removed from some jobs. Note that, as is typical of many real situations, some of the jobs in Table 11.13 cannot be expedited or extended, e.g., jobs B and D. And some jobs can be

Table 11.13. Manpower-time tableau.

JOBS	NORMAL MANPOWER		HIGH MANPOWER		LOW MANPOWER	
	NORMAL JOB DURATIONS	NORMAL MANPOWER COMPLE-MENT	EXPEDITED MANPOWER COMPLE-MENT	EXPEDITED JOB DURATIONS	REDUCED MANPOWER COMPLE-MENT	EXTENDED JOB DURATIONS
A	11	1 man	2 men	5	1 man	11
B	7	1 man	1 man	7	1 man	7
C	6	2 men	3 men	4	1 man	10
D	3	1 man	1 man	3	1 man	3
E	8	2 men	3 men	5	1 man	12
F	21	2 men	3 men	10	1 man	33
Totals =	56 days	9 men	13 men	34 days	6 men	76 days

expedited but not extended (job A). Also, as is typical of many real situations, the decrease or increase in the job duration is not linear with a decrease or increase in the manpower complement. For example, in job C the addition of one man (expediting the job) creates a 33% decrease in its duration. But the removal of one man (extending the job) creates a 66% increase in its duration.

Table 11.13 shows that if an additional four men become available, for a total manpower complement of 13 men, the total duration of the six-job set could be reduced to 34 days. The algorithms and procedures discussed earlier in this chapter could be applied to determine the best sequencing of these expedited jobs. However, instead of expediting all of the jobs at once, it may be more cost-effective to expedite some jobs while leaving others at their normal manpower loadings. For instance, since job F is the longest duration job it seems reasonable to expedite it. It may also be worthwhile to expedite job A, the next longest job. On the other hand, it is reasonable to consider extending some of the jobs by reducing their manpower complements, while expediting others. One might even consider extending all six jobs and accepting a total completion date of 76 days. Is there some way to determine the optimum manpower-time trade-off?

The answer is, "Yes, but not absolutely." The decision maker's value judgments and desires to finish ahead of schedule, the need to have a cushion against contingencies, the competing uses for the available manpower and many other circumstances may influence the final decision. However, diagrams like Figure 11.1 can be helpful to a decision maker. Enough points must be plotted to give a reasonable approximation to the actual curve. The slopes of the various line segments will then show the incremental completion time response for each increment of manpower

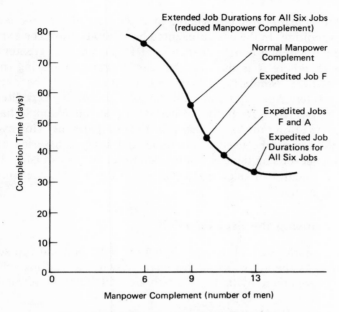

Figure 11.1. Manpower-time trade-off function.

that is applied. In general, the slope of the line segments in Figure 11.1 indicate that the addition of one more man to expedite job F from the normal case is a relatively productive choice. The Δ completion time = 56 − 45 = 11 days for a Δ manpower of 1 man, or a ratio of $\dfrac{11 \text{ days}}{1 \text{ man}} = 11$ days/man. But expediting both job F and A has a lower *incremental* benefit/cost ratio of $\dfrac{45 - 39 \text{ days}}{11 - 10 \text{ men}} = 6$ days/man. For all the jobs expedited the ratio is $\dfrac{39 - 34 \text{ days}}{13 - 11 \text{ men}} = 2.5$ days/man. Note that the *incremental changes* are used here instead of the overall changes. For example, to go from the normal to the all-expedited case, the overall average benefit/cost ratio is $\dfrac{56 - 34 \text{ days}}{13 - 9 \text{ men}} = 5.5$ days/man. However, this is *not* the correct ratio to use in deciding whether or not the case of all the jobs expedited is superior to expediting only jobs F and A. For that decision, the incremental changes in manpower and completion time must be used, as was done in the above calculations.

In general, if the ratio $\dfrac{\Delta \text{ completion time}}{\Delta \text{ manpower}}$ is greater than can be achieved by using the Δ manpower elsewhere, then the best alternative is to use them for expediting. In the case presented here, job F should be expedited only if the incremental benefit/cost ratio of 11 days/man is greater than a target rate R, where R is the rate that can be gotten by using that one person elsewhere. Similarly, jobs F and A should jointly be expedited only where 6 days/man $> R$, and all the jobs should be expedited only where 2.5 days/man $> R$. It should be noted that this example has used the total completion time as the basis for the comparisons. However, the above method could be used to compare and analyze a series of time-manpower trade-offs on the basis of net late time, number of late jobs, etc. It is simply a matter of selecting the manager's primary criterion as the basis for the analysis.

11.1.10 Choosing the Best Schedule

Table 11.14 summarizes all the scheduling procedures discussed so far in this chapter. As the above examples have shown, the various schedules that can be generated with these methods will differ in terms of the

Table 11.14. Simple single-station problems and their solution algorithms and procedures.

PROBLEMS	APPROPRIATE ALGORITHMS AND PROCEDURES
Minimize the Number of Late Jobs	Late-Job Schedule (Table 11.2)
Minimize the Maximum Job Tardiness	Due-Date Schedule (Table 11.4)
Minimize the Net Late Time	Late-Time Schedule (Table 11.5)
Minimize the Amount of Waiting Time	Late-Time Schedule (Table 11.5)
Minimize the Flowtime	Late-Time Schedule (Table 11.5)
Minimizing Maximum Job Tardiness with Least Flowtime	Slack-Time Schedule (Table 11.9)
Minimizing Maximum Job Tardiness with Precedence Constraints	Precedence-Constrained Algorithm (Table 11.11)
Satisfying Multiple Criteria	Combined Algorithms; Interchanging of Adjacent Jobs
Some Jobs are Deemed More Important Than Some Others	Importance-Weighting
Some Jobs Must Not Be Tardy	Priority-Constraining
Reducing Total Elapsed Time	Application of Additional Total Manpower; Use of Time-Manpower Trade-Offs
Selection of Satisfactory Time-Manpower Trade-Off	Application of Linear Approximations to Trade-Off Function (Figure 11.1)

number of late jobs and the earliness or lateness in the completion of these jobs.

In reality, it may be that none of the schedules which can be produced under a due-date, late-job, late-time or slack-time criterion are fully acceptable. Due-date schedules often result in too many late jobs. Late-job schedules usually result in one or more jobs which are extremely late. Late-time schedules may result in some very early and some very late jobs. Time weighting, priority-constraining and manpower reallocations among the jobs may also not lead to suitable schedules if there are many precedence constraints. But in most cases the procedures presented above will yield a feasible schedule. The decision maker may have to try several alternative schedules and hybrid modifications before a suitable one is found. In some cases the decision maker's aspirations and goals may simply be too high, and the decision maker may have to settle for something less than was originally desired. It will not be possible to minimize or maximize everything. It may not even be possible to achieve the desired levels on several schedule characteristics. Some compromises are usually inevitable.

11.2 DYNAMIC SINGLE-STATION PROBLEMS

In the static single-station problem, all the jobs are available or in the queue for processing. In the dynamic single-station problem, jobs may arrive and preempt the ongoing jobs. For instance, suppose the jobs are processed as received. It is not at all clear that this is optimal. It may be that when a job is received it should preempt an ongoing job, which is then restarted at the end of the preempting job. As it turns out, the rules for such dynamic problems are simple extensions of the static algorithms.

11.2.1 Preempting Rules

In many scheduling problems, the total duration of a job will be unaffected by the number of times it is interrupted. It can thus be interrupted and resumed at a later date. Preempting rules define the best way to conduct this interruption.

If the objective is to minimize the maximum job tardiness, then the optimum algorithm is given in Table 11.15. This algorithm states that the optimal rule is to give preference to whichever job has the earliest due-date.[5] This is nothing more than the due-date scheduling algorithm presented in a previous section of this chapter.

Table 11.16 presents the algorithm for minimizing net late time in

Table 11.15. Algorithm for minimizing maximum job tardiness in dynamic situations.

STEP	DECISION OR ACTION
1	At the time of arrival of a new job, compute $\Delta D = (d_j - d_i)$, where d_j is the due-date of the newly arrived job and d_i is the due-date of the job currently in-process.
2	If $\Delta D < 0$, preempt job i with job j, by ceasing work on job i and initiating job j.
3	If $\Delta D \geq 0$, simply add job j to the queue to be processed. At the time of each job completion, examine the queue and select as the next job the one with the earliest due-date.

dynamic cases. The rule is: always select the job with the least remaining processing time. Note that as a job is processed its priority increases under this rule, because its remaining processing time diminishes. In the extreme, one could continuously repeat the preempting decision at every time interval. In actual practice, either each job completion point or each job arrival point or both are specified as decision points. In other cases, arbitrary decision dates may be overlaid on the process. For example, at the end of each month, each year or each annual budgetary period the system could be "reoptimized." Thus the decision points may be selected so that they fit some chronologically-ordered and calendar-specified points in time, and are made on the basis of the then-current job system status. This decision-making structure is called dispatching and the rules that are used are called dispatching rules.[5]

To illustrate these ideas, recall that the optimum late-time schedule for the data in Table 11.1 was D-C-B-E-A-F (see Table 11.5). Now suppose that after job B has been started a new job G with $t_j = 7.5$ arrives. From Table 11.16 we see that job G can never preempt job B. This is because r_i

Table 11.16. Algorithm for minimizing net late-time in dynamic situations.

STEP	DECISION OR ACTION
1	At the time of arrival of a new job compute $\Delta T = (t_j - r_i)$, where t_j is the duration of the newly arrived job and r_i is the time remaining to complete the job currently in process. In general, $r_i = (t_i - a_i)$, where a_i is the amount of time already spent on job i and t_i is its duration.
2	If $\Delta T < 0$, preempt job i with job j, by ceasing work on job i and initiating job j.
3	If $\Delta T \geq 0$, simply add job j to the queue to be processed.
4	At the time of each job completion, examine the queue and select as the next job the one with the shortest remaining processing time.

$\leq 7 < t_j$, and hence $\Delta T = (7.5 - 7) > 0$. But suppose job G arrives when 2 days of work have been completed on the 11-day duration of job A. Then $\Delta T = (7.5 - 9) < 0$ and job G would preempt job A. The optimum late-time schedule would be D-C-B-E-A_1-G-A_2-F, where job A_1 represents the two days work on job A and job A_2 is the remaining nine days work on job A.

11.2.2 Handling Bundles and Strings

Sometimes bundles of jobs will be mixed in with the other individual jobs. For instance, a design shop manager may find that among his individual jobs are one or more contracts to perform a bundle of layout, artwork and specification jobs. Note that bundles do not contain technologically inter-related jobs. Rather, the jobs are simply *considered* as a bundle because of their source. Also, jobs in a bundle do not have any particular precedence ordering.

The optimum late-time schedule (see Table 11.5 and the associated discussions) can be determined for several bundles or a mixture of bundles and jobs using the following three-step procedure. In the first step, determine the optimum late-time schedule for each bundle by sequencing the jobs within each bundle in increasing order of their durations. Second, for each bundle compute the bundle duration $B_j = \sum_{i=1}^{n} t_{ij}$ for $i = 1, 2, \ldots,$ n jobs, where t_{ij} is the duration of the ith job within the jth bundle. In the third step, determine the late-time schedule for the bundles or the mixture of bundles and jobs based on the B_j numbers for the bundles and the job durations for the unbundled jobs. That is, determine the late-time schedule by treating the bundles as if they were individual jobs. The result will be a schedule of the form Job M-Job S-Job X-Job A-Job K-Job P, etc., where Job X-Job A-Job K is a bundle which was sequenced in the first step. Note that the due-date, late-job and other schedules discussed earlier in this chapter can be determined for mixed bundles and jobs in this same fashion.

A string differs from a bundle in that the jobs must be processed in a particular order. In effect, a string is a bundle of jobs with specified precedence relationships. The same approach used for bundles applies to a string. The only difference is that since a string is already sequenced, the first step in the above three-step procedure may be deleted.[5]

11.2.3 Handling Time-Variable or Stochastic Problems

Suppose that the duration of the ith job is randomly distributed, with a probability p_i of having an expected duration d_i^*. Optimum schedules can be devised using the importance-weighted approach described above, i.e., let $I_i = d_i^*/p_i$. When *both* the job durations and the target dates are randomly distributed, then the above algorithms still apply, but 95% confidence times should be used in the calculations. In general, $C_i = m_i + 2\sigma_i$ where C_i is a 95% confidence time or date for the ith job, m_i is the mean of the job times or dates, and σ_i is the standard deviation of these times or dates.[6,7] Thus, many dynamic problems can be handled as simple extensions of the static rules.[5,6,7]

11.3   MULTISTATION FLOW-SHOP PROBLEMS

In some scheduling problems there are m different stations or processing points and each job must be processed on each of the m stations. Moreover, each job must be processed in a preset technological order on the stations. That is, each job must first be processed at station 1, then at station 2, etc. (Jobs requiring fewer than m stations can be represented as taking zero times in those stations.)

11.3.1   *n*-Jobs, 2-Stations: Johnson's Rule

Suppose a decision maker wishes to schedule a series of jobs through two stations in such a way that the total time to complete all the jobs or the "makespan" is minimized. Table 11.17 presents the algorithm for minimizing makespan in the n-job, 2-station problem. This algorithm was originally developed by S. M. Johnson,[8] so that it has become known as "Johnson's Rule." Two assumptions must be met for Johnson's Rule to apply. First, the order of the stations is fixed and it is the same for all the

Table 11.17. Algorithm for Johnson's Rule.

STEP	DECISION OR ACTION
1	Develop a matrix showing the processing times for all the jobs within the two stations.
2	Circle the smallest job time duration in the matrix. If more than one job has this smallest time, circle all of these tied time values. Subscript the circle(s) with the numeral 1 to indicate the first pass through the data.
3	If the circled time is in the station 1 row, sequence the corresponding job in the first available position in the sequence. If the circled time is in the station 2 row, sequence the corresponding job in the last available position in the sequence. Eliminate that job from further consideration.
4	Repeat steps 2 and 3, subscripting the circles accordingly until all the available jobs have been sequenced (any ties may be broken arbitrarily).
5	Draw up a time schedule chart for the sequenced jobs.

Table 11.18. Example of the calculations for Johnson's Rule.

| | | | MATRIX OF PROCESSING TIMES (DAYS) | | | | | |

	Job I.D.	=	A	B	C	D	E	F	G
Step 1 through Step 4	Station 1 (Design)	=	8	10	11	$(8)_4$	$(15)_7$	$(9)_5$	12
	Station 2 (Costing)	=	$(3)_1$	$(5)_2$	$(6)_3$	10	20	12	$(10)_6$
	Optimum Job Sequence	=	D	– F	– E	– G	– C	– B	– A

jobs. For example, if the stations are "design" followed by "costing" it is assumed that all jobs will be processed in this order. Second, the processing times are assumed to be independent of their ordering or sequencing with the other jobs. That is, each job is independent of its preceding and succeeding jobs. The following example illustrates Johnson's Rule.

A service department that does design and costing work for the rest of the organization has seven jobs in its queue. The matrix of processing times is shown in Table 11.18, where the results from steps 1 through 4 of the algorithm are also shown. A time schedule chart of the optimum

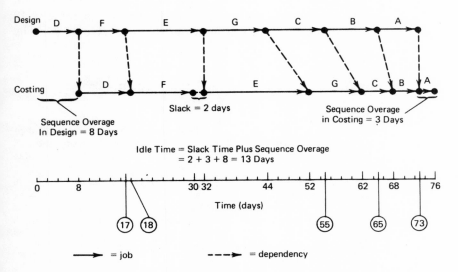

Figure 11.2. Time sequence schedule.

sequence is shown in Figure 11.2. This schedule may appear to be some-what inefficient because of the existence of some idle time. However, Johnson's Rule guarantees that a schedule with a lower makespan cannot be derived.

When more than two stations are involved, the number of combinations becomes very large and Johnson's Rule will not work. However, in the special case of n-jobs and 3-stations where the second station is domi-nated by *either* the first or the third station, then Johnson's Rule applies. The test of dominance is that either: (a) the shortest job duration in station 1 must be greater than or equal to the longest job duration in station 2, or (b) the shortest job duration in station 3 must be greater than or equal to the longest job duration in station 2. Then, the original 3-station problem may be collapsed into a 2-station problem by the relationships $D^*_{i1} = d_{i1} + d_{i2}$ and $D^*_{i2} = d_{i2} + d_{i3}$. Here, d_{ij} is the old duration of the ith job in the jth station in a 3-station problem, and D^*_{ij} is the corresponding new duration in the collapsed 2-station problem.[5, 8]

11.3.2 n-Jobs, 2-Stations with Orderings: Jackson's Rule

It is not unusual to have a mixed job queue in which some of the jobs must be processed first on station 1 and then on station 2, while others must be processed only at station 1, and still others must be processed only at station 2. If the objective is to schedule the jobs so as to minimize total processing time, J. R. Jackson has shown that the algorithm in Table 11.19 is optimal.[9] Let us illustrate its use with the data in Table 11.20. The

Table 11.19. Algorithm for Jackson's Rule.

STEP	DECISION OR ACTION
1	Sequence the jobs to be processed on only one station in the order of their increasing job durations. Do this for both the station 1 and station 2 jobs.
2	Use Johnson's Rule to optimally sequence the jobs that are to be processed in the following order: station 1 then station 2.
3	Use Johnson's Rule to optimally sequence the jobs that are to be processed in the following order: station 2 then station 1.
4	Combine these results as follows: (a) for station 1 the optimal sequence is the sequence resulting from step 2, followed by the sequence from step 1, followed by the sequence from step 3; (b) for station 2 the optimal sequence is the result from step 3, followed by the sequence from step 1, followed by the sequence from step 2.

Table 11.20. Data for Jackson's Rule problem.

	PROCESSING TIMES (DAYS)			
JOBS	IN STATION 1	IN STATION 2	TOTAL	TECHNOLOGICAL ORDERING
A	30	0	30	Station 1 only
B	70	35	105	Station 1 then Station 2
C	30	65	95	Station 1 then Station 2
D	0	75	75	Station 2 only
E	10	35	45	Station 1 then Station 2
F	30	5	35	Station 2 then Station 1
G	20	70	90	Station 2 then Station 1
H	0	45	45	Station 2 only
I	35	0	35	Station 1 only
		Total =	555	

Table 11.21. Example of the calculations for Jackson's Rule.

Step 1, for station 1: the optimal sequence = A-I
Step 1, for station 2: the optimal sequence = H-D
Step 2, for order station 1, station 2:

Job I.D.	=	B	C	E
Station 1	=	70	$(30)_2$	$(10)_1$
Station 2	=	$(35)_3$	65	35
Optimum Sequence	=	E – C – B		

Step 3, for order station 2, station 1:

Job I.D.	=	F	G
Station 2	=	$(5)_1$	70
Station 1	=	30	$(20)_2$
Optimum Sequence	=	F – G	

Step 4a, the optimum sequence at station 1 = E-C-B-A-I-F-G (225 days duration)
Step 4b, the optimum sequence at station 2 = F-G-H-D-E-C-B (330 days duration)

computations and results are shown in Table 11.21. The jobs are all completed in a total processing time of 330 days. "Jackson's Rule" guarantees this to be the minimum time possible with these data.

11.3.3 2-Jobs, *n*-Stations; Special Case for Akers-Friedman Rule

Consider the special case of two jobs to be processed by two or more stations, where the jobs are not processed in the same order but the

Table 11.22. Algorithm for Akers-Friedman Rule.

STEP	ACTION
1	Draw a set of orthogonal axes and set up the same time scale on each, running from zero to the durations of job 1 and job 2.
2	Lay out the processing times for one job (in its proper station order) along one of the axes, and the other job along the other axis. The longest total duration job should be laid out along the ordinate.
3	Block out the rectangular areas on the coordinate chart where a common facility is indicated on both axes.
4	Using only horizontal, vertical or 45° movements, draw a continuous line from the origin to the upper right-hand corner of the graph, all the time avoiding the blocked out areas generated in Step 3.
5	Determine the idle times for the jobs by adding the horizontal and vertical segments.
6	Select the sequence with the least total elapsed time.

ordering of the stations is fixed for each job. S. B. Akers and J. Friedman have shown that the algorithm in Table 11.22 is optimal for minimizing the elapsed time to process the two jobs.[10]

For simplicity, let us illustrate this algorithm when there are only three stations involved. Let the processing times for job A be 4 weeks, 8 weeks and 8 weeks respectively in stations 1, 2 and 3. Let the processing times for job B be 8 weeks each in stations 2 and 3, and 6 weeks in station 1. Figure 11.3 shows the layout of the jobs and station times according to the algorithm described in Table 11.22. The completion point is marked in Figure 11.3. All other points between the origin and this completion point are the coordinates of the state of completion. For example, point X in Figure 11.3 is the point at which job A has gone through stations 1 and 2, and job B has gone through stations 2 and 3, in that order. The shaded blocks represent the infeasible combinations where both jobs are being simultaneously processed. Five different alternative paths are shown in Figure 11.3. Each of these is a feasible time schedule for processing the two jobs. There are many others; only these five are shown here. Horizontal segments represent the processing of job A; vertical segments represent the processing of job B. A 45° segment represents the processing of both jobs A and B. To minimize the total duration, select the path with the most 45° segments. The effectiveness of each path is easily measured by tallying the total idle time along each path, which is represented by the horizontal and vertical segments. Of the five paths shown in Figure 11.3, path number 3 has the lowest total idle time of six days.

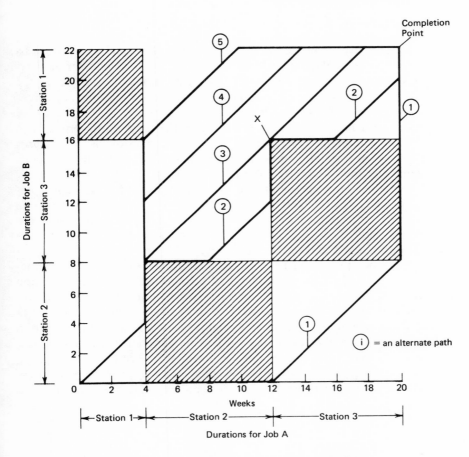

Figure 11.3. Akers-Friedman rule for 2-jobs, n-facilities.

11.3.4 *n*-Jobs, *m*-Stations

In general, as either n or m become very large, then the number of possible schedules increases geometrically. Even with very rapid computers, to search through all these schedules for the optimal one could take a very long time. Some sophisticated methods have been developed, but few of them are feasible for "back-of-the-envelope" use.[11] Acceptable solutions can sometimes be generated by the stepwise application of Johnson's Rule or Jackson's Rule in which the m-stations are nested and sequentially collapsed to smaller problems.[5]

11.4 SUMMARY

Selecting the best job processing sequence for more than four or five jobs can be a difficult analytical problem because of the large number of alternative schedules to choose from. The analytical problems of selecting the best schedule are often confounded by the presence of multiple objectives and constraints, some of which may be contradictory.

This chapter has presented and illustrated the most useful procedures for handling commonly encountered job scheduling problems. Procedures were presented for static and dynamic single-station job shop problems, deterministic and stochastic job shop problems, and multistation flow shop problems. These procedures cannot be expected to give highly precise and exact answers to complex sequencing problems that involve large numbers of jobs and processing stations. Such large-scale problems are notoriously difficult to solve, even with sophisticated mathematical programming methods and modern computers. However, the simplicity of the approaches presented here makes them amenable to "back-of-the-envelope" use. This becomes especially important when the decision maker is in the plant or at the field site where immediate answers are needed and sophisticated computers or mathematical models are not at hand. The procedures in this chapter can serve as a rapid "first cut" from which a decision maker can make on-the-spot generalizations about magnitudes or directions. This enables a decision maker to respond more quickly to time pressures and pressing clients who may only need to know if such-and-such targets are feasible, or who may only need approximate answers.

11.5 REFERENCES

1. Salvador, M. S. "Scheduling and Sequencing," in *Handbook of Operations Research: Models and Applications*, J. J. Moder and S. E. Elmaghraby (eds.), New York: Van Nostrand Reinhold Company, 1978, pp. 268–300.
2. Baker, K. R. *Introduction to Sequencing and Scheduling*. New York: John Wiley & Sons, Inc., 1974, pp. 43–58.
3. Heck, H. and Roberts, S. "A Note on the Extension of a Result On Scheduling With Secondary Criteria." *Naval Research Logistics Quarterly*, 9, No. 2: 403–405 (1972).
4. Woolsey, R. E. D. and Swanson, H. S. *Operations Research for Immediate Application*. New York: Harper & Row, 1975, pp. 31–37.
5. Baker, K. R. *op. cit.*, pp. 42–78; 144–162.
6. Crabhill, T. B. and Maxwell, W. L. "Single Machine Sequencing with Random Processing Times and Random Due-Dates." *Naval Research Logistics Quarterly*, 16, No. 4: 27–38 (1969).
7. For details, see any elementary statistics text, e.g., Spiegel, M. R. *Theory and Problems of Statistics*. New York: Schaum, 1961, pp. 69–84.

8. Johnson, S. M. "Optimal Two and Three Stage Production Schedules With Setup Times Included." *Naval Research Logistics Quarterly,* **1,** No. 1: 61–68 (1954).

9. Jackson, J. R. "An Extension of Johnson's Results on Job-Lot Scheduling." *Naval Research Logistics Quarterly,* **3,** No. 3: 201–204 (1956).

10. Akers, S. B. and Friedman, J. "A Non-Numerical Approach to Production Scheduling Problems." *Operations Research,* **4,** No. 3: 429–442 (1955).

11. Bansal, S. P. "Minimizing the Sum of Completion Times of *n* Jobs over *m* Machines In a Flowshop-A Branch and Bound Approach." *AIIE Transactions,* **9,** No. 3: 306–311 (1977).

11.6 BIBLIOGRAPHY

Baker, K. R. *Introduction to Sequencing and Scheduling.* New York: John Wiley & Sons, Inc., 1974.

Conway, R. W.; Maxwell, W. L.; and Miller, L. W. *Theory of Scheduling.* Reading, Massachusetts: Addison-Wesley Publishing Co., Inc., 1967.

Driscoll, W. C. and Emmons, Hamilton. "Scheduling Production on One Machine and Changeover Costs." *AIIE Transactions,* **9,** No. 4: 388–395 (1977).

Elmaghraby, S. E. "The Economic Lot Scheduling Problem (ELSP): Review and Extensions." *Management Science,* **24,** No. 6: 587–598 (1978).

Giglio, R. H. and Wagner, H. M. "Approximate Solutions to the Three-Machine Scheduling Problem," *Operations Research,* **12,** No. 2: 103–114 (1964).

Ignall, E. J. and Schrage, L. E. "Application of the Branch and Bound Technique to Some Flow-Shop Scheduling Problems." *Operations Research,* **13,** No. 3: 400–412 (1965).

Johnson, L. A. and Montgomery, D. C. *Operations Research in Production Planning, Scheduling, and Inventory Control.* New York: John Wiley & Sons, Inc., 1974.

Morton, T. E. and Dharan, B. G. "Algoristics for Single-Machine Sequencing With Precedence Constraints." *Management Science,* **24,** No. 10: 1011–1020 (1978).

Sidney, J. B. "Decomposition Algorithms for Single-Machine Sequencing with Precedence Relations and Deferral Costs." *Operations Research,* **23,** No. 2: 283–298 (1977).

Smith, W. E. "Various Optimizers for Single-Stage Production." *Naval Research Logistics Quarterly,* **3,** No. 1: 59–66 (1956).

Townsend, W. "Minimizing the Maximum Penalty in the Two-Machine Flow Shop." *Management Science,* **24,** No. 2: 230–234 (1977).

Vargas, G.; Hottenstein, M.; Aggarwal, S. "Using Utility Functions for Aggregate Scheduling in Health Maintenance Organizations (HMO's)." *AIIE Transactions,* **11,** No. 4: 327–335 (1979).

12

Project Scheduling

12.0 INTRODUCTION

The preceding chapter dealt with methods for scheduling recurring or repetitive jobs through one or more processing stations. This chapter deals with methods for scheduling nonrepetitive or one-time jobs within a total project. A project is a collection of several interdependent jobs which are jointly aimed at achieving some end item or objective. Examples would be a project to develop a new product or a project to achieve some targeted level of output. Many different jobs and activities must be performed by several different individuals, groups and organizations in order to meet such objectives. The project scheduling decision problem is thus concerned with finding the most cost-effective way to schedule and dovetail the necessary jobs to complete the project.

A large number of methods are available for project scheduling. Each has various advantages and disadvantages and each is best suited to different circumstances. This chapter reviews and illustrates these methods, showing how and when each can best be used.

12.1 DETERMINISTIC TIME SCHEDULING METHODS

Deterministic methods apply when the jobs, their interdependencies and their durations are known with relative certainty. For instance, if all the jobs within the project can be visualized, if their successor-predecessor orderings can be specified and their time durations are known, then deterministic methods apply. Deterministic project scheduling methods thus fall under the general category of decision making under certainty, as discussed in Chapter 4. Gantt charts, dependency diagrams, arrow networks, time-scaled networks and the critical path method (CPM) are the most commonly used deterministic techniques.

12.1.1 Gantt Charts

In the early 1900's, the industrial engineer Henry Gantt developed and applied a milestone chart that has continued to reappear in a variety of forms and applications.[1] Table 12.1 is a job list for a hypothetical project, project A. The Gantt chart in Figure 12.1 is developed from this list. The length of each rectangle is proportional to the duration of each job. The height of each rectangle is not meaningful; any suitable length may be chosen. For eye appeal and ease in conveying relationships, the jobs are usually arrayed in the approximate order of their completion dates. An often-used alternative form of the Gantt chart is to show the jobs as labeled lines instead of labeled boxes.

Gantt charts effectively communicate the durations and responsibility areas of the jobs. But they do not show the job interdependencies, or the successor-predecessor relations between them. This information is essential for time scheduling and resource allocation decision making.

12.1.2 Dependency Diagrams

It is a short step to go from the Gantt chart in Figure 12.1 to the dependency network in Figure 12.2. The only additional information required is the interjob dependencies shown in Table 12.2. A dependency diagram is constructed as follows. First, lay out two parallel vertical lines on each side of a large sheet of paper and label them "project start" and "project complete." The diagram is not drawn to scale, so the distance between these two lines bears no relationship to any job durations or to the total project duration. Second, from the predecessor-successor listing (Table 12.2), select all those jobs which have no predecessors. Using rectangles of any suitable size, diagram these jobs along the right-hand side of the "project start" line, as illustrated for jobs 1, 2 and 3 in Figure 12.2. Third, select those jobs which have no successors and diagram them along the left-hand side of the "project complete" line, as illustrated for jobs 6, 10 and 11 in Figure 12.2. Finally, using boxes to depict jobs and arrows to connect the dependent jobs, fill in the remainder of the diagram according to the predecessor-successor list (Table 12.2).

It is easy to gain the mistaken impression that the sizes of the boxes, the lengths of the arrows or the distances between the project start and completion lines are somehow meaningful in this diagram. They are not. A dependency diagram shows predecessor-successor relationships and nothing more. The arrows simply indicate the dependencies. However, dependency diagrams show many important job interrelations that Gantt charts do not. For instance, Figure 12.2 explains why some of the jobs in Figure 12.1 are scheduled earlier than others and why other jobs are

Table 12.1. Job list for project A.

JOB #	ACTIVITY	ANTICIPATED JOB DURATION, DAYS
1	Perform Process X	6
2	Physical Set-Up Work	7
3	Perform Process B	5
4	Conduct Analytical Work	4
5	Prototype Development Work	6
6	Technical Evaluation	4
7	System Cost Analyses	3
8	Component Development Work	6
9	Component Evaluation	2
10	Pad Design Work	2
11	System Design Work	5

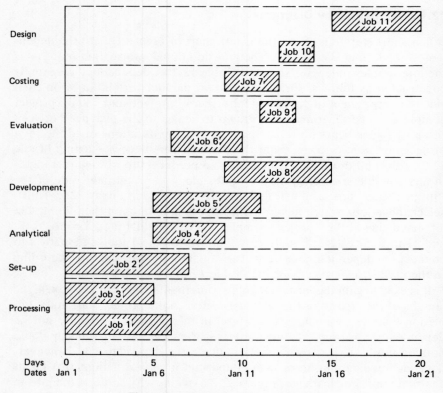

Figure 12.1. Gantt chart for project A.

Table 12.2. Predecessor-successor listing for project A.

JOB #	PREDECESSORS AND SUCCESSORS	
	PREDECESSOR JOB #	SUCCESSOR JOB #
1	None	6
2	None	7 and 8
3	None	4 and 5
4	3	7 and 8
5	3	9
6	1	None
7	2 and 4	10
8	2 and 4	11
9	5	11
10	7	None
11	8 and 9	None

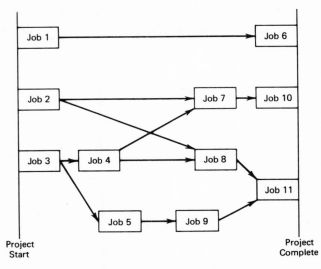

Figure 12.2. Dependency diagram for project A.

scheduled later. For example, Figure 12.2 shows that job 8 cannot start before jobs 2 and 4 are completed, thus explaining the position of job 8 in Figure 12.1.

12.1.3   Arrow Networks

While Gantt charts and dependency diagrams each display relevant information for decision making, both are inadequate relative to an arrow network. Figure 12.3 is the arrow network for project A. Note that the arrow network diagraming conventions are the reverse of those for dependency diagrams. In the arrow diagram, arrows represent jobs. The arrowheads eliminate any confusion about the direction of the various paths. Note that the lengths of the arrows are not necessarily proportional to the durations of the various jobs which they represent.

The important diagraming rules used in drawing up networks are presented and illustrated in Figure 12.4. Case 1 states that neither job C nor job D can start until both jobs A and B are completed. Contrast this with case 2. Case 2 states that job C cannot start until both jobs A and B are completed, and job D cannot start until job B is completed. Note how the dummy arrow is used in case 2 to show the dependence of job C on job B. A dummy arrow, unlike a job arrow, takes no time. It is a zero-time duration job that shows dependencies. Case 3 states that job D cannot start until both jobs A and B are completed, and job E cannot start until both jobs C and D are completed. Cases 4 and 5 illustrate an important distinction. In case 4, job D cannot be *started* until *both* jobs B and C are completed. In case 5, it is *job E* that cannot be started until *jobs B and D* are completed.

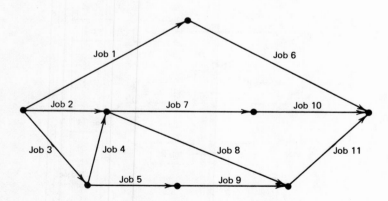

Figure 12.3. Arrow network for project A.

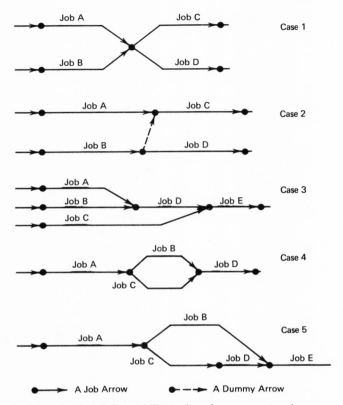

A Job Arrow   A Dummy Arrow

Figure 12.4. Rules and illustrations for arrow networks.

12.1.4 Time-Scaled Networks

A time-scaled network combines many of the advantages of Gantt charts, dependency diagrams and arrow networks. Figure 12.5 is the time-scaled version of Figure 12.3.

To draw up a time-scaled network, first lay out a suitable time scale on grid (or graph) paper. Second, from the predecessor-successor job list, select those jobs that have no predecessors and lay them out starting from the zero point on the time scale. Then lay out the successor jobs. Make the length of each arrow such that its *projection* on the time scale indicates the duration of the job. For example, note how jobs 3 and 2 are laid out in Figure 12.5. The measured length of the arrow which represents job 3 is longer than the measured length of the arrow which represents job 2. But their projections on the time scale are 5 days and 7 days, respectively, which are the durations shown in the job list in Table 12.1. Thus, the

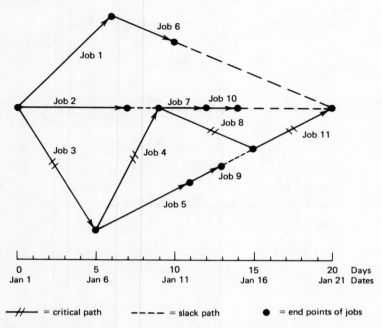

Figure 12.5. Time-scaled arrow network diagram for project A, with all jobs referenced at their earliest start.

actual length of the arrows in a time-scaled diagram is meaningless. It is their projection that matters. Broken lines or dummy jobs are used to show dependencies between the ends of predecessor jobs and successor jobs that do not meet. For example, job 9 follows job 5, but its duration does not run out to the start of its successor job 11. A dummy job is used to bridge this gap. It should be noted that arrowheads need not be shown in time-scaled networks, since the direction of work flow is always from left to right.

Most time-scaled networks will, like Figure 12.5, have various paths which include broken line portions. These broken line portions are called *slack* or *float*. The path(s) with zero slack are called *critical path(s)*, and jobs that lie on such paths are *critical jobs*. The essence of criticality is that any delay in any critical job will result in an equal delay to the project completion date. For example, Figure 12.5 shows that *either* job 1 or job 6 could be delayed for ten days without jeopardizing the January 21 project completion date. Or, *both* could be delayed for some time *combination* which *totals* ten days without jeopardizing the completion date. There is thus a total of ten days slack (or float) along the path from job 1 to job 6 to the end of the project. The slack runs from January 11 to January 21. Jobs 1 and 6 are called *slack jobs*. Similarly, jobs 2, 5, 7, 9 and 10 are slack jobs. But jobs 3, 4, 8 and 11 are critical jobs, since they lie on the path that has zero slack. This path is the critical path through the network plan for project A.

In drawing up Figure 12.5, all jobs were referenced at their earliest starting points. When this convention is used the slack will all be shown at the far right-hand side of the diagram. However, it should be apparent that the slack which is shown at the end of any path could be scheduled anywhere along that path. For example, the slack on the job 1 to job 6 path could be scheduled between jobs 1 and 6, so that job 6 started on January 17. There might be many reasons for scheduling the slack this way, such as the availabilities of manpower or materials. Similarly, the slack could be broken into smaller amounts and scheduled at various points throughout the path, to better accommodate the available manpower or the timing of arrivals of various materials.

Time-scaled networks provide a very complete picture of the overall project, the interrelations between the jobs, the slacks along each path and the various job durations. The time-scaled network is usually not difficult to draw up once an arrow diagram and the individual job times are established. No sophisticated calculations are required, and the resulting time-scaled network provides a comprehensive picture of the scheduling options open to the decision maker.

12.1.5 The Critical Path Method (CPM)

The Critical Path Method (CPM) was formally developed in 1957 for scheduling large-scale engineering projects in the chemical industry.[2, 3] Since then, CPM has evolved and been extended by various developers and users for many different applications. CPM and its family of variations have been very widely used in applications that range from scheduling the openings of Broadway plays to scheduling research projects and complex construction projects such as the St. Louis Gateway Arch Center.[4]

The CPM network time computations algorithm requires each job to start and end at a numbered node.[5] The node-numbered form of the arrow network for project A is shown in Figure 12.6. A numbered node is simply a placemarker; it occupies no time and takes no resources. Node numbers uniquely identify each job as "job *i-j*." It may be noted that in the original CPM terminology, a job was called an activity, a node was called an event, and slack time was termed float. Though these terms have not been

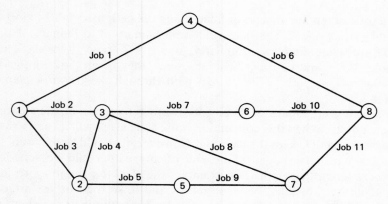

Figure 12.6. Node-numbered arrow network diagram for project A.

rigidly adhered to over the ensuing years, today most of the CPM computer programs use these labels in their printouts. To use the CPM time computations algorithm, either a predecessor-successor list or a node-numbered dependency diagram must be specified. Then the algorithm is used to make a *forward pass* calculation through the network to obtain the earliest start (ES) times for each job. The forward pass part of the algorithm is

$$ES_i = \max_k \left\{ ES_k + t_{ki} \right\}, \qquad (12.1)$$

for $i = 2, 3, \ldots, n - 1$ nodes, where t_{ki} is the duration of activity $k\text{-}i$, ES_k is the earliest start time for the kth activity, ES_i is the earliest start for all activities that begin with node i, and $ES_1 = 0$. Equation (12.1) is repeatedly applied to node numbers $i = 2, 3, \ldots, n - 1$ in the network. After the forward pass computations are completed, an analogous *backward pass* is made through the network to obtain the latest finish (LF) times for each job. This part of the algorithm is

$$LF_j = \min_k \left\{ LF_k - t_{jk} \right\}, \qquad (12.2)$$

for $j = n, n - 1, \ldots 2$ nodes, where LF_j is the latest allowable finish time for all activities that end in node j, where t_{jk} is the duration of activity $j\text{-}k$ and $LF_n = ES_n$. Equation (12.2) is repeatedly applied to node numbers $j = 2, 3, \ldots, n$ in the network. The path float part of the algorithm is given by

$$TF_{ij} = LS_{ij} - ES_i, \qquad (12.3)$$

or its equivalent,

$$TF_{ij} = LF_j - EF_{ij}, \qquad (12.4)$$

for any path $i\text{-}j$.

Table 12.3 presents an example of Equations (12.1), (12.2), (12.3) and (12.4) applied to the data in Tables 12.1 and 12.2. To illustrate the forward pass, let us find the earliest start time for job 11. Table 12.3 and Figure 12.6 identify job 11 as activity 7-8, and hence we are seeking ES_7. Equation (12.1) directs us to find the maximum value of the path times leading into node 7, which gives the starting point for job 11. That is, we are seeking

$$ES_7 = \max_k \left\{ (ES_3 + t_{3,7}), (ES_5 + t_{5,7}) \right\}. \qquad (12.5)$$

Here ES_3 is the earliest start of job 8 and ES_5 is the earliest start of job 9. Jobs 8 and 9 are the two predecessors to job 11. The reader may note that this information can be gotten from Table 12.2, though it is more readily apparent from Figure 12.6. The value of $(ES_3 + t_{3,7}) = 9 + 6 = 15$. The value of $(ES_5 + t_{5,7}) = 11 + 2 = 13$. The maximum of these two values is 15. Hence, 15 is the earliest start for node 7, which defines the start of job 11. Once the ES_i values are computed for all the jobs in the network, the EF_{ij} values can be computed directly by the relationship $EF_{ij} = ES_i + t_{ij}$. The fifth column of Table 12.3 displays these data for project A.

Let us illustrate the backward pass calculation by finding LF_3, which is the latest finish time for activities 1-3 and 2-3. From Equation (12.2):

$$LF_3 = \min_k \left\{ (LF_6 - t_{3,6}), (LF_7 - t_{3,7}) \right\}, \qquad (12.6)$$

$$LF_3 = \min_k \left\{ (18 - 3), (15 - 6) \right\} = 9. \qquad (12.7)$$

The latest finish data for each of the activities in the project A network are shown in the seventh column of Table 12.3. The latest start for job $i\text{-}j$ is then readily found from the relationship $LS_{ij} = LF_j - t_{ij}$. These data are shown in the sixth column of Table 12.3.

The total path float is readily computed by comparing the results from the forward and backward pass calculations. For example, using Equation (12.4) the total path float for job 1 is

$$TF_{1,4} = LF_4 - EF_{1,4} = 16 - 6 = 10. \qquad (12.8)$$

Table 12.3. CPM computations for project A.

JOB	ACTIVITY NUMBER $i\text{-}j$	DAYS DURATION t_{ij}	FORWARD PASS		BACKWARD PASS		PATH FLOAT	PATH I.D.
			EARLIEST START ES_i	EARLIEST FINISH EF_{ij}	LATEST START LS_{ij}	LATEST FINISH LF_j	FLOAT TF_{ij}	
1	1–4	6	0	6	10	16	10	
2	1–3	7	0	7	2	9	2	
3	1–2	5	0	5	0	5	0*	
4	2–3	4	5	9	5	9	0*	path 1-4-8
5	2–5	6	5	11	7	13	2	
6	4–8	4	6	10	16	20	10	
7	3–6	3	9	12	15	18	6	path 2-5-7
8	3–7	6	9	15	9	15	0*	
9	5–7	2	11	13	13	15	2	path 3-6-8
10	6–8	2	12	14	18	20	6	
11	7–8	5	15	20	15	20	0*	

* This is a critical job (on the critical path).

The last columns of Table 12.3 show the total path floats. Note that total floats are assigned to jobs in the computations, but the floats *do not* cumulate over several jobs in series. For instance, the entire path 1-4-8 *cannot* float out a *total* of the job 1-4 float plus the job 4-8 float (without delaying node 8). The TF_{ij} data for jobs 1-4 and 4-8 show the amount of the path 1-4-8 float that may be assigned to *either* jobs 1-4 or 4-8, but *not* to *both* of them at the same time. In most practical situations, the user will be interested in the total path float, from which a decision can be made about how to use this float on the various jobs in that path. For example, it may be decided to use the ten days of float by letting job 1 stretch out (or "float" out) seven days, and job 6 stretch out three days. Thus, the last column of Table 12.3 identifies all those paths where the TF_{ij} data occur. The TF_{ij} column shows the alternative jobs to which all this float may be assigned.

In the event that there is a target completion date D for the project such that $D > LF_n$ for n nodes in the network, then this introduces another float $F_n = D - LF_n$. This float is called the "free" float. It may be treated in the same way as regular float, in that it may be assigned to various jobs. Thus the free float F_n can be assigned to any job in the network or divided among them. It exists in addition to any regular float.

12.1.6 Using Deterministic Methods

Gantt charts are most useful for visual displays and the communication of the time-phasing of responsibilities. Dependency diagrams are most useful for working out the job interdependencies and deciding which jobs follow and precede others. For small projects, time-scaled network diagrams are much easier to work with than the CPM algorithm. In large projects, computerized CPM methods are almost mandatory to relieve the burden of hand calculations. But even then, the resolution of scheduling bottlenecks and the determination of the content of specific work packages is usually facilitated by drawing the time-scaled networks and subnetworks.

12.2 PROBABILISTIC TIME SCHEDULING METHODS

Probabilistic methods are required when the nature of the jobs, the job times or their interdependencies are uncertain. For example, this is often the case for research projects or new marketing efforts. Probabilistic methods thus fall within the general category of decision making under risk, as discussed in Chapter 4. The most common probabilistic methods are the Program Evaluation and Review Technique (PERT), the Decision

Box Network (DBN) and the Graphic Evaluation and Review Technique (GERT).

12.2.1   Program Evaluation and Review Technique (PERT)

At about the same time that the Critical Path Method (CPM) was being developed in industry, the Program Evaluation and Review Technique (PERT) was developed for managing the Polaris submarine project. Today, PERT and CPM have evolved and been further modified in their adoptions and applications to the point where the original distinctions between them have blurred.[4] It is not unusual to find the terms "CPM" and "PERT" being used interchangeably. However, the original developers of the two methods were interested in different types of management problems. The CPM developers sought a method for determining the best time-cost schedule of jobs with well-defined durations and manpower requirements. By contrast, the developers of PERT were interested in planning and coordinating jobs whose durations and outcomes were highly uncertain. They sought a method for planning and scheduling the work in such a way that there was a high probability of completing the Polaris project by a preselected date. Thus, the unique contribution of the PERT system is the ability to introduce uncertainty into the job durations and the project completion date. This permits the manager to use the statistical concepts of confidence completion times for scheduling jobs and projects.

The PERT system uses three time estimates for each job, instead of the single job duration used in the CPM system. The three time estimates which are solicited for each job are the optimistic time t_o, the most likely (modal) time t_m and the pessimistic time t_p. The t_o estimate is premised on an "everything goes right" assumption. It represents the shortest job duration that is likely to occur no more often than one time out of one hundred. The t_p value is premised on an "everything goes wrong" assumption. It represents the longest job duration that is likely to occur no more often than one time out of one hundred. The t_m estimate is the one used in the CPM system. Assuming that these three time estimates describe a Beta statistical distribution [6,7], then the expected or mean duration of the ith job t_{ie} is given by

$$t_{ie} = \left(\frac{t_{io} + 4t_{im} + t_{ip}}{6} \right). \tag{12.9}$$

When $t_{ip} - t_{im} = t_{im} - t_{io}$ the distribution is symetric and $t_{ie} = t_{im}$. The variance v_i of the ith job duration is given by

$$v_i = \left(\frac{t_{ip} - t_{io}}{6} \right)^2. \tag{12.10}$$

so that the standard deviation s_i of the ith job duration is

$$s_i = \sqrt{\left(\frac{t_{ip} - t_{io}}{6}\right)^2}, \qquad (12.11)$$

Thus, the confidence duration of any i^{th} job in a network may be found through the Central Limit Theorem of statistical theory [8] by computing the confidence time interval t_{ic}, where

$$t_{ic} = t_{ie} \pm k s_i. \qquad (12.12)$$

Here, $k = 3$ for the 99% confidence level, $k = 2$ for the 95% confidence level and $k = 1$ for the 68% confidence level. The expected completion time T_S for any set of jobs S in a path is given by

$$T_S = \sum_{i \ in \ S} t_{ie}. \qquad (12.13)$$

The extreme path in a PERT network (analogous to the critical path in a CPM network) is that path with the longest expected completion time T_N, as given by

$$T_N = max \ \{T_S\}. \qquad (12.14)$$

The confidence completion time $T_{c,S}$ for any set of jobs S is given by

$$T_{c,S} = T_S + k \sqrt{\sum_{i \ in \ S} v_i}. \qquad (12.15)$$

Note that $T_{c,S}$ is *not* simply $\sum_{i \ in \ S} t_{ic}$. Finally, the project confidence time $T_{c,N}$ is given by

$$T_{c,N} = max \ \{T_{c,S}\}. \qquad (12.16)$$

Figure 12.7 illustrates the use of these ideas for a hypothetical project B. Let us define the set S_1 to consist of job 1 and job 2, and the set S_2 to consist of job 3 and job 4. Then from Equation (12.13), $T_{S_1} = t_{1e} + t_{2e} = 4 + 7 = 11$ weeks, and $T_{S_2} = t_{3e} + t_{4e} = 5 + 4 = 9$ weeks. Then from Equation (12.14), the extreme path is the job 1-job 2 path, with a total expected completion time $T_N = 11$ weeks. But note that from Equation (12.15) for $k = 2$ ($c = 95\%$ confidence level) we find:

$$T_{c,S_1} = 11 + 2 \sqrt{0 + 1} = 13 \text{ weeks,} \qquad (12.17)$$

$$T_{c,S_2} = 9 + 2 \sqrt{9 + 1} = 15.3 \text{ weeks.} \qquad (12.18)$$

Hence, the path consisting of job 3 and job 4 has the *longer confidence time* because it contains jobs having relatively greater variances. Thus, from Equation (12.16) we find that the network confidence time for project B is:

$$T_{c,N} = max \ \{13, 15.3\} = 15.3 \text{ weeks} \qquad (12.19)$$

This is the target date which a conservative project manager would com-

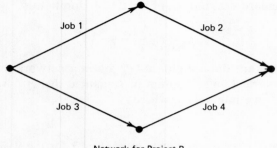

Network for Project B

Job $i =$	Job Time Estimate (weeks)			PERT Computations			
	t_{io}	t_{im}	t_{ip}	t_{ie}	v_i	s_i	t_{ic}, $c = 95\%$ $(k = 2)$
1	4	4	4	4	0	0	4
2	2	8	8	7	1	1	9
3	2	2	20	5	9	3	11
4	1	4	7	4	1	1	6

Network Extreme Path = Job 1 − Job 2; $T_N = 11$ weeks
$T_{c,N} = 15.3$ weeks (for $c = 95\%$ confidence)

Figure 12.7. PERT example for project B.

mit to, rather than the T_{S_1} or T_N date. The desired target date may be extended or shortened appropriately for the manager's risk propensity by suitably choosing $k = 3$ (99% confidence time) and $k = 1$ (68% confidence time). Specifically, if the project manager wants to be 99% confident of completing the project on time, then $9 + 3\sqrt{9 + 1} = 18.5$ weeks is the appropriate target date. If the project manager is willing to accept a one-in-three chance of *not* completing the project on time, then $9 + \sqrt{9 + 1} = 12.2$ weeks is the appropriate target date.

Let us compare these PERT results with those that would be obtained under the CPM approach. The CPM calculations yield $EF = 12$ weeks for the job 1-job 2 path and $EF = 6$ weeks for the job 3-job 4 path. Thus, the CPM critical path consisting of job 1 and job 2 is the same as the PERT extreme path. But the path completion times and other data are *not* the same. These differences are a direct result of the use of three versus one job time estimate, and the fact that the distributions of these time estimates are skewed so that $t_e \neq t_m$ for some jobs. Thus, depending on the direction of skewedness, and the combinations of these directions among the jobs in a network, the extreme path in a PERT network need not be the same as the CPM critical path in that same network.

12.2.2   The Decision Box Network (DBN)

Decision box networks provide a means for including decision tree elements in a regular PERT or CPM network.[9] This extends their applicability to situations where the outcomes of some jobs are uncertain. Figure 12.8 illustrates the decision box concept with a CPM arrow network. The decision box in Figure 12.8 indicates that the outcome of job 1-3 is uncertain. If the outcome is favorable, then the successor job 3-4 will require ten days to complete. But if the outcome is unfavorable, then the successor job 3-5 will take twenty days. There is a .80 probability that the outcome will be favorable and a .20 probability that it will be unfavorable. Thus, as shown at the bottom of Figure 12.8, there is a .80 probability that the project will be completed in thirteen days and there is a .20 probability that it will take as long as twenty-three days. The expected completion time, T_E, is given by

$$T_E = \sum_j p_j t_j, \qquad (12.20)$$

for $j = 1, 2, \ldots n$ critical jobs, where t_j is the duration of the jth critical job and p_j is the probability that it will occur. Denoting jobs by their ending node numbers, for the network in Figure 12.8, Equation (12.20) becomes

$$
\begin{aligned}
T_E &= p_3 t_3 + p_5 t_5 + p_4 t_4 + p_6 t_6 \\
&= (1.0)(2 \text{ days}) + (.20)(20 \text{ days}) + (.80)(10 \text{ days}) + 1.0 (1 \text{ day}) \\
&= 15 \text{ days}. \qquad (12.21)
\end{aligned}
$$

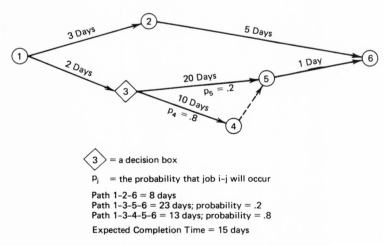

Figure 12.8. Illustration of a decision box network.

Thus, if the decision maker wishes to take the job outcome uncertainty into account, fifteen days is the appropriate target date for the completion of the project.

12.2.3   The Graphical Evaluation and Review Technique (GERT)

The Graphical Evaluation and Review Technique (GERT) extends the decision box method to cases of recycling through the same jobs.[10] As an illustration, let us take a drug research project, in which new chemicals are synthesized and tested in a search for an effective disease cure. This work consists of repeated trials of the same jobs until an effective drug is found. Figure 12.9 shows the network diagram for this project. Each trial consists of the synthesis and testing of a new drug, and many such trials may be made before an effective drug is found. In the case where the average probability of success on each trial p_s can be estimated, then the binomial expansion may be used to specify n, the number of trials needed. This approach was outlined in Equation (3.11) of Chapter 3. Given t and c, the respective duration and cost of one trial, then tn and cn are the respective expected duration and cost estimates for the project. In the case where p_s cannot be estimated with any degree of confidence, then simulation procedures may be used (as outlined in Chapter 8 for stochastic decision trees). In either case, GERT may be very useful. The GERT approach can handle situations where the durations of the jobs are random, the starting point or the completion point of any job is stochastic, and the time associated with any job is stochastic. GERT permits the user to specify any distribution the decision maker feels is reasonable for computing t_e. And relative frequency statistics can be collected on the occurrence of different paths in the network. Thus, GERT is especially useful

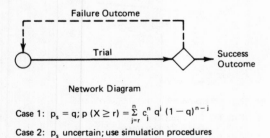

Figure 12.9. Illustration of two cases where GERT may be used.

for predicting the durations and the types of outcomes of projects where the basic input data is very sketchy and only a rudimentary network can be drawn up.

12.3   OTHER CHARTING AND SCHEDULING METHODS

12.3.1   Cause and Effect Diagrams

Cause and effect diagrams are useful preliminary tools for building up large network diagrams. To build up a cause and effect diagram, first start with the end objective as an ending node. Then work backward sequentially, from effects to possible causes. Finally, determine the appropriate jobs that will eliminate all the causes. This approach is a combined application of means-ends analyses (Chapter 6) and fault tree analyses (Chapter 8). Figure 12.10 illustrates how a cause and effect diagram can be used in the development of a decision box arrow network plan to solve a bearing wear problem.

12.3.2   DELTA Charts

DELTA charts are flow charts that portray activities, decisions, logic and feedback paths. Their principal virtue is their flexibility and extensive vocabulary. The acronym DELTA stands for Decision Event Logic Time

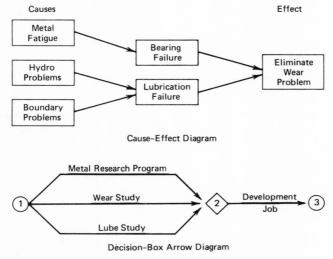

Figure 12.10. Illustration of a cause and effect diagram.

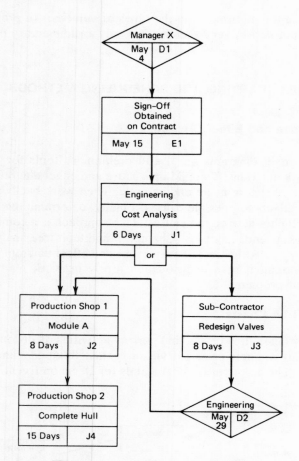

Figure 12.11. Example of a DELTA chart.

Activity. An example of a DELTA chart is presented in Figure 12.11. Diamond-shaped boxes are used to indicate decisions and rectangles are used for jobs. Decision makers are identified ("manager X," "engineering," etc.), job completion and decision dates are specified ("May 4," "May 15," etc.) and each job, event or decision has a unique identification ("J 1," "E 1," "D 1," etc.) which is keyed to a more detailed description list (not shown here).

12.3.3 Multiproject Scheduling

Where there are several projects to be scheduled, each project can be treated as a separate job and the entire set of projects may be diagramed and handled as one large network. A computer program called RAMPS has been designed for such applications.[11] The projects can be importance-weighted or priority-constrained so that some will necessarily be scheduled earlier. In general, the iterative use of multiproject level and project level network methods is one way that project and department level managers may devise integrated total plans. Individual project networks may be submitted by each project manager, which may then be merged into a multiproject network. Several alternative multiproject network schedules may be developed around various assumptions about priorities and resource availabilities. Each alternative multiproject schedule may then be examined as a basis for selecting the best one.[12]

12.3.4 Block Charts

The block chart is a simplistic, appealing graphical means of developing an approximate time-resource chart. A block chart can be converted to a more accurate PERT, CPM or Gantt chart, or left to stand as it is. The procedures for constructing a block chart are straightforward. First, identify the amount of time and resources available for the project. This step assumes that a block chart will be designed to fill the time and resources available. Second, identify the tasks to be performed in a job list. Third, determine blocks for each task. Finally, fit the blocks into the chart boundaries. Figure 12.12 is one of many alternative charts that could be developed from the block requirements shown at the bottom of Figure 12.12. Whether or not this chart is an acceptable plan will depend on the feasibility of parallel activities. For instance, if jobs 1, 2 and 3 can all be performed concurrently, then the manpower used in area A (one man-day) can be reallocated to the slack areas. This reduces the maximum number of men needed to 6. Alternatively, the duration could be reduced to 6 days if the manpower in area B (two man-days) can be reallocated to slack area 1. Several iterations and trials may be needed to produce a satisfactory block chart. However, the process of going through these exercises may help the decision maker to discover several new facets of the decision problem and several new alternatives that had not previously been considered. Thus, a block chart may be an excellent preliminary exercise to building a PERT or CPM program plan.

12.4 MANPOWER ALLOCATION METHODS

A network plan provides a very effective tool for optimizing the assignment of manpower to the various jobs within a project. Four kinds of manpower allocations can be performed: manpower leveling, excess manpower removal, manpower reallocation for time compression and

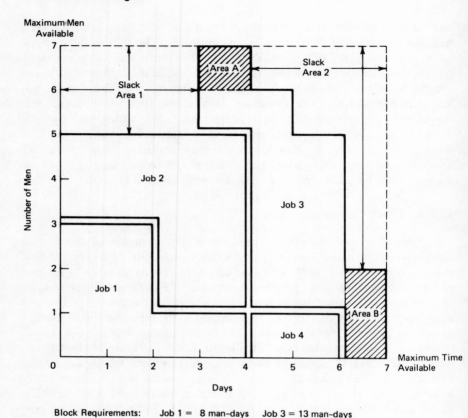

Figure 12.12. Illustration of a block chart.

time-cost expediting. All of these methods are based on ways of utilizing the slack (or float) in the network to either reduce the critical job durations, reschedule the critical jobs, or create a more acceptable manpower utilization pattern.

12.4.1 Manpower Leveling *

The manpower leveling problem exists where it is desired to smooth out the profile of manpower utilization within the given project duration. This

---

* Portions of the materials presented in this section are adapted from Souder, W. E., "Project Selection, Planning and Control," in *Handbook of Operations Research: Models and Applications*, J. J. Moder and S. E. Elmaghraby, (eds.), New York: Van Nostrand Reinhold Company, 1978, pp. 323–329.

Table 12.4. Manpower data for project A.

JOB	MANPOWER NEEDED
1	2 men
2	2 men *
3	1 man
4	Outside department **
5	2 men
6	Outside contractor **
7	Outside contractor **
8	2 men
9	Outside contractor **
10	2 men
11	2 men

* These men are not transferable and this job cannot be shortened or rescheduled.
** These men are not within the control of the project manager.

problem may occur where manpower availabilities are imposed, budgets are restricted or skill categories are constrained.

Table 12.4 and Figures 12.13 and 12.14 illustrate the manpower leveling approach for project A (see Figure 12.5). Table 12.4 lists the manpower needs for each job. To make the example more realistic, five of the jobs (jobs 2, 4, 6, 7 and 9) have been designated as outside the project manager's control. Figure 12.13 shows the unleveled manpower plan. In this plan, the total manpower utilization is heavy for the first six days, low during the last six days, and alternately high and low during the middle of the project. These peaks and valleys in manpower loading can result in periodic overuse and idleness in the staff. The periods of overuse may result in the unavailability of manpower for other jobs. Figure 12.14 shows one feasible manpower leveled schedule that brings the peak manpower needs down to a total of four men. This improved manpower profile is achieved by simply utilizing the available slack to reschedule slack jobs 1, 5, 6, 9 and 10. This is only one of many possible arrangements.

12.4.2 Manpower Removal

Further reductions in peak manpower utilization may be possible by allowing the slack jobs to float out, through the removal of excess manpower. Continuing with Figure 12.14, let us assume the following fortuitous circumstances. Let us suppose that job 5 will take two more days to complete if one man is removed from it. Then, let us assume that jobs 1 and 10 will each take one day longer to complete if one of the men

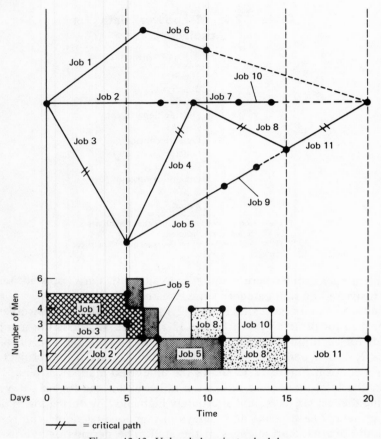

Figure 12.13. Unleveled project schedule.

assigned to each of those jobs is removed. Hence, three men may be removed from the original manpower plan without altering the project completion date. The result is shown in Figure 12.15. Note that some of the earlier (Figure 12.14) slack paths are now critical.

In general, all networks should be carefully examined for any excess manpower which can be removed without otherwise damaging the project. Considerable savings in manpower may be possible, as the above illustration has suggested.

12.4.3   Manpower Reallocation for Time Compression

If men are transferable from one job to another, then transfers from slack to critical paths may be effected to compress the project completion date.

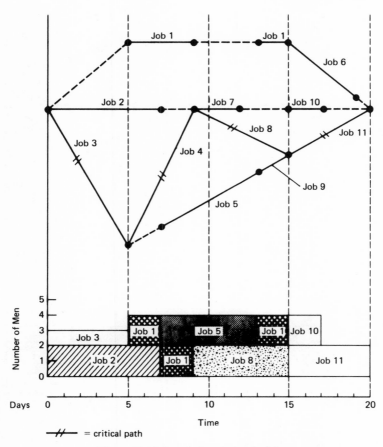

Figure 12.14. Leveled project schedule.

Figure 12.16 illustrates this idea, based on the hypothetical data shown in Table 12.5, and starting from the network plan in Figure 12.13. In Figure 12.16, jobs 1, 5 and 10 are allowed to float out, and critical jobs 3, 8 and 11 are compressed a total of five days. Hence, the total project completion date is reduced by five days. Note that several new paths become critical under this reallocation.

The optimum compressed schedule is reached when either no men can be reallocated, all slacks have been absorbed or the critical path cannot be further reduced through a reallocation of resources from a slack to a critical job. However, compressed schedules usually exhibit large manpower peaks. It is sometimes difficult to have both an acceptable compressed schedule and an acceptable smoothing of manpower.

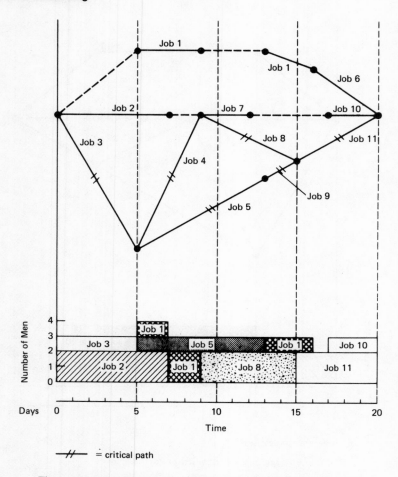

Figure 12.15. Manpower reduced network with three men removed.

12.4.4   Time-Cost Expediting and Contractor Incentives

A further way to reduce the critical paths after all slack to critical reallocations have been made is to apply additional resources from outside the project. For example, suppose a particular critical job n which normally costs C_n and takes t_n time units can be expedited to be completed in t_i units with cost C_i, where $t_i < t_n$ and $C_i > C_n$. Then, suppose another critical job m which normally costs C_m and takes t_m time units can be expedited to be completed in t_j time units with cost C_j, where $t_j < t_m$ and $C_j > C_m$. Then job m should be expedited in preference to job n where

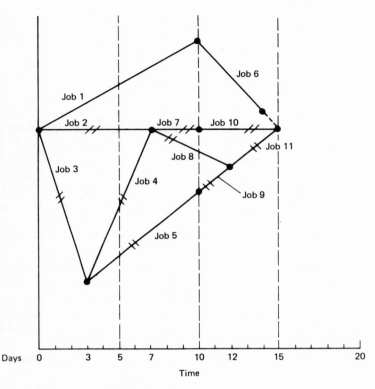

Days 0   3   5   7   10   12   15   20

Time

Transfers			Network Time Reduction
Number of Men	From Job	To Job	
1	1	3	2
1	5	8	1
1	10	11	2
			5 days

—//— = critical path

Figure 12.16. Illustration of manpower reallocation.

Table 12.5. Job durations for various manpower complements.

JOB	DURATION WITH ONE LESS MAN	DURATION WITH ONE MORE MAN
1	10 days	—
5	7 days	—
10	5 days	—
3	—	3 days
8	—	5 days
11	—	3 days

$$\frac{t_m - t_j}{C_j - C_m} > \frac{t_n - t_i}{C_i - C_n},$$ (12.22)

and where

$$\frac{k_t(t_m - t_j)}{C_j - C_m} > R.$$ (12.23)

Here, k_t is either the cost saving or the reward gained, per time unit saved, and R is the organization's average return on investment. For example, k_t might be either the dollar penalty per time unit or the dollar incentive per time unit that is part of an incentive clause in the project contract. Equation (12.23) states that no expenditure that lowers the organization's average return on its investments should be made. Equation (12.23) may be repeatedly applied to several critical jobs to determine a priority order for expediting. [12]

As an example, suppose the duration of project A in Figure 12.16 can be reduced to 14 weeks in two alternative ways. The first way is to spend $1,000 on job 10 plus $400 on job 11, for a total cost of $1,400. The other alternative is to spend $1,000 on job 2 plus $800 on job 3, for a total of $1,800. Note that both jobs 2 and 3 must be expedited to achieve the one-day compression in the total project, because they are on separate critical paths. The $1,400 expenditure is clearly the more cost-effective choice.

Equation (12.23) is very useful for setting contract incentives. A contractee wants to set a large enough incentive rate k_t that the contractor is induced to expedite the work, but not so large that the contractor profits handsomely. In general, with appropriate intelligence and the use of learning curve models (discussed in Chapter 3), the contractee may be able to estimate an R value for the contractor. Then the size of the incentive payment k_t required to induce the contractor to meet a job target date t_j by expediting is given by:

$$k_t \geq \left(\frac{C_j - C_m}{t_m - t_j}\right) R.$$ (12.24)

12.5 SUMMARY

Table 12.6 is a guide to the selection and use of the various project scheduling methods described in this chapter. Most users will find that the ideas behind several of the above methods can profitably be combined and mixed. An almost infinite number of variations, combinations and extensions of these basic methods could be devised.

Table 12.6. Summary of project scheduling methods.

WHEN THE SCHEDULING PROBLEM IS CHARACTERIZED BY A NEED FOR:	THE MOST EFFECTIVE METHODS TO USE ARE:
A quick analysis of a simple problem; a "first cut" is needed to develop a PERT or CPM chart	Block charts; dependency diagrams; arrow networks; cause-effect diagrams
A detailed time schedule; target dates are being set; it is desired to determine what jobs are critical and where slacks exist, and:	
(a) all variables are deterministic	CPM; time-scaled networks; DELTA charts
(b) the job durations are distributed over a range from optimistic to pessimistic	PERT
(c) the outcomes of some jobs are uncertain	Decision-box networks; GERT
A way to handle stochastic situations; job times and/or event occurrences are uncertain and/or there are loopbacks in the network	GERT simulation or GERT stochastic computations
A display of information to other groups in order to communicate deadlines and commitments	Gantt charts; DELTA charts; CPM diagrams; PERT charts, time-scaled networks
A quick and approximate technique that can be used in a group setting	Block charts; dependency diagrams; cause-effect diagrams; arrow networks
Communications to top management	Gantt charts; DELTA charts; time-scaled networks; CPM; PERT
Multiproject prioritizing; manpower allocations; multiproject scheduling; incentive-setting	RAMPS; manpower leveling; manpower removal; manpower reallocation; time-cost expediting

12.6 REFERENCES

1. Cleland, D. I. and King, W. R. *Systems Analysis and Project Management.* New York: McGraw-Hill, 1975, pp. 342–347.
2. Mauchly, J. W. "Critical-Path Scheduling." *Chemical Engineering.* April 16, 1962, pp. 139–154.
3. Kelley, J. E., Jr. "Critical-Path Scheduling and Planning: Mathematical Basis." *Operations Research,* **9,** No. 3: 296–320 (1961).
4. Lerda-Olberg, Sergio. "Bibliography on Network-Based Project Planning and Control Techniques: 1962–1965." *Operations Research,* **15,** No. 6: 925–931 (1966).
5. International Business Machines Corporation. "Project Control System 360 Program Description and Operations Manual." IBM Corporation, White Plains, New York, 1976.
6. McBride, W. J., Jr. "PERT And The Beta Distribution." *IEEE Transactions on Engineering Management,* EM-14, No. 4: 166–169 (1967).
7. King, W. R. and Lukas, P. A. "An Experimental Analysis of Network Planning." *Management Science,* **19,** No. 2: 307–317 (1973).

8. See any basic statistical text, e.g., Robert Schlaifer. *Probability and Statistics for Business Decisions*. New York: McGraw-Hill, 1959, pp. 285–427.
9. Eisner, Howard. "A Generalized Network Approach to the Planning and Control of a Research Project." *Operations Research*, **10**, No. 10: 115–125 (1962).
10. Pritsker, A. and Happ, W. "GERT: Graphical Evaluation and Review Technique-Part I, Fundamentals." *Journal of Industrial Engineering*, **17**, No. 5: 267–274 (1966).
11. Moshman, Jack; Johnson, J.; and Larson, M. *RAMPS: A Technique for Resource Allocation and Multi-project Scheduling*. Arlington, Virginia: CEIR, Inc., 1963.
12. Souder, W. E. "Project Selection, Planning and Control," in the *Handbook of Operations Research: Models and Applications*, J.J. Moder and S. E. Elmaghraby (eds.), New York: Van Nostrand Reinhold Company, 1978, pp. 330–333.

12.7   BIBLIOGRAPHY

Clark, C. E. "The PERT Model for the Distribution of an Activity Time." *Operations Research*, **10**, No. 4: 405–408 (1962).
Fulkerson, D. R. "A Network Flow Computation for Project Cost Curves." *Management Science*, **8**, No. 2: 51–60 (1961).
Kwak, N. K. and Jones, L. "An Application of PERT to R&D Scheduling." *Information Processing and Management*, **14**, No. 2: 121–131 (1978).
Levy, F. K. and Wiest, J. D. *A Management Guide to PERT/CPM*. Englewood Cliffs, New Jersey: Prentice-Hall, Inc., 1969.
Moder, J. J. and Phillips, C. R. *Project Management with CPM and PERT*. New York: Van Nostrand Reinhold Company, 1970.
Patterson, J. H. and Huber, W. D. "A Horizon-Varying, Zero-One Approach to Project Scheduling." *Management Science*, **20**, No. 6: 990–998 (1974).
Warfield, N. N. and Hill, J. D. "The DELTA Chart: A Method for R&D Project Portrayal." *IEEE Trans. on Eng. Mgt.*, **EM-18**, No. 4: 132–139 (1971).
Wiest, J. D. "Project Network Models: Past, Present and Future." *Project Management Quarterly*, **3**, No. 4: 120–124 (1977).
Yoshida, T. and Katsundo, H. "Optimal Two-Stage Production Scheduling with Set-Up Times Separated." *AIIE Transactions*, **11**, No. 3: 261–268 (1979).

Part VI
Resource Management

The optimum management of resources is one of the most difficult kinds of decision problems. Such problems are usually characterized by many uncertainties, by many constraints and restrictions, and by a scarcity in the amount and types of resources available to achieve the objectives. Two of the most commonly encountered resource management problems are inventory decision making and resource programming problems. In inventory decision making, the manager desires to balance the costs and risks of being out of stock against the costs and risks of carrying too much stock. In programming decision problems, the manager seeks the best allocation of the available resources and funds among several alternatives. The two chapters in this part of the book present the state-of-art methods in these two areas. Chapter 13 presents the most useful inventory decision making methods, and Chapter 14 presents some mathematical programming methods for resource allocation decison making.

13

Inventory Decision Making

13.0 INTRODUCTION

Nearly all organizations have inventories. Retailers and wholesalers purchase and store finished goods for sale. Manufacturers have raw materials, work-in-process and finished goods inventories. Even a commission agent or a broker who serves as an order-taker and does not take physical possession or title to goods has an inventory of supplies.

The amount and composition of the inventories carried will vary greatly with the nature of the technologies employed, the nature of the business, the level of demand, the availability of supplies, the frequency of sales and the general economic conditions. Maintaining an optimum level of inventories in the face of these factors is vital to the organization. Too little inventory can result in lost sales, inability to take advantage of market opportunities and a possible permanent loss of market share. Too much inventory may result in high carrying costs, excess interest charges and opportunities foregone because otherwise available funds were tied up in inventory. If the inventory is perishable or subject to obsolescence, then holding excess inventory can entail great risks of losses.

Several different models and methods have been developed to assist the decision maker in maintaining an optimum level of inventories. This chapter illustrates these approaches.

13.1 THE INVENTORY MANAGEMENT CYCLE

13.1.1 The Inventory Flow Process

The inventory cycle consists of the sequence of events from the expected or actual sales order to the delivery of the finished goods that fill this order. For example, in a typical manufacturing business the expected or actual sales demands trigger the issuance of work orders, from which raw materials are ordered and production is planned. When the work orders and production plans are implemented the raw materials are converted to work-in-process. Stock ledgers and other documents are used to control and track man-hour, machine-hour and other values which go into work-in-process. Completed goods are transferred to a finished goods inventory, which is subsequently delivered to the customer to complete this cycle.

Figure 13.1 traces the flow of inventory costs through a typical manufacturing cost accounting system. In this hypothetical example, four different lots of 100,000 units of the same raw material are purchased at four different points in time over a year. The increased dollar amounts

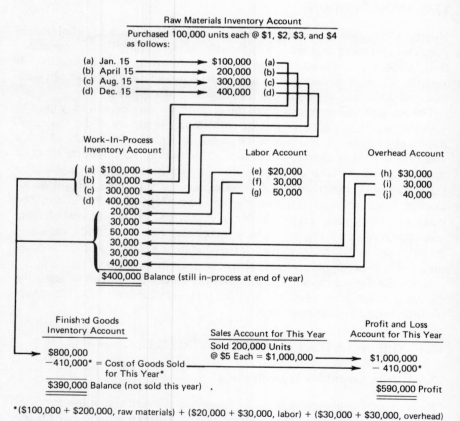

*($100,000 + $200,000, raw materials) + ($20,000 + $30,000, labor) + ($30,000 + $30,000, overhead)

Figure 13.1. Typical annual flow of inventory through the accounts of a manufacturing firm.

reflect price increases of $1 per unit at each new purchase. Significant value is added during the production and transformation processes which move the goods from the raw materials state to the finished goods state. Salaries and wages, supplies, heat and lighting, storage costs, the share of investment and other overhead costs go into the value-adding process. Thus, the value of the finished goods inventory may be many times the value of the original raw materials that are applied. The actual sale of the finished goods inventory replenishes the cash balance, so that the cycle can begin again.

13.1.2   Accounting for Inventory: FIFO *vs.* LIFO

Either of two alternative cost accounting assumptions may be adopted: FIFO or LIFO. These assumptions bear no necessary relation to the actual physical flow of the goods. Rather they are accounting assumptions that may be used in determining taxable profits and net incomes. The FIFO (first-in, first-out) accounting system assumes that the oldest inventory is used up first. By contrast, the LIFO (last-in, first-out) system assumes that the last unit put into inventory is the first unit used.

The choice of one accounting system over the other can have a dramatic effect on a firm's financial vitality, especially under a situation of rising prices. Table 13.1 illustrates this. When the FIFO system is applied to the data in Figure 13.1 the 200,000 units sold during the year are costed at the old first-in raw material cost of $1 per unit. Thus, the total cost of goods sold is the $200,000 of raw materials plus the $110,000 of labor and overhead value added (items [e], [f], [h] and [i] in Figure 13.1). This gives a total of $310,000. When the LIFO system is used the 200,000 units are costed at the last-in raw material cost of $4 per unit. Thus, the total cost of goods sold is the $800,000 of raw materials plus the $110,000 of value added or $910,000. As summarized in Table 13.1, it may be said that the

Table 13.1. Relative impacts of different accounting procedures on profits.

	PHYSICAL COUNT	FIFO SYSTEM	LIFO SYSTEM
Sales	$1,000,000	$1,000,000	$1,000,000
Cost of Goods Sold	410,000	310,000	910,000
Profit	590,000	690,000	90,000
"False" Profit	500,000	600,000	0
Excess Income Taxes (at 50% *)	$ 250,000	$ 300,000	$ 0

* The combined state and federal corporate taxes total to about 50% for many firms.

physical count and the FIFO systems create "false" profits. And these accounting systems result in the firm having to pay excess income taxes on these false profits. The FIFO and physical system profit figures have failed to take into account the fact that the replacement inventory will cost more than the old inventory. To the extent that profits are thus overstated, taxes will be higher. A more accurate picture of profits is, therefore, provided under a rising-price situation if LIFO is used. In an analogous way, FIFO may produce a more accurate profits picture in the case of falling prices. Over the years, a firm that pays excess taxes on false inventory profits may eventually find that its long term profits have silently eroded.

13.1.3 Influence of Decision Making Practices

Figure 13.2 illustrates a well-managed in-phase inventory condition, a level inventory and a poorly-managed out-of-phase inventory condition. In the in-phase case the cyclical sales pattern is anticipated, and inventories are managed in such a way that they are adequate to meet the sales demands with only a small amount of lead and lag over the demand cycle. From time t_0 to t_3 inventory is being built up in anticipation of the sales surge. By time t_4 the inventory buildup is purposely being diminished in anticipation of falling sales demand. Then at some subsequent point t_7 the cycle repeats. This ideal state of inventory management is often extremely difficult to achieve. It depends on being completely accurate in

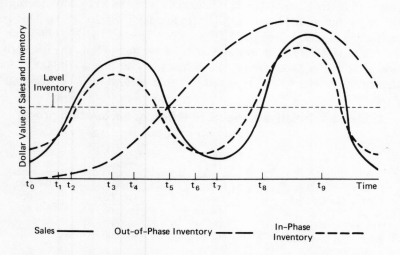

Figure 13.2. Illustration of in-phase and out-of-phase inventory management.

forecasting future sales and sales periodicity. In the out-of-phase case the awareness of the coming boom in demand during the t_0 to t_4 time frame stimulates a buildup of inventory. But by the time this is achieved the demand has fallen. Consequently, excess inventories must be carried along until a new surge of demand reduces them during the t_7 to t_9 time frame. Such out-of-phase inventory behaviors can create severe economic boom and bust conditions for the enterprise. The level inventory condition is only a partial improvement on the out-of-phase condition. Excess carrying costs are incurred during the t_0 to t_2 time frame, shortages occur from t_2 to t_5, etc.

Maintaining an in-phase inventory is the fundamental inventory management decision problem. However, the organizational locus of this responsibility is often very diffuse and splintered. Purchasing and production personnel may jointly be responsible for raw materials inventories. Production may be responsible for work-in-process inventories, as well as the finished goods inventory. But since each party normally has different goals, implementing a coordinated inventory policy may be difficult. Sales personnel want as much finished goods inventory on hand as possible. Production normally wants as much raw material on hand as possible. And purchasing usually wants the best price, sometimes without too much concern for quality and delivery dates.

13.2 INVENTORY DECISION PROBLEMS

13.2.1 Decision Variables and Parameters

The optimum inventory decision is the one that minimizes the total inventory cost. This total cost is the sum of the set-up cost (for a manufacturer) or reordering cost (for a retailer), the holding cost and the shortage cost. The set-up or reordering cost is the cost of obtaining the goods, e.g., the dollar cost of purchasing or manufacturing the goods. The holding (or carrying) cost is a function of the quantity of inventory on hand and the duration it will be held. Holding costs include such out-of-pocket costs as insurance, taxes, warehouse rental, heating and lighting. Holding costs also include the opportunity cost or value of opportunities lost because the capital tied up in inventories is unavailable for other uses. The shortage (or stockout) cost is the amount of the sales opportunity foregone or the economic loss associated with delays in meeting the demand. The seriousness of being short depends on the value of the item, its perishability, the nature of its demand and the presence or absence of competitors and substitute products. It might be that a stockout would drive customers to adopt a substitute, with the consequent complete loss of the firm's market position in that product. Overstocking thus results in excess investment and high opportunity costs. Understocking incurs a high production run or reordering frequency and associated high set-up costs, in addition to the risk of stockouts. An optimum decision balances off these costs and risks.

13.2.2   Types of Decision Problems

Figure 13.3 presents the family tree of inventory decision problem settings. In the deterministic case the demand is known with certainty. In the stochastic case the demand is a random variable. A static situation is one where demands are the same in each time period. In dynamic situations the demand may vary from one time period to the next, e.g., seasonality.

Decisions are required within each of these settings with respect to the size of the inventory to keep on hand, how much to order (or produce) and when to order. These decisions usually need to be made continuously, because the factors that influence them are dynamic and ever-changing. Moreover, these decisions usually need to be made for all types of inventories: raw materials, work-in-process and finished goods. The determination of the optimum size of the inventory to keep on hand is the *control policy decision*. The determination of the optimum size of inventory to reorder (or produce) is the *lot size decision*. And the determination of the optimum time to reorder is the *review point decision*. These three decisions are interdependent; a decision about any one of these three aspects usually influences the other two aspects.

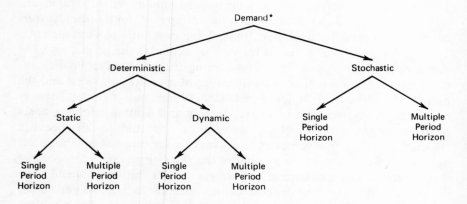

*An analogous diagram could be developed for inventory costs

Figure 13.3. Major types of inventory decision problem settings.

13.2.3 Financial Control Policy Decision Methods

Table 13.2 presents several financial ratios that are commonly used to measure and control the size of inventories. The %ASVR is for finished goods inventories, and the %CGSR is for work-in-process inventories. The inverse of the %ASVR is the turnover index, which shows the extent to which the firm is generating sales dollars per inventory investment dollar. The higher the turnover index the greater is the productivity of the inventory investment dollar. The days sales in inventories ratio (DSIIR) gives the number of days sales that are "on the books" or tied up in inventory. A large number implies that a long time period may be needed to clear out the excess inventory. In extreme cases, production may have to be shut down and labor may have to be laid off while the inventory recedes to a normal level. It must be noted that such ratios are only a guide to judgment. Published statistics and long term industry averages are available from trade sources that are often of value in determining whether or not a particular ratio is out of line.

Most inventory systems involve some classification by item value. An ABC system is typical, where the A, B and C classes designate value categories. The high-value items are placed in Class A, the medium-value items in class B and the low-value items in class C. Normally, class A will have the smallest number of items and class C will have the largest number. This system permits the grouping of items by like value without regard to what these items are. For example, class C items could include paper clips, rubber bands, pencils and pens. The classification system permits the decision maker to allocate attention and control to the high-valued items, thereby facilitating control policy decision making. Differ-

Table 13.2. Some commonly used inventory financial control ratios.

$$\%\text{ASVR}^* = \frac{\text{Dollar Value of End of Year Inventories}}{\text{Dollar Sales For That Year}} \times 100\%$$

$$\%\text{CGSR}^{**} = \frac{\text{Dollar Cost of End of Year Inventories}}{\text{Cost of Goods Sold For That Year}} \times 100\%$$

$$\text{Turnover} = \frac{1}{\%\text{ASVR}} \times 100$$

$$\text{DSIIR} = \left(\frac{\text{End of Year Inventory Value}}{\left[\dfrac{\text{Sales Dollars for Last Year}}{365} \right]} \right)$$

* Annual Sales Value Ratio.
** Cost of Goods Sold Ratio.

ent reorder points, lot sizes and control policies are usually established for each class.

13.2.4 Review Point Methods

There are two basic methods for monitoring inventories and determining when reordering is warranted: the periodic review or two-bin method, and the continuous review or perpetual method. The label "two-bin" derives historically from the earlier practice of keeping two inventory storage bins. The depletion of the first bin triggered a reorder, and the demand was supplied from the second bin during the leadtime required to replenish the first bin. Today, the two-bin or periodic system reviews the stock on hand each week or month and a reorder is placed when the stock falls to a one-week or one-month supply.

By contrast, a perpetual system records every transaction in and out of the inventory. This approach provides an up-to-date running account of all stock movements over time. It is the ultimate in management information for decision making. But it also may be a costly and time-consuming system to maintain, unless automated and computerized facilities are available. Many manufacturing firms use a continuous review method called the materials requirements planning system (MRPS). This type of system coordinates inventories with production through demand forecasting and production control methods.[1]

13.2.5 Ordering Policies: R, r and Q, r

The lot size decision (how much to order) and the review point decision (when to order) are interrelated. Joint policies can be specified for determining the optimum lot size at each review point. There are two fundamental models for doing this: the R, r model and the Q, r model. The former is appropriate for periodic review situations; the latter is appropriate for continuous review situations.

Figure 13.4 illustrates the R, r policy. In this policy the inventory is observed at equally spaced time points t_1, t_2, etc. Here T is the *review period*, each t_i is a *review point*, r is the *reorder point*, I_i is the *observed inventory* on hand, R is a *target level* of inventory and q_i is the *lot size* (order size) at the ith review point. The R, r policy decision rule is to order

$$q_i = \begin{cases} R - I_i \text{ when } I_i \leq r, \\ \text{zero when } I_i > r. \end{cases} \tag{13.1}$$

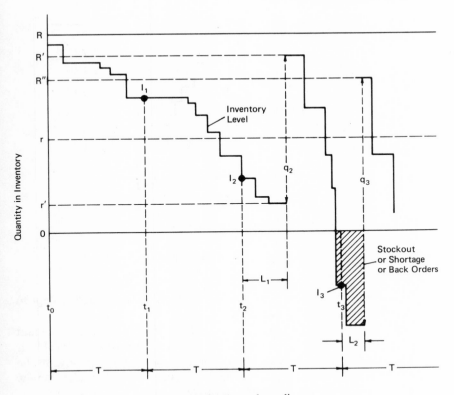

Figure 13.4. The R,r order policy.

For example, no order is placed at review point t_1 in Figure 13.4 because $I_1 > r$. At t_2 we see that $I_2 < r$ and Equation (13.1) indicates that an amount $q_2 = R - I_2$ should be ordered. However, during the leadtime L_1 while this order is arriving the inventory falls to r'. Hence, when the order arrives at time $t_2 + L_1$ the inventory on hand will recover to $q_2 + r' = R - I_2 + r' = R' < R$. Each reorder will thus fall increasingly short of recovering the inventory level to R, with a consequent risk of stockout in some subsequent period. Moreover, if the inventory depletion rate is quite rapid, a stockout could occur prior to the next review point, as illustrated in Figure 13.4 for t_3. Even with the relatively short leadtime L_2 shown after t_3 the R, r policy only recovers the inventory to $R'' < R' < R$. This biases the inventory level toward another subsequent stockout. To avoid this, an "order up to D" policy (discussed under the dynamic models section of

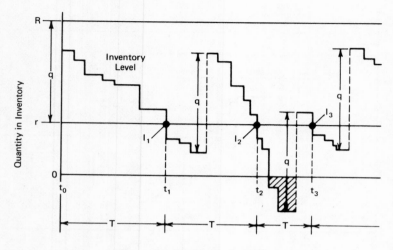

Figure 13.5. The Q,r order policy.

this chapter) may be used in which a buffer stock or base stock is kept to compensate for the leadtime demand.

Figure 13.5 illustrates the Q, r order policy. In this policy a constant sized lot $q = R - r$ is always reordered whenever the inventory level falls to r. Note the difference between this approach and the R, r policy. In the R, r policy the lot size q_i can vary at each ith review point but each review period T is always the same length. In the Q, r policy a fixed amount q is always ordered at each review point, but the review periods may vary in their durations. Like the R, r policy, the Q, r policy can also lead to stockouts, as illustrated in Figure 13.5 between review points t_2 and t_3.

13.3   A STATIC MODEL: EOQ

13.3.1   Definitions and Terms

The economic order quantity (EOQ) model is one of the most basic inventory models. First developed by Ford Harris around 1915, it was later popularized during the 1930's by H. R. Wilson. Though the assumptions which underlie this model are highly unrealistic, it oftens leads to very useful insights. Moreover, the concepts and ideas behind this model are universal.

Several kinds of EOQ models will be presented here. The following notations and definitions will be used throughout these presentations, as well as the remainder of this chapter. Let: q = the lot size, the size of the production run, or the size of the reorder; q^* = the optimum q, or the economic order quantity (EOQ); D_i = the quantity demanded during the ith period, where $D_1 = D_2 = \cdots = D_i = \cdots = D_n = D$ for static models; H = the length of the total planning horizon consisting of $i = 1, 2, \ldots, n$ review points; Q = the total demand or requirements over the planning horizon; T = the length of the review period or the interval between review points; t_i = the ith review point; c = the set-up or procurement cost per run or order; h = the holding (or carrying) cost per unit of inventory per unit of time; s = the shortage cost per unit of inventory stocked-out; R = the desired inventory level at the start of the cycle; p = the replenishment rate or production rate to replenish the inventory.

13.3.2 Model A: EOQ when Stockouts are not Allowed

In the simplest situation only one product is stocked, there is a static demand for this product, the leadtime is zero, there is a policy of not permitting shortages and all costs are known with certainty. This inventory situation is thus a case of decision making under certainty, as discussed in Chapter 4. The behavior of this inventory situation is depicted in Figure 13.6. Note that this is a Q, r policy system in which the reorder point is $r = 0$ with a constant order quantity $q = D$ in each period. The objective is to determine the optimum review point and lot size.

To solve this problem, note that the average inventory during any review period T within the horizon H is $q/2$. If h is the cost of holding one unit of inventory per time interval, then hT is the total holding cost per

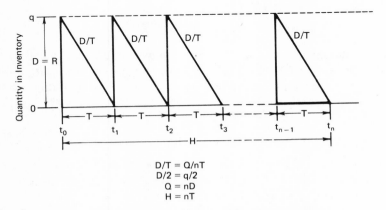

$$D/T = Q/nT$$
$$D/2 = q/2$$
$$Q = nD$$
$$H = nT$$

Figure 13.6. Illustration of model A inventory behavior.

unit of inventory for each period. The unit inventory cost C for each period is then given by

$$C = (q/2)hT + c. \tag{13.2}$$

If D units are demanded and sold during the ith period then the total average cost TAC of the inventory during that period is given by

$$TAC = C(D/q) = \frac{hDT}{2} + \frac{cD}{q} \tag{13.3}$$

But since $q = D$ then

$$TAC = \frac{hTq}{2} + \frac{cD.}{q} \tag{13.4}$$

By the methods of differential calculus, the minimum of Equation (13.4) is found by taking its first derivative, setting the result to zero and solving.[2, 3] This yields:

$$\frac{d(TAC)}{dq} = \frac{hT}{2} - \frac{cD}{q^2} = 0 \tag{13.5}$$

$$\frac{hT}{2} = \frac{cD}{q^2} \tag{13.6}$$

$$q^* = \sqrt{\frac{2cD.}{hT}} \tag{13.7}$$

Equation (13.7) gives the optimum lot size or EOQ value q^*. Equation (13.7) is often called the "square root rule." Substituting q^* for q in Equation (13.4) gives the minimum cost TAC^* of supplying the inventory during the review period T:

$$TAC^* = \sqrt{2\,cDhT}. \tag{13.8}$$

In the multiple period case, D is replaced by Q and T is replaced by H in Equations (13.7) and (13.8). Then q^* and TAC^* are for the entire horizon H rather than for simply one review period T. Then the optimum length of the review period T^* is given by

$$T^* = \sqrt{\frac{2cH}{hQ}}. \tag{13.9}$$

As illustrated in Figure 13.7, the EOQ model finds the trade-off between increasing carrying (or holding) costs and decreasing set-up costs as q increases. Carrying costs increase with an increase in the order size or run size q, since more inventory will be carried on hand. Set-up costs de-

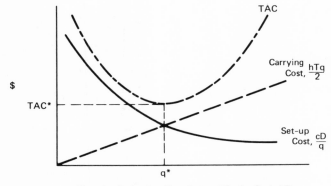

Figure 13.7. The EOQ cost functions for the period T.

crease with the order or run size, since fewer orders or runs are made over the time period T.

13.3.3 Model B: EOQ when Stockouts are Allowed

Figure 13.8 depicts the case where shortages are permitted. This is a two-bin review system where the point $q = 0$ is the start of the second bin. To derive the model for this case, let R be the inventory level desired by management, let s be the shortage costs per unit time and let the other notations be the same as in model A. To derive this model, we note from Figure 13.8 that $T_1/T = R/q$ and that $T_2/T = (q - R)/q$ by the geometry of similar triangles. Then

$$TAC = C(D/q) = \left(\frac{R \ hT_1}{2} + \left[\frac{q - R \ sT_2}{2}\right] + c\right) D/q, \qquad (13.10)$$

and by the same approach used above we derive[3]

$$q^* = \sqrt{\frac{2cD}{hT}} \ \sqrt{\frac{h + s,}{s}} \qquad (13.11)$$

$$T^* = \sqrt{\frac{2cH}{hQ}} \ \sqrt{\frac{h + s,}{s}} \qquad (13.12)$$

$$TAC^* = \sqrt{2cDhT} \ \sqrt{\frac{s}{h + s.}} \qquad (13.13)$$

Thus, model A in the preceding section is simply a special case of this model B.

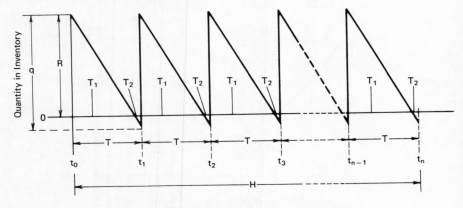

Figure 13.8. Illustration of model B inventory behavior.

13.3.4   EOQ Model C: Noninstantaneous Replenishment Rate

If the replenishment is not instantaneous, then as illustrated in Figure 13.4, the leadtime demand may effectively keep the desired level R from being achieved. To derive this model, let p be the replenishment rate. The other notations here will be the same as in models A and B. Then, it can be deduced that

$$C = \frac{cD}{q} + \frac{hTq}{2p}(p - D),\qquad(13.14)$$

from which we may derive [3]

$$q^* = \sqrt{\frac{2cD}{hT(1 - D/p),}}\qquad(13.15)$$

$$TAC^* = \sqrt{2cDhT(1 - D/p)}.\qquad(13.16)$$

Equations (13.16) and (13.8) can be used to compare the cost of a "make $vs.$ buy" decision, where Equation (13.16) gives the lowest cost to make the units and Equation (13.8) gives the lowest cost to buy the units. In general, where

$$\sqrt{2cDhT(1 - D/p)} < \sqrt{2cDhT}\qquad(13.17)$$

it is cheaper to make the product. Equation (13.17) suggests that, all other things being the same, it will always be cheaper to make the product if the replenishment rate (or production rate) is greater than the rate of demand, since D/p will then be less than 1.0. On the other hand, it is apparent from

Equation (13.17) that whenever $D > p$ then purchases should be made to make up the difference between the two rates.

13.3.5 When to Use EOQ Models

EOQ models often give surprisingly good results, even in the face of large errors in estimating the c, h, D and T input data. However, if the TAC curve is not flat in the region of q^*, then EOQ models can give very poor results. Similarly, if the demand fluctuates from period to period, EOQ models may lead to an out-of-phase inventory condition (see Figure 13.2). EOQ models will also give very poor results where there are joint products or where the demand in each period is not independent of the demand in prior periods. EOQ models may give incorrect results where either the demand or the leadtime is stochastic. On the other hand, it must be noted that these situations where EOQ models are ineffective are often very complex and difficult to model by other means. Thus, an EOQ model can usually prove to be very useful as a first approximation or as a starting point solution to be improved upon by other methods.[4]

13.4 SOME COMMON DYNAMIC MODELS

In dynamic situations the demand may cycle from period to period due to seasonal fluctuations, competitive factors, changing tastes or other forces. Though such situations can be modeled, dynamic models often require a great deal of quantitative data that are not readily available.[4] For instance, some dynamic models require the decision maker to accurately specify the demand for all future time periods within the planning horizon, the holding costs for each of those same periods, and the stockout costs for periods when the demand is extremely high. In many cases, if these data could be accurately estimated the optimum inventory policies could be deduced without a model. However, there are some periodic review rules and order policies that are very helpful under dynamic situations. We shall examine two of these: the order up to D policy and the moving average rule.

The "order up to D" policy is:

$$q_i = \begin{cases} D_i - I_i \text{ if } D_i > I_i + b, \\ \text{zero if } D_i \leq I_i + b, \end{cases} \tag{13.18}$$

where q_i is the reorder quantity (lot size), I_i is the inventory on hand at the start of the ith review period, D_i is the expected demand during the ith period and b is a buffer stock. The buffer stock accounts for variations in the demand from one period to the next and it may be set according to some appropriate rule that reflects the decision maker's willingness to take the risk of a stockout. The "moving average rule" is:

$$q_i = \begin{cases} D_a - I_i + (D^*_{-1} - q^*_{-1}) \text{ if } D_a > I_i, \\ \text{zero if } D_a \leq I_i \end{cases} \qquad (13.19)$$

where $D_a = (D^*_{-1} + D^*_{-2} + D_{L+1})/3$, where D^*_{-j} is the actual demand j periods previous to this one, where D_{L+1} is the forecasted demand for the leadtime L plus 1 period hence, and where q_{-1} is the lot size actually ordered during the immediately preceding period. Either of these rules may help to smooth out gyrations in the lot size, which would otherwise occur.

13.5   SOME COMMON STOCHASTIC MODELS

Stochastic models are useful when demand is uncertain. In these models, demand is treated as a random variable that can be analytically approximated using probability concepts. Thus, stochastic models are useful in cases of decision making under risk and uncertainty, as discussed in Chapter 4. Like dynamic models, stochastic models can be very complex and demanding in their data requirements. Only the most widely applicable models and heuristics are thus presented and discussed here.

13.5.1   The Critical Item Model for Avoiding Stockouts

This model is especially applicable to cases where a stockout has a very high penalty. Though estimating this penalty with precision may be difficult, this model permits the decision maker to get a good idea of the cost of a stockout and its implication.

To derive this model let: c = the cost of obtaining each unit for inventory; s = the stockout cost, or the penalty for being out of stock; q = the number of items in stock; q^* = the particular value of q which minimizes the total inventory cost; d = the number of items demanded or required and $P(d)$ = the probability that d will in fact be required. Then the expected cost $EC(q)$ of keeping q units in stock is

$$EC(q) \begin{cases} P(d)(q - d)c, \text{ for } d < q, \\ P(d)(d - q)s, \text{ for } d > q, \text{ and} \\ \text{zero for } d = q. \end{cases} \qquad (13.20)$$

The total expected cost TEC (q) of meeting the demand by keeping q units in inventory is given by

$$TEC(q) = c \sum_{d=0}^{q} P(d)(q - d) + s \sum_{d=q+1}^{\infty} P(d)(d - q), \qquad (13.21)$$

where the last term in Equation (13.21) gives the total stockout cost.
Now consider a particular value of q, say q_0 such that

$$[c + s]P(d \leq q_0) > s \qquad (13.22)$$

and such that

$$[c + s]P(d \leq q_0 - 1) < s. \qquad (13.23)$$

Then Equations (13.22) and (13.23) may be combined and rearranged to obtain

$$P(d \leq q_0 - 1) < \frac{s}{c + s} < P(d \leq q_0). \qquad (13.24)$$

The optimum stock level q^* is therefore that value of q_0 which satisfies Equation (13.24). Table 13.3 presents the algorithm for this model.

To illustrate this model, suppose the problem is determining how many replacement servomechanisms to stock in a computer center. The purchased cost of each extra servo is \$475. If no servos are on hand when one is needed, the downtime cost and lost business may approach \$14,000. The data in Table 13.4 are needed to solve this problem. These data show that of 100 servomechanisms, 90 did not fail at all, 4 of them failed one time, 3 failed on two occasions, 1 failed on three occasions, etc. Using the algorithm in Table 13.3, from step 1 we obtain the results in Table 13.5. Then from step 2 of the algorithm we obtain the critical ratio:

$$s/(c + s) = \$14,000/(\$475 + \$14,000) = .967. \qquad (13.25)$$

Table 13.3. Critical item algorithm.

STEP	ACTION OR DECISION
Step 1	From the historical data on past demands or requirements, assemble a table of cumulative probabilities of the requirements being less than or equal to selected inventory levels. These data are $P(d \leq q)$.
Step 2	Compute the value of the critical ratio, $s/(c + s)$.
Step 3	From the table developed in step 1, find that value q_0 which satisfies: $P(d \leq q_0 - 1)$ $< \dfrac{s}{c + s} < P(d \leq q_0)$. This value is q^*.
Step 4	Check for alternate optima, where the alternate optima are: $P(d \leq q_0) = s/(c + s)$; $q^* = q_0$ and $q_0 + 1$. $P(d \leq q_0 - 1) = s/(c + s)$; $q^* = q_0$ and $q_0 - 1$.
Step 5	Calculate the total expected cost of stocking q^* items, $TEC(q^*)$, by substitution into Equation (13.21).

Table 13.4. Data for the critical item algorithm.

NUMBER OF SERVOMECHANISMS	HISTORICAL DATA ON THE FREQUENCY OF FAILURE
90	0
4	1
3	2
1	3
1	4
1	5
Total 100	

From step 3, we set up the rule for finding q_0:

$$P(d \leq q_0 - 1) < .967 < P(d \leq q_0). \qquad (13.26)$$

The appropriate q_0 is $q_0 = 2$, since $P(d \leq 2-1) < .967 < P(d \leq 2)$ from Table 13.5. Hence, $q^* = 2$ servomechanisms.

The appropriate value of s can seldom be specified with complete accuracy. But, the critical item model can be used for estimating the value that s would have to take in order to justify various policies. For example, let us suppose there is a policy of keeping three servos in stock at all times. Then from Table 13.5 this policy implies that:

$$P(d \leq 2) < \frac{s}{\$475 + s} < P(d \leq 3), \text{ so that} \qquad (13.27)$$

$$.970 < \frac{s}{\$475 + s} < .980, \text{ and for } q = 2 \qquad (13.28)$$

$$s = \frac{(.970)(\$475)}{(1 - .970)} = \$15,358.33. \qquad (13.29)$$

Table 13.5. Results from step 1 of the critical items algorithm.

q	d	$P(d)$	$P(d \leq q)$
0	0	.90	.900
1	1	.04	.940
2	2	.03	.970
3	3	.01	.980
4	4	.01	.990
5	5	.01	1.000
		1.00	

Similarly, the maximum value of s to justify $q = 3$ is:

$$s = \frac{(.980)(\$475)}{(1 - .980)} = \$23,275. \tag{13.30}$$

Hence, the $q = 3$ policy is tantamount to saying that the regret is between a minimum of \$15,358.33 and a maximum of \$23,275. This approach can be expanded to develop a table of minimum and maximum regret values for each decision policy $q = 1$, $q = 2$, etc. At some point, say q_i, management will decide that the risk of a loss has been sufficiently covered. The corresponding s_i value that management is willing to pay is the amount of "insurance" they want to take out.

13.5.2 Using the Critical Item Model: Obtaining Risk Profiles

Converting the decision policy to s values and thinking in terms of the insurance cost is often a revealing way to think about an inventory problem. Sometimes a policy of having q_x units on hand, which seems reasonable from a physical count standpoint, becomes quite unreasonable from an insurance standpoint. For instance, it may be concluded that the corresponding s_x value is far in excess of the expected cost of a stockout, and therefore a policy of keeping q_x units in stock is far too conservative and costly. In other words, an examination of the s_x value has led to the realization that a policy of carrying q_x units actually "overinsures" the firm against the expected regrets of a stockout.

In an organizational setting, it is sometimes very useful and informative to compute the complete range of s_i values for the full range of q_i policies. Then, solicit each decision maker's s_i cut-off value, e.g., the topmost s_i insurance value which each decision maker feels should be bought. Then, an NI-type meeting (see Chapter 5) can be held to discuss and resolve any differences. Risk-avoidance oriented decision makers will opt for high s_i (and q_i) values. And risk-taking decision makers will select much lower s_i values. The decision makers can thus use this meeting to exchange perceptions and work toward a consensus on the appropriate inventory policy for the organization.

Another useful approach is to think of s as the incremental cost of the incremental inventory unit $(q + 1) - q$, or the insurance benefit value of this unit. Then the ratio s/c is the insurance benefit per dollar outlay. For example, from Table 13.5 and Equation (13.29) we find that the maximum value of s to justify $q = 2$ is \$15,358.33. Then the incremental benefit per dollar outlay in going from $q = 2$ to $q = 3$ is

$$\frac{\$23,275 - \$15,358.33}{\$475} = 16.7. \tag{13.31}$$

By comparison, the comparable ratio for the change from $q = 1$ to $q = 2$ is also 16.7. The ratio for the change from $q = 0$ to $q = 1$ is 6.7. Thus, there appears to be little incremental advantage of $q = 3$ over $q = 2$, though there is an advantage of $q = 2$ over $q = 1$.

13.5.3   Reorder Point Model for Reducing Leadtime Stockout Risks

Stockouts are an ever-present possibility when the demand is stochastic. When the leadtime is also stochastic a two-bin policy may not avoid stockouts since the second bin could be exhausted before the order arrives. Carrying a large buffer stock can create excessively high carrying costs, and it may not even avoid a stockout. However, one very simple approach that sometimes works well here is the reorder point model. To derive this model, let r be the reorder point. Then the objective is to set r such that the probability of a stockout is less than α, some small number. More formally, the objective is to set r such that

$$P(D > r) \leq \alpha. \tag{13.32}$$

where D is demand and P is a probability.

To illustrate the use of this simple rule, let the decision maker be willing to accept a 10% risk of a stockout. Then, this means that the decision maker is willing to accept an average of one stockout in ten leadtime periods. In terms of Equation (13.32), this means that $\alpha = .10$. Now suppose that past data shows that out of ten cases the total leadtime demand was 2 units in seven of those ten cases, 3 units in two of those ten cases and 4 units in one of those ten cases. Then from these data it is apparent that $P(D > 3) = 1/10 = .10$ and $P(D > 2) = (2 + 1)/10 = .30$. Thus, when $r = 3$ the decision maker's risk tolerance is just met. A policy of reordering when the stock level falls to three units is appropriate. Note that if the decision maker is willing to accept a 30% risk of stockout (an average of three stockouts in ten periods), then a policy of $r = 2$ is appropriate.

13.5.4   The Critical Ratio Reorder Model

Let the total expected shortage cost be given by

$$P_i(s) \times \left(\frac{sD_i}{I_i}\right), \tag{13.33}$$

where s is the cost per unit stocked-out, $P_i(s)$ is the probability of being stocked-out, D_i is the number of units expected to be demanded, and I_i is the number of units on hand at the start of the ith horizon. Let the total expected holding cost be given by

$$h I_i [1.0 - P_i(s)], \tag{13.34}$$

where h is the cost per unit held and $1.0 - P_i(s)$ is the probability of not having a stockout in the ith horizon. As in the above EOQ models, total costs are minimized where holding costs and shortage costs are equated. Letting $r = I_i$ and equating Equations (13.33) and (13.34) and solving for $P_i(s)$ gives

$$P_i(s) = \left(\frac{hr}{\dfrac{sD_i}{r} + hr} \right) \tag{13.35}$$

Equation (13.35) tells us to set the reorder point r such that the probability of having a stockout is equal to the ratio of the total holding costs to the sum of the total shortage and total holding costs. The ratio in the right-hand side of Equation (13.35) is called a "critical ratio" because it defines the critical point for optimality.

13.5.5   The "Overproduce" Rules

A simple but effective common sense approach is to produce (or order) only when there is a demand D_i, but to overproduce (or overorder) by a controlled amount. The set of rules is:

1. If $D_i - x_i \le 0$ fill the order from the stock, where x_i is the on-hand inventory or stock;
2. If $D_i - x_i > 0$ and if $D_i - x_i \ge q_i^*$, then produce or order an amount $D_i - x_i$ to complete the order, where q_i^* is the EOQ;
3. If $D_i - x_i < q_i^*$, then produce or order an amount q_i^* and place any remainder in stock.

This approach can be surprisingly effective in reducing carrying costs while not incurring excessive stockout penalties.

13.5.6   Using Stochastic Models

Many real-world inventory situations are stochastic. Unfortunately, these situations are often extremely difficult to model, to obtain data for, and to solve with great precision.[4] In any stochastic situation, the risks of stock-outs and overstocking are major considerations. Models and heuristics that can assist the decision maker in obtaining a better picture of these risks are valuable aids to decision making. Thus, the use of critical ratios and other simple rules can often help the decision maker test out many alternative policies and evaluate their "goodness." In this way, a decision maker can narrow down the number of choices that should be seriously considered in making a final policy decision.

13.6   SOME COMMON QUESTIONS AND THEIR ANSWERS

Should the item be stocked at all? This is a common question when the number of items proliferate. An answer can be found by comparing K_s with K_n, the respective average costs of stocking and nonstocking the item, where

$$K_n = L(p - c) + (1.0 - L)c_s n, \tag{13.36}$$

$$K_s = h(d/n) + c_s(q/n). \tag{13.37}$$

It is only justifiable to stock when $K_s < K_n$. In the above equations p and c are the unit price and production (or ordering) cost, d is the annual number of units demanded, n is the number of orders per year, h and c_s are the unit holding and set-up costs, q is the annual production or procurement rate and L is the percentage sales dollars lost from not stocking (the stockout penalty).

Is the demand large enough to warrant producing this item? This question often arises where the demand is sporadic in pattern and small in total. On the one hand, there may be a desire to have a complete line of goods. But there is also a proclivity to eliminate such items, to economize on set-up and holding costs. Following some ideas developed by Fred Hanssmann (see Bibliography), let

$$TEC = \left(\frac{Hh}{2}\right)(k - 1) + \frac{cD}{k}, \tag{13.38}$$

where k is an integer, h is the holding cost per unit, c is the set-up cost per unit and D is the expected demand over the horizon H. Taking the derivative of Equation (13.38) with respect to k and solving for D at the minimum of TEC gives

$$D = (k^2 hH)/2c. \tag{13.39}$$

Equation (13.39) says that any low-demand item whose expected demand is not at least equal to the ratio of its total holding costs to twice its set-up cost should not be produced and stocked. The value of k can be varied to allow for special circumstances. Note that from Equation (13.38) it can be seen that when $k = 1$ this is the policy of not producing and not stocking the item.

How much should be allowed for shrinkage, rejects, obsolescence or decay in the inventory? One way is to set the EOQ equal to $q^* (1.0 + S)$, where S is the percentage reject rate and q^* is the lot size from an EOQ model. However, if the number of rejects is stochastic or if the cost of replacing the rejects is very much different from the usual set-up costs, then the above rule is not sufficient. In that case, we can devise an approximate rule as follows. Let x be the number of items in stock, let D be the number of items demanded, let $p(r)$ be the probability that r rejects will occur and let r be the number of items rejected. To avoid a stockout, $r + D$ must not exceed $x + q^*$, where q^* is the EOQ lot size. Then the rule $P(D \geq x + r + q^*) \leq \alpha$ may be formulated following the procedures outlined for Equation (13.32) in section 13.5.3 of this chapter. This rule may then be solved for r, given various values of α.

13.7 SUMMARY

Maintaining an adequate but not excessive level of inventories is a difficult decision problem. An incorrect decision can lead to either high opportunity costs in lost sales due to a stockout, or high carrying and storage costs due to excess inventories. The choice of an optimum inventory level is deeply influenced by the risk-taking propensity of the decision maker. The cost of carrying excess inventories is the cost of insurance against a stockout. And the opportunity loss from a stockout is the potential regret from not having adequate insurance.

This chapter has presented several simple models for comparing and analyzing these costs and risks, as an aid to the decision maker. The greatest difficulty with any inventory model is obtaining the input data: demand forecasts, cost estimates and probabilities. In most cases, exact data and precise estimates are not easy to obtain. Thus, the simple models and approaches presented here will often be sufficient, given the crudeness of the decision data that are available. If more exact answers are needed, then more precise data and more sophisticated methods are required. Even then, the basic methods discussed here embody the fundamental logic which is used in these more sophisticated approaches. Thus, the simple methods presented here can often serve as a first approximation or as part of a quick "what if" analysis.

13.8 REFERENCES

1. Brown, R. G. *Management Decisions for Production Operations*. Hinsdale, Illinois: Dryden, 1971.
2. See any standard differential calculus text.
3. Nearly every text does these algebraic derivations differently, thus making comparisons among the texts rather difficult. For a treatment that is consistent with the equations here

see; Churchman, C. W.; R. L. Ackoff; and E. L. Arnoff. *Introduction to Operations Research.* New York: John Wiley & Sons, Inc., 1957, pp. 224–232.
4. Nahmias, S. N. "Inventory Models," in *Encyclopedia of Computer Science and Technology: Volume 9,* Jack Belzer, A. G. Holzman and Allan Kent (eds.), New York: Marcel Dekker, Inc., 1978, pp. 446–482.

13.9 BIBLIOGRAPHY

Akturk, Cetin and Jucker, J. V. "The Robustness of the Variable S Inventory Model: Some New Results." *AIIE Transactions,* **9,** No. 4: 382–386 (1977).

Bechtold, S. E. and Nast, D. A. "A Comparison of Two Inventory Decision Models." *Journal of Management,* **4,** No. 1: 85–95 (1978).

Brown, R. G. *Decision Rules for Inventory Management.* Hinsdale, Illinois: Dryden, 1967.

Brown, R. G. "Inventory Control," in *Handbook of Operations Research: Models and Applications,* J. J. Moder and S. E. Elmaghraby (eds.), New York: Van Nostrand Reinhold Company, 1978, pp. 173–212.

Gross, D. and Ince, R. "A Comparison and Evaluation of Approximate Continuous Review Inventory Models." *International Journal of Production Research,* **10,** No. 2: 201–232 (1975).

Hadley, G. J. and Whitin, T. M. *Analysis of Inventory Systems.* Englewood Cliffs, New Jersey: Prentice-Hall, Inc., 1963.

Hanssmann, Fred. *Operations Research in Production and Inventory Control.* New York: John Wiley & Sons, Inc., 1962, pp. 20–22.

Johnson, L. A. and Montgomery, D. C. *Operations Research, Production Planning, Scheduling and Inventory Control.* New York: John Wiley & Sons, Inc., 1974.

Ward, J. B. "Determining Reorder Points When Demand is Lumpy." *Managment Science,* **24,** No. 6: 623–632 (1978).

Wecker, W. W. "Predicting Demand from Sales Data in the Presence of Stockout." *Management Science,* **24,** No. 10: 1043–1054 (1978).

Zalkind, David. "Order-Level Inventory Systems with Independent Stochastic Leadtimes." *Management Science,* **24,** No. 13: 1384–1392 (1978).

14

Mathematical Programming and Resource Allocation

14.0 INTRODUCTION

The word "programming" refers to the process of planning and allocating scarce resources. All programming problems are characterized by the following attributes. There are several alternative actions that can be taken. Each action is expected to result in some degree of goal achievement. Each action has a cost in terms of using up some of the available resources. And there is a limited amount of resources available. Thus, the best utilization of the limited resources among the alternative actions is sought, in terms of maximizing the total goal achievements.

Programming problems can become quite complex if there are many alternative actions and several cost-achievement trade-offs among them. Mathematical programming methods are available to handle some of these complexities. This chapter reviews and discusses these methods.

14.1 PROGRAMMING PROBLEMS

14.1.1 Handling Trade-Offs

To illustrate the effects of trade-offs in a programming problem, let us take the following example. Suppose there is a total of $100,000 available to be allocated to two areas, A and B. The funds can be apportioned between the two areas in $20,000 increments, with the resulting percentage goal achievements shown in Table 14.1. It is obvious that both areas cannot achieve 100% of their goals with the limited funds available. However, management desires at least 35% goal achievement in each area. The problem is to find the optimum allocation: the one which gives the largest

Table 14.1. Illustration of programming problem solution.

FUNDS AVAILABLE = **$100,000**

ALLOCATE:		RESULTING PERCENTAGE GOAL ACHIEVEMENT IS:	
TO A	TO B	ON A	ON B
$ 0	$100,000	0%	100%
20,000	80,000	50	85
40,000 *	60,000 *	75	80
60,000	40,000	85	50
80,000	20,000	95	20
100,000	0	100	0

* Optimum allocation = $40,000 on A plus $60,000 on B; total percentage goal achievement = 75% + 80% = 155%

total percentage goal achievements with the available funds. The solution to this problem is indicated in Table 14.1.

The optimality of this solution can readily be verified by examining the results from incremental reallocations on either side of the optimum $40,000/$60,000 split. Table 14.2 shows the results of reallocating $20,000 (the smallest increment possible, as noted above) first from area A to B, and then from area B to A. In both cases the resulting loss exceeds the gain. Note that a $40,000 incremental reallocation is not feasible because of the constraint that at least 35% goal achievement must be made in each area (see Table 14.1).

Table 14.2. Results of incremental reallocations, starting from the $40,000 on A and $60,000 on B allocation.

	INCREMENTAL AMOUNT REALLOCATED	FROM	TO	RESULTING TOTAL ALLOCATIONS		RESULTING LOSS (−) OR GAIN (+) IN PERCENTAGE GOAL ACHIEVEMENTS *	
				A	B	ON A	ON B
Case 1:	$20,000	A	B	$20,000	$80,000	−25%	+5%
Case 2:	20,000	B	A	$60,000	$40,000	+10%	−30%

* Loss or gain from the optimal 75% and 80% goal achievements on areas A and B

14.1.2 Mathematical Programming Formulation

The mathematical programming formulation of the above problem is:

$$max \quad Z = \sum_{i=1}^{2} G_i \tag{14.1}$$

$$s.t. \quad G_i \geq 35\% \tag{14.2}$$

$$\sum_{i=1}^{2} d_i \leq b \tag{14.3}$$

where "s. t." is the abbreviation for "subject to the constraints that," where G_i is the percentage goal achievement in the ith area, b is the total amount of funds available ($b = \$100,000$), d_i is the amount of funds allocated to the ith area, and Z is a parameter which measures the magnitude of the achievements. Equation (14.1) is the objective function, Equation (14.2) is the minimum achievement constraint and Equation (14.3) is the total funding or budget constraint. The usual nonnegativity constraint $d_i \geq 0$ is redundant here and is not included because Equation (14.2) insures that none of the d_i will be negative in the solution.

To solve this programming problem, the optimum values of the decision variables d_i must be found. These optimum values d_i^* are the ones which result in the maximum value of Z, denoted by Z^*. As presented in the preceding section, $d_1^* = \$40,000$, $d_2^* = \$60,000$ and $Z^* = 75\% + 80\% = 155\%$. This solution can be arrived at by the following algorithm. First, define the feasible alternatives. There are only three: \$20,000 on A plus \$80,000 on B; \$40,000 on A plus \$60,000 on B; \$60,000 on A plus \$40,000 on B. There are no other alternatives which meet the 35% minimum goal achievement constraint Equation (14.2). Second, select any one of these three feasible alternatives as a starting point. Compute the resulting gain and loss in percentage goal achievements for an incremental reallocation between the starting point and its nearest neighboring alternative, as illustrated in Table 14.2. If the gain exceeds the loss then that adjacent alternative is better than the starting point. Third, replace the starting point alternative with the *best* adjacent alternative and repeat the second step until no better alternative is found. This is essentially the approach that is used to solve all mathematical programming formulations. And the fundamental condition that must exist at the optimum point is the one illustrated in Table 14.2. Let us state this condition formally:

The Fundamental Condition for Optimality: the value of the objective function cannot be improved by any internal reallocation of resources among the decision alternatives.

This is a fundamental condition that holds for all programming problems. It is the basic rule that is used to determine whether or not an optimum solution has been reached. And it is the basic rule that is used to search for the optimum solution point.

In some real decision problems it is not practical to look for the one best solution. As discussed in Chapters 4 and 5, the problem may be so complex that any feasible solution is acceptable, and the decision maker may not feel it is worthwhile to search for anything better. Though mathematical programming methods seek the one best solution, they can also be quite useful in narrowing down the number of alternatives and in locating satisfactory solutions to complex problems.

14.2   CLASSICAL PROGRAMMING METHODS

The "classical" methods of programming date from the work of the 16th and 17th century mathematicians and the 18th and 19th century economists.[1] These methods are based on differential calculus and they apply only where the decision problem can be formulated in terms of continuous-valued functions. To find the optima (maxima and minima of the function), take the first derivative of the function, set it to zero and solve for the optimum values of the decision variables. Then take the second derivative of the function and evaluate it at the optimum values of the decision variables. A negative-valued result indicates a maximum; a positive-valued result indicates a minimum. These rules are effective for functions of order n, where $n \leq 3$; extensions of these rules are used for higher order functions.[1]

14.2.1   Classical Methods for Unconstrained Optimization

Suppose we have the planning model $\Pi = 27p - p^3$ relating the net price p for an item to its profit Π, as determined by an analysis of available data. Here $p = g - c$, where g is the gross selling price and c is the cost to produce and sell the item. To find the profit-maximizing net price level p^*, we formulate the programming problem

$$max \ \Pi = 27p - p^3. \tag{14.4}$$

Applying differential calculus methods, the optima are

$$\frac{d\Pi}{dp} = 27 - 3p^2 = 0, \tag{14.5}$$

$$p^* = +\$3 \text{ and } -\$3. \tag{14.6}$$

To show that $p^* = +\$3$ is a profit-maximizing price, take the second derivative $d^2\Pi/dp^2$ of Equation (14.4) and evaluate it at $p^* = +\$3$. The result is

$$\frac{d^2\Pi}{dp^2} = -6(p) = -6(\$3) = -18, \qquad (14.7)$$

and the negative value for Equation (14.7) indicates a maximum. The profit for the horizon will be 27 ($3) − ($3)^3 = $54. By similarly testing the other root $p^* = -\$3$ it may be seen that it is the profit-minimizing value.

To illustrate the multivariate case, let $q = f(x_1, x_2)$ be a production function where x_1 and x_2 are two resources or inputs and q is the output. Let the total production cost be $C = r_1 x_1 + r_2 x_2 + b$ where r_1 and r_2 are the respective unit costs of the inputs x_1 and x_2 and b is a fixed cost. Then the profit equation is $\Pi = pq - C$ where p is the unit selling price of the output q. The programming problem and its solution are:

$$max\ \Pi = p(f\,[x_1, x_2] - (r_1 x_1 + r_2 x_2 + b), \qquad (14.8)$$

$$\frac{\partial\Pi}{\partial x_1} = p(f'[x_1]) - r_1 = 0, \qquad (14.9)$$

$$\frac{\partial\Pi}{\partial x_2} = p(f'[x_2]) - r_2 = 0, \qquad (14.10)$$

$$p(f'[x_1]) = r_1, \qquad (14.11)$$

$$p(f'[x_2]) = r_2. \qquad (14.12)$$

Here, $\partial\Pi/\partial x_1$ and $\partial\Pi/\partial x_2$ are the respective partial derivatives of Equation (14.8) with regard to variables x_1 and x_2. The notations $f'(x_1) = \partial q/\partial x_1$ and $f'(x_2) = \partial q/\partial x_2$ are the first partial derivatives of the function $f(x_1, x_2)$ with regard to the variables x_1 and x_2, respectively. The quantity $p(f'[x_1])$ is the rate by which revenues will increase with each incremental application of the ith input resource. The quantity $f'(x_i)$ is the "marginal" or incremental contribution of the ith resource to output q. The quantity $p(f'[x_i])$ is the "value" of this marginal product. The results in Equations (14.11) and (14.12) are fundamental to programming problems. These results say that at the optimum point the value of the marginal product of each resource will be equal to its input cost. Let us examine the logic of this result. If $\partial\Pi/\partial x_i < r_i$ then it would be economical to use *less* of the ith resource. But if $\partial\Pi/\partial x_i > r_i$ it would be economical to use *more* of the ith resource. Where $\partial\Pi/\partial x_i = r_i$ for all inputs $i = 1, 2, . . . n$, the system is in economic equilibrium. This simple idea is the rule which drives most linear programming and nonlinear programming algorithms. And it is the rule that is used to assure that an optimum policy has been reached by these algorithms.

14.2.2   Classical Methods for Constrained Optimization

To illustrate the constrained case, let the revenue equation be $R = p_1 q_1 + p_2 q_2$ for two outputs q_1 and q_2 which are sold at respective prices p_1 and p_2. For simplicity, suppose that only one input, x, is used to produce these two outputs and the implicit production function is $x = f(q_1, q_2)$. Then the programming problem is

$$max\ R = p_1 q_1 + p_2 q_2 \tag{14.13}$$

$$s.t.\quad x - f(q_1, q_2) = 0 \tag{14.14}$$

The mathematician Lagrange[1] showed that such problems can be solved by converting the constrained problem to an equivalent unconstrained problem, using a Lagrangian equation and a Lagrange multiplier, λ. The Lagrangian for Equations (14.13) and (14.14) is

$$R_L = p_1 q_1 + p_2 q_2 + \lambda(x - f[q_1, q_2]). \tag{14.15}$$

The solution to Equation (14.15) is

$$\frac{\partial R_L}{\partial q_1} = p_1 - \lambda f'(q_1) = 0, \tag{14.16}$$

$$\frac{\partial R_L}{\partial q_2} = p_2 - \lambda f'(q_2) = 0, \tag{14.17}$$

$$\frac{\partial R_L}{\partial \lambda} = x - f(q_1, q_2) = 0. \tag{14.18}$$

Simultaneously solving Equations (14.16) and (14.17) yields the fundamental result

$$\lambda = p_1 \frac{\partial q_1}{\partial x} = p_2 \frac{\partial q_2}{\partial x}. \tag{14.19}$$

Note that $p_j(\partial q_j / \partial x_i) = \partial R / \partial x_i$, for any i^{th} input used in producing any j^{th} output. Hence, it follows from Equation (14.19) that:

$$\frac{\partial R}{\partial x_i} = \lambda \tag{14.20}$$

at the optimum point x_i^*. Equation (14.20) says that revenues can be increased by an amount λ when the total amount of the input resource x_i is increased by an incremental amount.

In general, $\lambda \geqslant 0$ in Equation (14.20). The $\lambda = 0$ case is easily illustrated by referring to Table 14.1 and its associated discussions. Suppose the funds available = \$200,000. Then $d_1^* = \$100,000$ and $d_2^* = \$100,000$ and $Z^* = G_1 + G_2 = 200\%$. Now let b be increased by a small amount $\Delta b = \$1$. This additional \$1 cannot be used because Z is already at the maximum total achievement level possible. Hence, the impact on Z is $\Delta Z = 0$, so that $\Delta Z / \Delta b = \lambda = 0$ when there are excess total funds available. However, when the available funds are inadequate to fund all the alternatives at their highest contribution level then $\Delta Z / \Delta b = \lambda > 0$. To show this, suppose $b = \$120,000$ and again refer to Table 14.1. The optimal allocation of \$120,000 is $d_1^* = \$60,000$ and $d_2^* = \$60,000$, which yields $Z^* = 85\% + 80\% = 165\%$. Recall that when $b = \$100,000$, then $Z^* = 155\%$ as shown in Table 14.1. Thus when b is increased from \$100,000 to \$120,000 it is apparent that $\Delta Z / \Delta b = (165\% - 155\%)/\$20,000 = \lambda > 0$.

As an illustration of the application of the Lagrangian, take the general resource programming problem

$$max \; Z = f(d_1, d_2) \tag{14.21}$$

$$s.t. \qquad d_1 + d_2 = b, \tag{14.22}$$

where b is the total amount of resources available, d_1 and d_2 are the respective amounts of resources allocated to two competing alternatives, and the optimum allocations d_1^* and d_2^* are sought. The solution is given by

$$Z_L = f(d_1, d_2) + \lambda(b - d_1 - d_2) \tag{14.23}$$

$$\frac{\partial Z_L}{\partial d_1} = f'(d_1) - \lambda = 0 \tag{14.24}$$

$$\frac{\partial Z_L}{\partial d_2} = f'(d_2) - \lambda = 0 \tag{14.25}$$

$$\frac{\partial Z_L}{\partial \lambda} = b - d_1 - d_2 = 0. \tag{14.26}$$

Noting that $f'(d_i) = \partial Z / \partial d_i$ and simultaneously solving Equations (14.24) and (14.25) leads to the mathematical statement of The Fundamental Condition for Optimality:

$$\frac{\partial Z}{\partial d_1} = \frac{\partial Z}{\partial d_2}. \tag{14.27}$$

The notations ∂d_1 and ∂d_2 denote incremental changes in d_1 and d_2, the resources allocated to the two competing alternatives. Equation (14.26) restricts such changes to offsetting internal reallocations, i.e., a decrease in one must result in a corresponding increase in the other since b is not changed. Thus, Equation (14.27) states that at the optimum point it will not be possible to increase Z by an internal reallocation. Any gain in Z by increasing d_1 to the level $d_1 + \Delta d$ will be offset by an equal loss in Z, due to the decrease in d_2 to the level $d_2 - \Delta d$. This was precisely the result in Table 14.2 where it was found that $\Delta Z/\Delta d_1 = (-25\% + 5\%)/\$20{,}000 = \Delta Z/\Delta d_2 = (+10\% - 30\%)/\$20{,}000$.

14.2.3   General Form Programming Problem

The general form of all mathematical programming problems is:

$$max\ Z = f(\bar{x}) \tag{14.28}$$

$$s.t. \qquad g_i(\bar{x}) \le b_i, i = 1, 2, \ldots k - 1, \tag{14.29}$$

$$g_i(\bar{x}) \ge b_i, i = k, k + 1, \ldots m, \tag{14.30}$$

where b_i is a resource limit or budget and where $\bar{x}$ is a shorthand notation for the vector $(x_1, x_2, \ldots x_n)$. The inequality constraints, Equations (14.29) and (14.30), must be converted to their "augmented" equality forms by respectively adding slack, $+ s_i$, and surplus, $- s_i$, variables before the Lagrangian approach can be applied. The augmented forms of Equations (14.29) and (14.30) are:

$$g_i(\bar{x}) + s_i = b_i, i = 1, 2, \ldots k - 1, \tag{14.31}$$

$$g_i(\bar{x}) - s_i = b_i, i = k, k + 1, \ldots m, \tag{14.32}$$

and the Lagrangian form of this problem is:

$$max\ Z_L = f(\bar{x}) + \sum_{i=1}^{k-1} \lambda_i (b_i - s_i - g_i[\bar{x}])$$

$$+ \sum_{i=k}^{m} \lambda_i (b_i + s_i - g_i[\bar{x}]). \tag{14.33}$$

Note that $b_i - s_i - g_i(x) = 0$ and $b_i + s_i - g_i(\bar{x}) = 0$, so these equations can be added to Equation (14.28) to form the Lagrangian without changing the value of Equation (14.28). If the slack and surplus variables were not added then the constraint equations would not be equal to zero. Then they could not be added to Equation (14.28), and the Lagrangian approach would not work.

In general, some of the constraints will usually be "active," in that the solution will lie on that constraint. Others may be "inactive," i.e., the solution will not be restricted by the constraint. The solution to the Lagrangian will indicate which constraints are active and which are not. It will work out that when $\lambda_i = 0$ and $s_i > 0$ then the constraint will be inactive. When $\lambda_i > 0$ then $s_i = 0$ and the constraint will be active. These ideas are extensively used in linear programming (LP) methods and nonlinear programming (NLP) methods. To illustrate these ideas consider the two cases shown in Figure 14.1. In case 1, the available resources b_1 are inadequate to permit the unconstrained optimum point R^* to be reached on the revenue function $f(R)$. Only a suboptimal point R_1 can be achieved. The constraint is active, and $\lambda > 0$ because an increase in b_1 will permit a higher point to be reached on $f(R)$. The constraint becomes $b_1 - a + mx = 0$ in the Lagrangian, so the slack variable $s = 0$. But $\lambda = 0$ in case 2 because increasing b_2 cannot increase revenues beyond R^*. But note that $s > 0$ in case 2. Why? The answer is that a variable $s > 0$ must be added to the inequation $a - mx \leqslant b_2$ to take up the slack and bring it to the form $b_2 - a + mx - s = 0$ so it can be used in a Lagrangian. Note that, as shown in Figure 14.1, the equation $a - mx = b_2$ and $f(R)$ do not intersect: they have no feasible solution. However, the augmented form $a - mx + s = b_2$ does have a feasible solution in common with $f(R)$. Thus, this illustration shows that the product of λ and s will always be zero because either one or the other is always zero. That is

$$\lambda s = 0 \qquad\qquad (14.34)$$

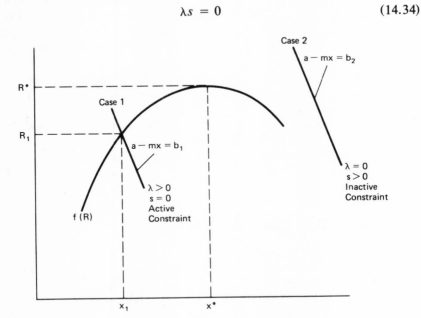

Figure 14.1. Illustration of active and inactive constraints.

Equation (14.34) is another fundamental relationship which has a very important use in linear programming (LP), as discussed below in this chapter.

14.2.4 Duality and Saddle Points

The duality concept says that any constrained maximization problem has a dual minimization problem that lies behind it or "shadows" it. And any constrained minimization problem has a dual maximization "shadow" problem. Looked at from one direction, the problem is to maximize some function. Looked at from another direction, this same problem can be treated as a minimization problem. The solution to the minimization problem is also the solution to the maximization problem. The coordinates of the solution are referred to as a "saddle point."

To illustrate these ideas consider

$$max \; Z_L = f(x_1, x_2) + \lambda(g[x_1, x_2]), \text{ and} \tag{14.35}$$

$$min \; X_L = h(x_2, \lambda) + x_1(g[x_2, \lambda]). \tag{14.36}$$

Equation (14.35) is a *primal* problem and Equation (14.36) is a *dual*. The solution to the primal yields a coordinate (x_1^*, x_2^*) which is the maximum of the function $f(x_1, x_2)$. The solution to the dual problem yields a coordinate (x_2^*, λ^*) which is the minimum of the function $h(x_2, \lambda)$. Figure 14.2 depicts these ideas where the functions $f(x_1, x_2)$ and $h(x_2, \lambda)$ are parabolas. Curve $A'B'$ is the function $f(x_1, x_2)$. Curve $C'D'$ is the function $h(x_2, \lambda)$. The Lagrangian is the saddle function $ABCD$. Viewed from one direction, the saddle function is Equation (14.35). Viewed from the other direction, the saddle function is Equation (14.36). The solution to either the primal or the dual yields the saddle point $(x_1^*, x_2^*, \lambda^*)$. The primal gives the values x_1^* and x_2^*, with the value λ^* as a shadow value. The dual gives the value x_2^* and λ^*, with the value x_1^* as a shadow value. These ideas are very basic to all programming problems, but especially to linear programming (LP) problems.

14.3 LINEAR PROGRAMMING (LP)

To illustrate the LP approach, suppose the problem is ascertaining the optimum allocation of efforts in the production of speedboat and sailboat hulls. Sailboat hulls sell for $400 apiece and speedboat hulls sell for $300 apiece. Each sailboat hull requires five man-hours of labor and three machine-hours of shop time. Each speedboat hull requires two man-hours

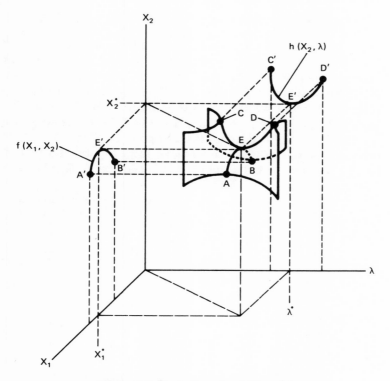

Figure 14.2. Illustration of a saddle point.

of labor and three machine-hours of shop time. Production is limited to a total of 60 hulls, and 135 machine-hours and 195 man-hours are available over the production horizon. The mathematical programming formulation of this problem is

$$max\ \Pi = \$400x_1 + \$300x_2 \tag{14.37}$$

$$s.t.\ 5x_1 + 2x_2 \le 195\ \text{hrs.} \tag{14.38}$$

$$3x_1 + 3x_2 \le 135\ \text{hrs.} \tag{14.39}$$

$$x_1 + x_2 \le 60\ \text{hulls} \tag{14.40}$$

$$x_1, x_2 \ge 0, \tag{14.41}$$

where Π is the total sales revenues, x_1 is the number of sailboat hulls, x_2 is the number of speedboat hulls and Equation (14.41) is the nonnegativity constraint. Note that all the equations are linear.

14.3.1 Graphical Approach

Equations (14.38), (14.39) and (14.41) define the feasible space $ABCD$ in Figure 14.3. The solution must lie within this space (or on its perimeter). It now becomes obvious that Equation (14.40) is redundant and it may be eliminated. Equation (14.37) represents a family of isorevenue lines, each with a slope of $-4/3$. When $\Pi = 0$ the line for Equation (14.37) goes through point B in Figure 14.3. When $\Pi = \$13,500$ the line goes through point A. When $\Pi = \$15,600$ it goes through point C. When $\Pi = \$17,000$ it goes through point D. Thus, it is obvious from Figure 14.3 that $\Pi^* = \$17,000$, $x_1^* = 35$ sailboat hulls and $x_2^* = 10$ speedboat hulls, where Π^*, x_1^* and x_2^* denote optimum values.

Note that point D represents the solution to the set of simultaneous Equations (14.37) through (14.41). Any point to the left of point D is an

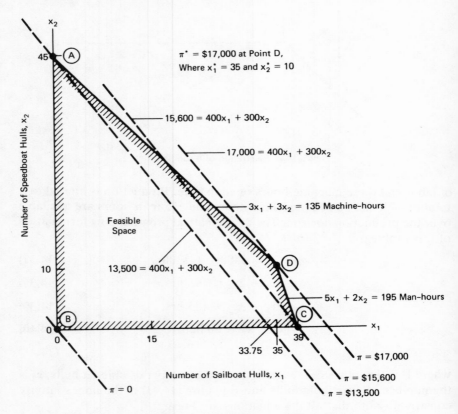

Figure 14.3. Solution to the primal LP problem.

inferior revenue solution and any point outside region $ABCD$ is not a feasible solution to this equation set. Note also that the solution point D lies on both constraints, i.e., 195 man-hours and 135 machine-hours are used in this solution.

14.3.2 Post-Optimal Analysis

If $\Pi = \$15,600$ then any combinations of x_1 and x_2 values lying along the line $400x_1 + 300x_2 = 15,600$ are feasible solutions. All such coordinates will give a total profit $\Pi = \$15,600$. Point C is one such point. Here, $x_1 = 39$ and $x_2 = 0$. In this case, the man-hour constraint is active but the machine-hour constraint is inactive. That is, point C lies on the man-hour constraint. Point C is the case where $5x_1 + 2x_2 = 195$ and $3x_1 + 3x_2 < 135$. Another feasible point is the coordinate $x_1 = 36$ and $x_2 = 4$. At this point, both constraints are inactive. That is, $5x_1 + 2x_2 < 195$ and $3x_1 + 3x_2 < 135$. Similarly, for $\Pi = \$13,500$ point A is a feasible solution. Here, $x_2 = 45$ and $x_1 = 0$ and the man-hour constraint is inactive.

A post-optimal analysis of this type may be especially useful when the decision problem is somewhat fuzzy. For example, the budget may not be rigidly fixed, the constraints may be somewhat flexible or the decision maker may be content with a "good" decision rather than the "best" decision. A post-optimal analysis can provide a more complete picture of the problem alternatives and their interrelationships. For example, the decision maker may purposely decide to operate at point C instead of point D in Figure 14.3 as the result of a post-optimal analysis. Point C may be a better choice if the market demand for speedboat hulls is uncertain relative to sailboat hulls. In selecting point C over point D the decision maker will have to balance off the profit difference of $\$1,400$ between points D and C against the estimate of the relative market risks involved. But without the post-optimal analysis the proximity of point C to point D might not be discovered.

14.3.3 The Simplex Method

The graphical method is limited to linear programming problems in which there are only two dimensions or activities. When there are more than two dimensions a mathematical approach such as the simplex method must be used. A simplex is a closed geometrical polyhedron. The polyhedron $ABCD$ in Figure 14.3 is a simplex. The simplex method or algorithm is a step-by-step method of selecting an initial basic solution and then moving to successively better solutions until the best one is found.

The initial solution to the boat problem is found from the "augmented"

Table 14.3. Initial basic feasible solution simplex tableau.

	Column Numbers				
	1	2	3	4	5
Headings	−400	−300	0	0	0
Row 1	5	2	1	0	195
Row 2	3	3	0	1	135

form of the original problem statement, Equations (14.37) through (14.39). The augmented form of these equations is:

$$\Pi - 400x_1 - 300x_2 = 0 \qquad (14.42)$$

$$5x_1 + 2x_2 + 1s_1 + 0s_2 = 195 \qquad (14.43)$$

$$3x_1 + 3x_2 + 0s_1 + 1s_2 = 135. \qquad (14.44)$$

One obvious simultaneous solution to this set of equations is $x_1 = 0$, $x_2 = 0$, $s_1 = 195$ and $s_2 = 135$. At this point $\Pi = 0$, no hulls are produced ($x_1 = x_2 = 0$), and there are slacks of 195 man-hours ($s_1 = 195$) and 135 machine-hours ($s_2 = 135$). This initial basic solution is thus the origin point B in Figure 14.3, which can surely be improved upon.

Table 14.3 presents the simplex tableau for this initial basic feasible solution. The tableau is comprised of the problem variables and constants arranged as shown in Table 14.4. The $-p_1$ and $-p_2$ variables are referred to as "indicators." The μ_1 and μ_2 variables are referred to as "shadow variables" or "shadow prices." The reader who is familiar with matrix algebra will recognize that rows 1 and 2 of the tableau are simply the coefficients and constants from the constraint Equations (14.43) and (14.44) written in matrix form. The negative indicators in Table 14.3 show that the profit of $\Pi = 0$ can be improved by an amount equal to $\Pi - p_1 x_1 = $

Table 14.4. Layout of the initial tableau.

	Column Numbers				
	1	2	3	4	5
Headings	$-p_1$	$-p_2$	μ_1	μ_2	Π
Row 1	a_{11}	a_{12}	1	0	b_1
Row 2	a_{21}	a_{22}	0	1	b_2

Table 14.5. Adjusted tableau.

	Column Numbers				
	1	2	3	4	5
Headings	0	−140	80	0	15,600
Row 1	1	2/5	1/5	0	39
Row 2	0	9/5	−3/5	1	18

$0 - (-\$400)x_1$ in the x_1 direction and by an amount $\Pi - p_2x_2 = \$0 - (-300)x_2$ in the x_2 direction. The greatest opportunity for profit improvement thus lies in the x_1 direction. Then by examining the rows in the tableau of Table 14.3 we see that row 1 is the most limiting constraint, since $b_1/a_{11} = 195/5 = 39$ sailboat hulls and $b_2/a_{21} = 45$ sailboat hulls. Thus, the most profitable move from the initial solution of $x_1 = x_2 = 0$ is to the solution $x_1 = 39$ and $x_2 = 0$, where $\Pi = \$400(39) + \$300(0) = \$15,600$. This is point C in Figure 14.3.

Each of the numbers in row 1 of the tableau in Table 14.3 must now be adjusted by dividing them by a_{11} to account for the resources used up in producing the 39 sailboat hulls. The adjusted results are shown in row 1 of Table 14.5. The other numbers must also be adjusted proportionately. For example, the old $-p_1$ value of -400 becomes $-400 - (-400 \times 1) = 0$; the old $-p_2$ value of -300 becomes $-300 - (-400 \times 2/5) = -140$; the old μ_1 value of 0 becomes $0 - (-400 \times 1/5) = 80$; the old a_{21} value of 3 becomes $3 - (3 \times 1) = 0$; etc. Table 14.5 shows the results of all these adjustments. The procedures for making the adjustments are formalized in the algorithm presented in Table 14.6.

Table 14.6. Simplex algorithm.

STEP	DECISION OR ACTION
1	Select the most negative p_j indicator and call this the *pivotal column*, column J.
2	Select the row with the lowest b_i/a_{ij} value and call it the *pivotal row*, row I. Call the corresponding a_{IJ} value the *pivotal element*.
3	Divide all the v_{Ij} entries in I^{th} row by a_{IJ} to obtain the adjusted entries $\hat{v}_{Ij} = v_{Ij}/a_{IJ}$, where $\hat{v}_{Ij}$ is an adjusted value.
4	For each ith row other than row I obtain the adjusted entries $\hat{v}_{ij}$ from the old entries v_{ij} by computing $\hat{v}_{ij} = v_{ij} - (a_{iJ} \times \hat{v}_{Ij})$.
5	Repeat steps 1–4 until no negative indicators remain.

Table 14.7. Final tableau for the primal problem.

	Column Numbers				
	1	2	3	4	5
Headings	0	0	33.34	77.77	17,000
Row 1	1	0	1/3	−2/9	35
Row 2	0	1	−1/3	5/9	10

The negative indicator in column 2 of the tableau in Table 14.5 shows that the machine-hour limit has not yet been used up. That is, the profit could be increased to $\Pi - p_2 x_2 = \$15,600 - (-\$140)x_2$ by moving in the x_2 direction. Therefore, the above procedure is repeated using a_{22} as the pivotal element (as indicated in step 2 of the algorithm in Table 14.6). The resulting final tableau is shown in Table 14.7. Note that no further incremental reallocations are possible since $p_1 = p_2 = 0$. The optimal values are $x_1^* = 35$ sailboat hulls and $x_2^* = 10$ speedboat hulls. The optimum profit Π^* = is $17,000. These values appear in the last column (column 5) of the tableau. Note that this last incremental reallocation from $x_1 = 39$ and $x_2 = 0$ (Table 14.5) to $x_1^* = 35$ and $x_2^* = 10$ resulted in a loss of $4 \times \$400 = \$1,600$ in sailboat hull profits, and a gain of $10 \times \$300 = \$3000$ in speedboat hull profits. This is a net gain of $1,400 in profits, which is precisely the difference in the Π values of $17,000 and $15,600 in Tables 14.5 and 14.7. The optimum values of the "shadow prices," $\mu_1^* = 33.34$ and $\mu_2^* = 77.77$ appear in the headings in columns 3 and 4, respectively. These values show that labor and machine time are valued, at their optimal levels, at $33.34 per hour and $77.77 per hour, respectively.

Many modifications and extensions have been made in LP methods since their early development by George Dantzig and his associates during the 1950's. The revised simplex, dual simplex, composite simplex, primal-dual and decomposition methods which have subsequently been developed have all increased the capability of LP to solve larger and more challenging problems.[2]

14.3.4 The Dual

Equations (14.37) through (14.41) are the primal LP problem. The dual of this problem is:

$$min\ C = 195\mu_1 + 135\mu_2, \tag{14.45}$$

$$s.t. \ 5\mu_1 + 3\mu_2 \geqslant 400, \tag{14.46}$$

$$2\mu_1 + 3\mu_2 \geqslant 300, \tag{14.47}$$

$$\mu_1, \mu_2 \geqslant 0 \tag{14.48}$$

Note how the b_i's and p_j's are interchanged, and how the matrix of a_{ij} values are transposed in the primal and the dual. The graphical solution to the dual is shown in Figure 14.4. Note that the feasible space for this problem is unbounded to the right. In this dual problem the lowest point in this region is sought, relative to the isocost line Equation (14.45). This is just the inverse of the primal problem, where the highest point in the feasible region was sought relative to an isorevenue line. With one modification, the algorithm in Table 14.6 applies to minimization problems just as well as to maximization problems. This modification involves step 1 of the algorithm. In minimization problems, the *least* negative indicator is chosen instead of the most negative indicator. This is because the iso*cost* line is moved *down* to the *lowest* point of the simplex. Note that $C^* =$

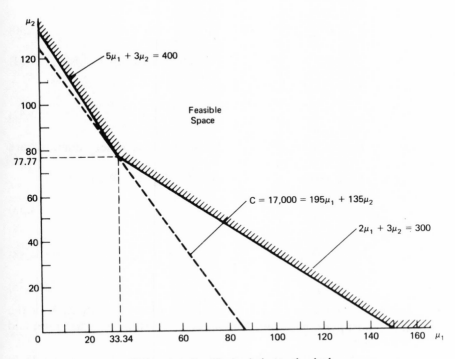

Figure 14.4. Graphical solution to the dual.

$17,000 = \Pi^*$. And note that $\mu_1^* = \$33.34$ and $\mu_2^* = \$77.77$, the same values that appeared in the final primal tableau shown in Table 14.7. Thus, as noted in a previous section of this chapter, the solution is a saddle point.

14.4 INTERPRETING AND USING LP

14.4.1 Meaning of the Variables

Let p_j be the unit profit for j^{th} output or activity, let b_i be a resource availability or limit (e.g., a budget), let a_{ij} be the activity coefficient which specifies how much of the ith resource is required to produce one unit of the jth activity or output, and let x_j be the amount of the jth activity to be determined from the LP solution. Then, the primal LP problem statement is:

$$max \ \Pi = \sum_{j=1}^{n} p_j x_j \tag{14.49}$$

$$s.t. \quad \sum_{j=1}^{n} a_{ij} x_j \leq b_i, i = 1, 2, \ldots m \text{ resources} \tag{14.50}$$

$$x_j \geq 0, j = 1, 2, \ldots n \text{ products or outputs.} \tag{14.51}$$

In the case of cost minimization, Equation (14.49) becomes

$$min \ Z = \sum_{j=1}^{n} c_j x_j, \tag{14.52}$$

where c_j is the unit cost of the jth activity and the other equations are unchanged.

The dual of the problem in Equations (14.49), (14.50) and (14.51) is:

$$min \ C = \sum_{i=1}^{m} b_i \mu_i \tag{14.53}$$

$$s.t. \quad \sum_{i=1}^{m} a_{ji} \mu_i \geq p_j, j = 1, 2, \ldots n \tag{14.54}$$

$$\mu_i \geq 0, i = 1, 2, \ldots m \tag{14.55}$$

The variable p_j is the unit profit contribution of the jth output, μ_i is the accounting cost per unit of the ith input, e.g., the standard wage rate, and C is a parameter.

In a linear programming problem all the equations are linear. That is, p_j is both the marginal (or incremental) and the average profit contribution (or the price) of the jth output. Similarly, μ_i is both the average and the marginal (or incremental) accounting cost or value of the ith input. In the augmented form of the primal, as in Equations (14.43) and (14.44), the slack variable s_i represents the unused capacity in input resource i. In the augmented form of the dual, the surplus variable s_j is the opportunity cost per unit of product j. As an example, the augmented form of Equation (14.54) is:

$$\sum_{i=1}^{m} a_{ji}\mu_i - s_j = p_j. \tag{14.56}$$

With these concepts in mind, let us now examine some important implications and uses of the outputs from an LP model.

14.4.2   Using the Outputs from an LP Model

In general, at the optimum LP solution

$$x_j s_j = 0 \text{ for all } j, \tag{14.57}$$

$$\mu_i s_i = 0 \text{ for all } i. \tag{14.58}$$

These equations say that either x_j or s_j must be zero and either μ_i or s_i must be zero in the optimum solution. Equation (14.57) says that if any j^{th} product is produced ($x_j > 0$), then its opportunity cost must be zero ($s_j = 0$). When its opportunity cost is not zero ($s_j > 0$), it should not be produced ($x_j = 0$). Now, when $x_j > 0$, it must be that the corresponding dual surplus variable $s_j = 0$. This means that there is some corresponding i^{th} input that is used to capacity. Or, in other words, some i^{th} input lies at the constraint in the dual. Similarly, Equation (14.58) says that when any input is not fully utilized ($s_i > 0$) then it is a free good ($\mu_i = 0$) with no value. The reader should note that Equation (14.58) is identical to Equation (14.34), where $\mu_i = \lambda$ and $s_i = s$. Thus, all the interpretations given above for λ and s may be fully applied here for μ_i and s_i, respectively. The implications of these relationships are very significant for decision making. Without the benefit of the knowledge that comes from the LP type of analysis, it is possible to produce too many products. Products with large opportunity costs may be difficult to spot. A product line analysis with an LP model may identify many products that should not be produced at all. Similarly, many inputs may be used to capacity that should not be used at all, from an economic standpoint. The results from a dual LP analysis can show which inputs should and should not be used. Thus, an LP analysis can often increase profits and decrease costs through a more effective reallocation of resources and a better choice of inputs.

At the optimum point The Fundamental Condition for Optimality (see Section 14.1.2) must hold. In the LP case of two outputs x_1 and x_2 the Fundamental Condition is

$$\frac{\Delta\Pi}{\Delta(a_{i1}x_1)} = \frac{\Delta\Pi}{\Delta(a_{i2}x_2)} \tag{14.59}$$

Note that Equation (14.59) and (14.27) both express the same idea. This idea was used in moving from point C to point D in Figure 14.3, or in moving from the tableau in Table 14.5 to the tableau in Table 14.7. This move involves an incremental reallocation of a total of 20 man-hours of shop time along the active constraint $5x_1 + 2x_2 = 195$. The move from point C involves a loss of $\Delta\Pi/\Delta(a_{i1}x_1) = (\$400[39 - 35])/(5)(-4) = -\$80$ per man-hour. The gain is $\Delta\Pi/\Delta(a_{i2}x_2) = (\$300[0 + 10])/(2)(+10) = +\$150$ per man-hour. Thus the gain from moving to point D exceeds the loss that is incurred; point D is thus preferred.

The shadow price μ_i indicates the incremental change in profit for each incremental addition of the ith resource. In general

$$\frac{\Delta\Pi}{\Delta b_i} = \frac{\Delta C}{\Delta b_i} = \mu_i \tag{14.60}$$

for the ith input resource, where b_i is the amount of that resource which is available. The b_i values are usually called the "right-hand" side. Equation (14.60) is a very useful relationship to have as part of a post-optimal analysis. If any μ_i are positive, then an increase in the corresponding right-hand side variable would be profitable. Such an analysis can often show that budgets have been set too low or that insufficient resources have been provided. The reader should note how Equation (14.20) earlier in this chapter and Equation (14.60) both express the same ideas.

The dual slack variables, the s_j's are often termed the "reduced costs." They indicate the amount by which the cost (or profit) of the associated x_j variable would have to decrease (or increase) in order for that variable to come into the solution. For example, if the value of $s_j = 6$ then this says that the profit on product x_j would have to increase by \$6/unit before it would be profitable to produce it. This type of information can tell a decision maker a great deal about the decision policies. For instance, if the market price for x_j is not expected to rise more than \$6 above the current level, then x_j should never be produced. However, if prices may rise more than \$6/unit then the decision maker should consider the prospects of including product x_j in the production plans during the coming horizon.

The shadow price μ_i may be used as the focal point for allocating resources in a large hierarchical organization. The parent company can permit the divisions to have as much of each ith resource as they desire at the optimum price μ_i^*. Then, since each division must make enough profit to cover μ_i^*, they will each produce the x_j^* amounts that result from an LP analysis. Thus, simply charging the optimum shadow price level for each resource will automatically result in an optimal allocation of the firm's resources. This assumes that all the firm's decision makers are behaving according to the economic model discussed in Chapter 4. The mix and levels of activities will be economically guided by the shadow prices in such a way that profits are maximized. Though these ideas have been applied with some success, the fact that the economic model is not always an accurate description of decision behaviors accounts for some failures in these decentralized organizational decision making LP methods.[2,3]

14.4.3   Performing Sensitivity Analyses

In a sensitivity analysis an attempt is made to systematically examine the influence of changes in various variables on the optimal solution. A sensitivity analysis is quite useful because in many practical applications some of the problem data are not known with great precision. A sensitivity analysis is also very useful for finding new optimal solutions as new estimates of the data become available. A comprehensive sensitivity analysis will consider changes in the right hand side, changes in the constraints, changes in the costs or profits, the addition or deletion of a product or resource, and the addition or relaxation of one or more constraints. All these changes can be tested and evaluated by simply modifying the existing rows or introducing new rows into the LP tableau. A technique known as parametric programming can be used to systematically change the problem variables in a way that shows the effects of combinations of changes.[2] Such a comprehensive "what if" analysis can reveal a great deal about the suitability of various policies and the effects of various decisions. A thorough sensitivity analysis can often reveal the presence of constraints that are too restrictive or a problem definition that is too narrow.

14.4.4   Some Problems and Limitations

If any of the p_j indicators in the simplex tableau are of the same magnitude, and are therefore tied for the honor of being the Jth column, either can be chosen. But if two or more rows are tied for the honor of being the Ith row then the LP algorithm may oscillate endlessly between them. This is "degeneracy," and there are special rules to prevent it. Special rules are also available for finding alternate optima, such as when the objective function and one of the constraints are congruent.[2]

Equality constraints of the form

$$\sum_{j=1}^{n} a_{ij}x_j = b_i \tag{14.61}$$

may create some problems because $s_i = 0$, and an initial basic solution is not obvious. However, by suitably chosen mathematical rearrangements, Equations like (14.61) can be converted to their equivalent less-than-or-equal-to forms like Equation (14.50), which can then be solved by a conventional LP approach.[2] Similarly, equations of the form

$$\sum_{j=1}^{n} a_{ij}x_j \geqslant b_i \tag{14.62}$$

can be converted to their more conventional form, Equation (14.50). These arrangements depend on the use of what is called the "big M" method of LP.[2]

The LP method has four basic assumptions which limit its applicability to specific kinds of problems. These are the assumptions of linearity, divisibility, additivity and finiteness. The linearity assumption states that for LP to be applicable, the ratio of each input to each output must be constant, for all levels of output. This is the economic assumption of constant returns to scale. The divisibility assumption states that LP is only applicable where the process can be used to any degree or scale of operation. The additivity assumption states that the quantities of inputs used at some output level, say $2x$, must be the same as the sum of the quantities of inputs used at $x + x$. The finiteness assumption means that the simplex must not have an infinite number of vertexes, thus leading to the possibility of a nearly infinite number of solutions. Though LP can often be usefully applied to help the decision maker analyze problems and gain insights, when the above assumptions are not met the LP solution may not be optimal. Nonlinear and integer programming methods should be used when precise solutions are needed and the LP assumptions are not met.

14.5   INTEGER AND NONLINEAR PROGRAMMING

14.5.1   Integer Programming (IP)

In some types of LP problems only integer (whole number) solutions are sensible. For instance, one can produce only whole autos, only whole people can be assigned, etc. Rounding off the optimal LP solution to the nearest whole number seldom works because the nearest whole number may be outside the feasible region. On the other hand most approaches to the solution of integer problems either begin with the LP solution or use some of the LP procedures. The standard LP may be solved and checked to see if integer solutions result. If not, then integer programming (IP) procedures must be used. These IP approaches include the introduction of modified constraints and cutting planes, the use of branch and bound methods, the separation of the LP into descendent problems, piecewise linear approximation methods, ranking and indexing methods, and combinatorial matching methods.[4] Many capital budgeting problems, manpower assignment problems and production planning problems require integer solutions. Some of these problems are so large and complex that they are difficult to solve without the aid of fast computer codes.

14.5.2 Nonlinear Programming (NLP)

The LP linearity assumption often does not hold in many real world situations. For example, in a maximization problem when there are increasing returns to scale (the ratio of outputs to inputs increases with more inputs) the LP solution will lead to the production of too many products. Several different kinds of mathematical methods have been developed for handling various types of NLP problems. The most frequently used nonlinear approaches are gradient or hill-climbing methods, quadratic programming, separable programming and dynamic programming.[5]

Gradient methods are a variant of classical programming procedures that are very useful for multivariate functions. The problem is visualized as finding the pinnacle of a hill (maximization) or the lowest point in a depression (minimization) on an n-dimensional surface. Zigzag steps are taken, with each subsequent step being the one with the highest incremental value at each point. Quadratic programming is a particular NLP problem where the objective function is a quadratic equation. In separable programming, approximately optimal solutions are obtained by a modified simplex approach. From the original objective function, two sets of functions are devised that are equivalent to the original problem. These two functions may then be jointly solved by integer or other NLP methods, or sometimes by a standard LP. Dynamic programming involves the calculus of variations. The problem is solved sequentially or stagewise, in such a way that the combined optima at each stage yield the overall optimum of the problem.[6]

14.6   SUMMARY

Decision problems which involve the optimum allocation of scarce resources among competing alternatives are often very complex and difficult to solve. Mathematical programming methods can be used to assist in formulating and solving such problems. Depending on the nature of the problem, either linear programming (LP), nonlinear programming (NLP) or integer programming (IP) methods may apply. In some cases, the decision data and the problem formulation may be defined with great precision and exact solutions may thus be sought. In other cases where the objectives or constraints are fuzzy or the data inputs are imprecise, only approximate solutions may be possible. Sensitivity analyses, post-optimal analyses and parametric approaches may be especially useful under these circumstances. These techniques permit the decision maker to examine a range of decision alternatives, and to test several "what if" situations, as a guide to the choice of the overall most suitable decision.

14.7   REFERENCES

1. Hancock, Harris. *Theory of Maxima and Minima*, New York: Dover, 1960, pp. 1–42; 96–164.
2. Bazaraa, M. S. and Jarvis, J. J. *Linear Programming and Network Flows*. New York: John Wiley & Sons, Inc., 1977.
3. Sweeney, D. J.; Winkofsky, E. P.; Roy, Probir; and Baker, N. R. "Composition vs. Decomposition: Two Approaches to Modeling Organizational Decision Processes." *Management Science*, **24**, No. 14: 1491–1499 (1978).
4. Glover, Fred "Integer Programming and Combinatorics," in the *Handbook of Operations Research: Foundations and Fundamentals, Volume 1*, J. J. Moder and S. E. Elmaghraby (eds.), New York: Van Nostrand Reinhold Company, 1978, pp. 120–146.
5. Mangasarian, Olvi L. "Nonlinear Programming" in the *Handbook of Operations Research: Foundations and Fundamentals, Volume 1, op. cit.,* pp. 245–265.
6. Rosen, E. M. and Souder, W. E. "A Method for Allocating R&D Expenditures," *IEEE Trans. on Eng. Mgt.*, **EM-12** No. 3: 87–93 (1965).

14.8   BIBLIOGRAPHY

Barnes, J. W. and Crisp, R. M. "Linear Programming: A Survey of General Purpose Algorithms." *AIIE Transactions*, **7**, No. 3: 212–220 (1975).
Bazaraa, M. S. and Shetty, C. M. *Nonlinear Programming*, New York: John Wiley & Sons, Inc., 1977.
Cooper, L. L. and Steinberg, David. *Introduction to Methods of Optimization*. Philadelphia: W. B. Saunders Company, 1970.
Dantzig, G. B.; Orden A; and Wolfe, P. "The Generalized Simplex Method of Minimizing a Linear Form Under Linear Inequality Restraints." RAND Memorandum RM-1264, 1954.
Hadley, G. *Linear Programming*. Reading, Massachusetts: Addison-Wesley Publishing Co., Inc., 1962, pp. 1–272; 429–487.

Henderson, J. M. and Quandt, R. E. *Microeconomic Theory*. New York: McGraw-Hill, 1958, pp. 42–84; 241–255; 257–277.

Kantorovich, L. *Mathematical Methods in the Organization and Planning of Production*. The Leningrad State University Press, 1939; translation in *Management Science*, **6**, No. 3: 366–422 (1958).

Moder, J. J. and Elmaghraby, S. E. (eds.) *The Handbook of Operations Research: Foundations and Fundamentals, Volume 1*, New York: Van Nostrand Reinhold Company, 1978, pp. 85–294.

Riley, V. and Gass, S. I. *Linear Programming and Associated Techniques: A Comprehensive Bibliography on Linear, Nonlinear and Dynamic Programming*. Baltimore: Johns Hopkins Press, 1958.

Schruben, L. W. "Assignment of Primary Response Zones to Emergency Medical Units." *AIIE Transactions*, **11**, No. 2: 30–36 (1979).

Part VII

Managing the Decision System

The decision making process does not come to an abrupt end once a decision is made. All decisions must be implemented. They must also be controlled to insure that they do not get out of date. And they must be constantly evaluated and checked for their continuing effectiveness over time. Moreover, the overall decision making process must be maintained by keeping the various decision support systems up to date. The one chapter in this part of the book, Chapter 15, discusses these aspects.

15
Evaluating, Implementing and Controlling the Decision

15.0 INTRODUCTION

The effectiveness of any decision is a function of three things: its quality, its implementation and its control. Fundamentally,

$$E = f(Q, I, C), \tag{15.1}$$

where E = the effectiveness of the decision, Q = the quality of the decision, I = the extent to which it is implemented and C = the degree to which it is controlled. A high-quality decision is one that solves the problem in a timely, economical fashion. A well-implemented decision is accepted by all the involved parties, and they are enthusiastically committed to carrying it out. A well-controlled decision is carefully monitored, followed up and fine tuned to adjust it to changing circumstances over time. Because decisions often get out of date, an important part of the control function includes sensing and signaling the need for a revised decision to cope with the changed circumstances.

Though it may not be possible to apply Equation (15.1) with great rigor and precision, this equation provides an overall guide to the factors which control the effectiveness of a decision. This chapter discusses these factors and the ways in which modern managers can maximize each of them.

15.1 THE QUALITY OF A DECISION

15.1.1 Quality Factors[1]

The seven factors listed in Table 15.1 collectively determine the quality of a decision. Though trade-offs among these factors are possible, the high-

Table 15.1. Factors which determine the quality of a decision.

Potency
Cost-Effectiveness
Flexibility
Generality
Timeliness
Forward-Focus
Feasibility

est quality decision occurs when all seven factors are achieved. Let us briefly examine these factors.

A potent decision eliminates the limiting factor or the critical cause of the problem. Every problem will have one most critical cause or limiting factor (see Chapter 10). Eliminating this factor will solve the problem. A cost-effective decision has the highest possible potency/cost or benefit/cost ratio (see Chapters 7 and 8). A flexible and general decision covers a range of circumstances and situations that may occur over time. Timeliness refers to the time-phasing of the decision. In a properly timed decision, the solution will not occur after the problem has taken a heavy toll, nor will it occur so early that its potency is dissipated before the problem fully emerges. A forward-focused decision will be oriented to solving future problems as well as the particular one that is at hand. This is a very important aspect. A problem that "won't stay dead" or a problem that keeps reappearing in derivative forms often results when the solution is not sufficiently forward-focused. The feasibility of a solution refers to whether or not it fits within the existing constraints and restrictions. Two common reasons why a solution may not be feasible are an inadequacy of resources and an inconsistency between the solution and the desires of some members of the organization.

15.1.2 Quality Evaluation Approaches

The list of factors in Table 15.1 provides a handy checklist for evaluating the quality of any decision. A scoring model could be developed around these factors to facilitate the analyses (see Chapter 9). Dominance analyses (Chapter 4), parametric analyses (Chapter 8) and cost-benefit methods (Chapter 7) could be used as part of these evaluations. GEMPA charts (Chapter 10), fault trees (Chapter 8) and means-ends analyses methods (Chapter 6) could also be applied to assist in the evaluations. Brainstorming, purge or tear-down methods (Chapter 6) and group evaluation techniques (Chapter 5) may be especially useful in quality evaluations, since much of the evaluation data is necessarily judgmental.

A pilot test of the decision on a subpopulation of users or problems can identify weaknesses that must be corrected prior to implementation. If a pilot test is not possible, simulation is the next best approach. If precise data are available, it may be possible to develop a computer simulation code or to model the situation with one of the existing simulation languages like *GASP, Simscript* or *GPSS*. The economic and cost-effectiveness aspects of a decision can often be simulated in this fashion. However, the ways in which the potency, feasiblity, timeliness and generality of the decision can be enhanced or diminished by various human reactions can seldom be modeled so precisely. Thus, role-playing and "what if" speculations about human behaviors have a proper place in the simulations. In order for this kind of analysis to be effective, the role-player must have accurate insights into the "palace politics" of the organization as well as a good understanding of human behaviors and motives. The role-player must be able to identify and empathize with others, and to extrapolate by analogy from previous experiences.

15.1.3 Quality Limitations

The quality of a decision is sometimes rather naturally limited by a variety of human, organizational, resource, legal and economic constraints. Individual values and personalities may restrict the decision to a scope or quality that is below the maximum level. Similarly, the quality and quantity of resources available may not be sufficient to meet the demands of a high-quality solution. The absence of a risk-taking, venturesome climate can impede the quality of a decision. High-quality decisions often involve some exposure of individuals and organizations to the risk of failure, embarrassment, conflict and stress. Unless the climate rewards individuals for taking such risks, higher-quality decisions may be shunned.

In the short run, there may be no way around such quality limitations. However, their existence poses longer run problems for the organization and its decision makers. Building and maintaining high quality human resources, a venturesome climate and a willingness to accept change is vital to the long run quality of decision making. Though many methods and techniques are available to assist in these endeavors, sound long term management is required in order to achieve them.[2, 3]

15.2 IMPLEMENTATION

15.2.1 Implementation Barriers

Because decisions must often be carried out by others, or because all the resources to implement the decision are not fully controlled by the decision maker, problems in implementation may arise. Gaining individual

304 VII / Managing the Decision System

and organizational acceptance and commitment to carry out a decision is often a major hurdle. Table 15.2 lists nine most frequently encountered barriers to implementation. Let us briefly examine each of them.

Rationalistic naïveté refers to the blind belief that all one needs to do is present the decision in a purely rational way and it will be implemented. This approach is naïve because it neglects the fact that while people are often rational they are also emotional. Any decision maker or implementer who fails to properly appeal to human motives will usually fail to get the decision implemented, no matter how rational it is. This is especially true when there is a lack of a perceived problem or a felt need for a decision. Simply put, you cannot sell the product when there is no demand for it. In this case, the decision maker may have to devote time to sales, promotion and the creation of a demand.

The fear that the decision will destroy the power base, the power status or a comfortable status quo is often foremost in the minds of individuals. Even when there is a desire to move away from the status quo, the fear that the new decision may somehow result in even worse conditions may make people reluctant to accept it. Thus, any decision that appears to be irreversible will naturally be resisted. A flexible decision which permits individuals the option of returning to the old status quo will always have more appeal.

The feelings of trust and openness toward the decision maker are often important factors in implementation. A lack of trust and faith in the decision maker naturally clouds how individuals feel about any new actions and decisions which the decision maker is advocating. Trust-based relationships and a strong achievement orientation often go hand-in-hand. A trusting climate fosters a sense of confidence and a willingness to take on new challenges and changes. A climate that lacks a strong achievement motivation will generally be resistant to change.

Self-interests often get in the way of a decision. Many illustrations of how self-interests can block decisions can be found in the various com-

Table 15.2. Barriers to implementation.

Rationalistic Naïveté
Lack of a Perceived Problem
Fear of Inability to Reverse the Decision
Perceived Disruptions to Status Quo
Lack of Trust
Lack of Achievement Orientation
Conflicts With Self-Interests
Lack of Consensus Agreement
Lack of a Systems Approach

munity action movements that have been formed to block the building of new expressways, dams and other public programs. In general, a lack of consensus agreement and an unwillingness to acquiesce to the larger needs and goals is a frequent barrier to implementation. Many such obstacles arise because the decision maker has failed to take a systems perspective toward the implementation problems. Any decision maker who fails to carefully look beyond the immediate impacts of the decision may overlook many important longer-range second-order and third-order impacts.

15.2.2 Reducing the Barriers

Table 15.3 lists several approaches to reducing the implementation barriers. Let us discuss each of these and note how they may be used.

The use of participation and involvement strategies may be an effective approach for overcoming resistances. When individuals are given the opportunity to help formulate and influence decisions they generally feel more committed to them. Moreover, the quality of the decision may be improved by the collective wisdom and debates that have been brought to bear on it. On the other hand, modern managers have come to recognize that participation in decision making is not the cure-all that it was once thought to be. Many studies have shown that people do not always want to participate in the decision formulation process.[4] Moreover, if the decision conflicts with their self-interests, the participants will surely attempt to defeat or alter it. The result may be a decision that solves the wrong problem. In general, the participants may go away with the feeling that the decision maker is ineffectual, and that they should be consulted on other matters which are actually none of their concern.

Interactive modeling methods involve procedures for measuring the specific individual and organizational barriers that inhibit the adoption of a particular decision. These barriers are then compared to the particular features of the decision that are being resisted by the adopters. Sequential

Table 15.3. Barrier reducing strategies.

Participation and Involvement
Interactive Modeling
Tailoring the Decision to the Climate
Taskforces and Group Methods
Trials and Parallel Pilot Tests
Facilitative Assistance
Reeducative Programs
Persuasion
Appeals to Logic, Fear, and Regret Avoidance

adjustments are then made in both the decision features and in the barriers until the decision and the willingness to adopt are in harmony. A similar approach is used in tailoring the decision to the climate of the organization, except that here the changes are made primarily to the decision. These approaches are relatively new. They involve the use of negotiation, bargaining and post-optimal analysis methods, usually with the aid of interactive computer terminals to obtain rapid answers to "what if" questions, and with the aid of group sessions to achieve consensus.[5, 6]

The use of taskforces to study the decision and nominal-interacting group sessions to debate the alternatives can be effective (see Chapter 5). Group settings may be especially useful for conducting pilot studies, and for carrying out parallel trials of the proposed decision vis-à-vis established procedures. Side-by-side comparisons of the old and new procedures may not only be used to prove the superiority of a decision, but also to obtain implementation and use at the same time.

Facilitative, reeducative, persuasive and appeal approaches are all "selling" strategies. The facilitative approach helps the individual to see how his or her own self-interests can be achieved by adopting the decision. A reeducative program attempts to alter the individual's perception of the decision by more fully explaining its logic, rationale and impacts. A persuasive approach is the "hard sell," often involving some appeal to emotion, fear or regret avoidance. Often, all three must be used in some joint way in order to increase the willingness of various parties to adopt the decision.[7, 8]

15.2.3 Four Steps to Implementation

There are four basic steps to implement any decision. The first step is to assess the implementation problems and the implementability of the decision. The barriers to implementation should be enumerated, using Table 15.2 as a checklist to aid in this process.

The second step is to carry out a situation status check. This step answers the following three questions: Where are we now with regard to the degree of implementation? What are the needs, desires and goals of those who are expected to adopt the decision? What will motivate the adopters?

The third step is to develop the implementation plan. Program planning and budgeting techniques (see Chapters 9, 10 and 11) may be usefully applied at this point in working out the details of the plan. However, the fundamental concern in this step is the selection of the appropriate barrier reducing strategies. Though this is largely an art, there are some useful approaches that can guide the decision maker in selecting appropriate strategies.[9, 10]

The fourth step is selecting the leadership plan to carry out the implementation. Real implementation occurs only when individuals carry out the decision with a determined commitment and enthusiasm. To achieve this, individuals who command the trust and respect of the users must be selected to lead the implementation effort. In some cases, the decision maker may not have the sensitive interpersonal touch or the leadership qualities required. Thus, a "neutral" third party may be selected as the change agent in charge of implementation. This third party may be either a competent individual or a team of persons. Participation, interactive modeling, pilot tests, facilitative, reeducative and persuasive methods may all be used. But the essential requirement is that the third party be an authority figure and a leader who can create a lasting atmosphere of trust and confidence.[7, 9]

15.3   CONTROL

Modern decision makers need timely and accurate control information on how well their decisions are performing over time. The most effective approach to collecting such information is to use separate but related control methods for routine, recurrent and nonroutine decisions. Routine decisions can be effectively controlled by policies, rules and decision tables. Management need only get involved when the policy is violated or when an exceptional case occurs. Cost-progress methods can be used for recurrent decisions on projects. These approaches effectively free up top management's time, permitting them to focus on their proper role as strategic planners and handlers of nonroutine problems. The three levels of decisions—routine, recurrent and nonroutine—can be linked through an integrated planning and control system (see Section 15.3.3).

15.3.1   Policies, Rules and Decision Tables

Many routine decisions can be preprogrammed. Policies and rules can be established that specify the appropriate action for every outcome. An example of this approach is presented in Table 15.4. The decision table shown there defines an appropriate decision rule for every possible outcome that is expected to occur. Management does not need to become involved unless a new condition should occur or some exceptional case should arise.

Table 15.4. Example of a decision table.

CONDITIONS			OUTCOMES	
Chances of rain ≥ .60	yes	...... yes	no	...... no ...
Chances of cold wind ≥ .40	no	...... yes	yes	...... no ...
Chances of sunshine ≥ .50	no	...... no	yes	...... yes ...

Rule 1: Take
Umbrella
　　　　Rule 2: Wear
　　　　Raincoat
　　　　　　Rule 3: Wear
　　　　　　Overcoat
　　　　　　　　Rule 4: Wear
　　　　　　　　Jacket

15.3.2 Cost-Progress Control *

Keeping a project on schedule can be a difficult task unless achievements and expenditures can be carefully related. The cost-progress approach permits the project manager to relate achievements with expenditures and to obtain early warning indicators of pending overruns.

To illustrate the cost-progress approach, let us assume that a time-scaled network plan has been developed (see Chapter 12). Then let t = the time period, $t = 1, 2, \ldots n$; E_t = the cumulative dollars actually expended by the end of time period t; $\hat{E}_t$ = the cumulative dollars forecasted to be expended by the end of time period t; $\Delta E_t = (\hat{E}_t - E_t)$ = the cost variance for t; Φ_t = the cumulative actual output at the end of time period t; $\hat{\Phi}_t$ = the cumulative forecasted output at the end of time period t; $\Delta\Phi_t = (\Phi_t - \hat{\Phi}_t)$ = the progress variance for t; $\hat{C}_t$ = the total *forecasted* cost of the total *actual* output at the end of t; $\Delta C_t = (\hat{C}_t - E_t)$ = the cost/progress variance for t. Let the output be measured as the percentage of the nodes completed in the network diagram. Then $\hat{\Phi}_t$ is the percentage of the nodes expected to be completed at the end of time period t and Φ_t is the actual percentage of the nodes completed. The variances ΔE_t, $\Delta\Phi_t$ and ΔC_t are the information feedbacks that monitor costs and achievements over time. When these variances become large enough they trigger a control action by the project manager, e.g., reallocations of resources, replanning of the project, etc.

* Portions of the material in this section are based on Souder, W. E. "Project Selection, Planning and Control," in the *Handbook of Operations Research: Models and Applications*, J. J. Moder and S. E. Elmaghraby (eds.), New York: Van Nostrand Reinhold Company, 1978, pp. 334–344.

These ideas are illustrated in Table 15.5 and Figure 15.1. To visualize how this model functions, suppose that at the end of time period 5 the actual output has been determined to be .40 (40% of the nodes have been achieved) and the total actual amount expended has been determined to be $100,000. Therefore, a mark X_5 was made at the coordinates $E = 100$ and $\Phi = 0.4$ in Figure 15.1, ignoring for the moment the time scale. The appropriate values of the parameters $\hat{E}_5$, E_5, $\hat{\Phi}_5$, Φ_5, and $\hat{C}_5$ were entered in the "Analysis of Budget Variance Table" shown in Table 15.5 and the respective variances were computed. Likewise, the marks X_1, X_2, X_3, . . . X_n were made in Figure 15.1 for months 1, 2, 3, . . . n and the corresponding variances were similarly computed and entered in Table 15.5. Note that the forecast line in Figure 15.1 is simply a graphic portrayal of the time-scaled network plan, and is developed by simply plotting the $\hat{\Phi}_t$ values against the corresponding budgeted $\hat{E}_t$ and t values. Thus, Figure 15.1 is simply a way of depicting the time-scaled network plan and recording actual cost and progress through it. The time and expenditure scales in Figure 15.1 are those from the network plan, e.g., the expenditure scale is developed by adding up the cost for each time point or at each node.

This model enables project management to see variances as they occur, categorize their causes and determine the appropriate control action to be taken. For example, the data in Table 15.5 and Figure 15.1 show that the manager should not be concerned about the overspending indicated by the negative cost variance at the end of the second month ($\Delta E_2 = -10$). The cost/progress variance is positive ($\Delta C_2 = +20$), indicating that the extra expenditure has "bought" more than a proportionate achievement. Note the location of X_2 in Figure 15.1. In other words, running over budget will not matter if the overexpenditure is "buying" proportionate achievements. But, now consider the data for the third, fourth and fifth months in

Table 15.5. Analysis of budget variance table.

t	EXPENDITURE			OUTPUT			COST/ PROGRESS	
	E_t	$\hat{E}_t$	ΔE_t	ϕ_t	$\hat{\phi}_t$	$\Delta\phi_t$	$\hat{C}_t$	ΔC_t
1	20	20	0	0.10	0.10	0	20	0
2	50	40	−10	0.25	0.15	+0.10	70	+20
3	60	70	+10	0.35	0.25	+0.10	85	+25
4	75	90	+15	0.40	0.40	0	90	+15
5	100	120	+20	0.40	0.65	−0.25	90	−10
6	130	140	+10	0.70	0.75	−0.05	130	0
7	180	160	−20	0.70	0.85	−0.15	130	−50
8	230	180	−50	0.70	0.87	−0.17	130	−100

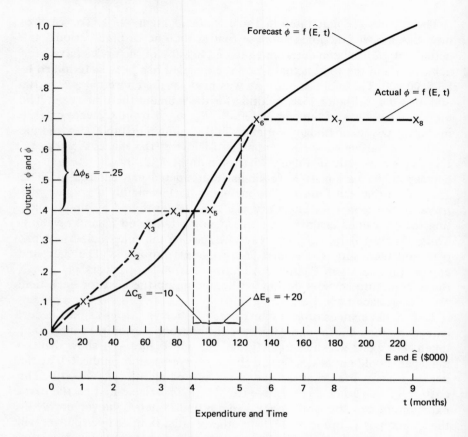

Figure 15.1. Cost-progress control model example.

Table 15.5 and Figure 15.1. The absolute level of achievement is slipping at an increasing rate, as shown by the entries in the $\Delta\Phi_t$ column changing from $+0.10$, through 0, to -0.25. And the level of achievement per amount of expenditure is also slipping, as shown by the entries in the ΔC_t column. Not only is the project achieving less with each passing month, but it is also achieving less per dollar with each passing month. But none of this "bad news" shows in the "budget" or cost variance, the ΔE_t column in Table 15.5. In fact, the project shows a favorable status in budgetary control (positive entries in the ΔE_t column) over these three months!

The conclusion is that controlling by "budget" overruns and underruns *only* can be seriously misleading. Cost (or budget) variances and achievement variances can balance out, as shown at the end of the sixth month in Table 15.5 and Figure 15.1. Or they may reinforce each other, as shown at the end of months seven and eight in Table 15.5 and Figure 15.1. In any event, it is the interaction of both the cost and achievement variances that determines the actual status of the project. This simple fact is often obscured in many project control situations. As a result, an inordinate amount of significance is generally attached to project cost overruns, while some projects running under their budgeted costs often fail to attract badly needed attention. For example, even under fixed manpower assignments, misalignments may occur because a manager may choose to underconsume a "fair share" of outside services, e.g., analytical services, in the interest of staying under budget. Or the manager may underconsume in the hope of reserving some funds for other projects. The cost-progress approach makes the effects of such misalignments immediately apparent.[11, 12]

15.3.3 Integrated Methods for Nonroutine Decision Control

Planning premises and other informational inputs to the planning process are often highly tenuous and subject to rapid change. The technical status of the ongoing activities may change rapidly, competition may introduce a similar product, the price of an essential raw material may change, etc. Changes in these planning premises can necessitate a reperformance of the planning and control functions in order to adapt to these changes. The dynamic impacts of these changes on other existing programs or the anticipated reactions of competitors and suppliers may cause further changes which necessitate additional adaptive planning and control actions. Thus, an iterative planning and control cycle may be performed over time, as illustrated in Figure 15.2. A planning model, e.g., a project

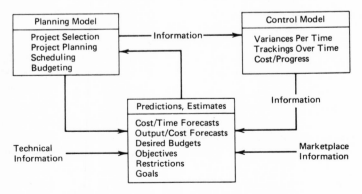

Figure 15.2. Integrated planning and control system.

selection-resource allocation and network scheduling package, may be used to arrive at a satisfactory plan. After the plan is implemented, actual events may cause a change in the original predictions and estimates sufficient to warrant a replanning and iterative repetition of the planning model. That is, things have changed to the degree that a new set of projects, funding allocations and time schedules must be devised. The planning and control cycle thus repeats, with the planning and control models continuously reused in these fashions as analytic aids to decision making.

This system combines centralized and decentralized decision making. Control is decentralized in that it takes place at the lowest possible level. Policies, decision tables and rules are used at the lowest levels of activity control within the organization. Cost-progress methods are used at the project level of control, where the project manager keeps the project within the planned limits by making minor adjustments that are within the given budget. However, changes in total project budgets, changes in the number or types of personnel, or any major replanning that affects other projects involves management at levels above project supervision. This is the strategic control-decision making level. Thus, this integrated system interfaces planning and control at the activity level with planning and control at the project level, with planning and control at the multiproject or area level, and with planning and control at the strategic level of the organization.

15.4. DECISION SUPPORT SYSTEMS

No decision making system is complete if it does not have a decision support system. Modern computerized decision support systems can reduce the time lag between problem recognition and decision implementation. Management information systems (MIS) can store and retrieve many different kinds of valuable decision data. Large-scale information banks like the *Dialog, Orbit, Mead, New York Times* and *Dow Jones* data bases can provide a variety of data to assist in the definition of the problem, the generation of alternatives and the analysis of these alternatives. Modern computer technologies provide the library capability to browse, have access to, search and retrieve an enormous amount of information on a wide variety of technical and nontechnical topics in only a few minutes. Computerized economic analysis methods, decision tree models, mathematical programming models and cost-progress control methods can be linked to these data bases to carry out rapid "what if" analyses, post-optimal analyses and other exercises aimed at finding the most feasible decision. Previous problem situations and their solutions can be stored for future recall and consultation in like situations. Modern computer methods can even tell the decision maker whether or not a problem like this has ever arisen before, and what was done about it. Today's modern decision maker can have all these capabilities in a small portable computer terminal that can be used anywhere there is a telephone.

Today's state-of-the-art in decision support systems is in its infancy. Significant changes are imminent that may make traditional information handling processes and decision making styles obsolete. Modern managers must keep alert to these changes and developments.

15.5 SUMMARY

The overall effectiveness of any decision is a product of its quality, implementation and control. This chapter has reviewed several approaches that may be used to maximize the effectiveness of a decision. A manager who follows these approaches in using the structured decision making process and the techniques discussed in this book should be able to dramatically improve the overall effectiveness of the decision making process.

However, a mechanical approach to the application of the structured decision making process and the techniques discussed in this book will lead to many disappointments. The key to effectiveness in decision making is the style, leadership, risk-taking, boldness, judgment, assertiveness and decisiveness qualities of the decision maker. There is no substitute for "taking the bull by the horns," so to speak. The techniques and approaches presented in this book can significantly augment these qualities. But they can never substitute for them. It is the synergism of the structured decision making methods and the qualities of the decision maker that make the difference between an effective and ineffective decision.

15.6 REFERENCES

1. This section is based on Souder, W. E. "A Scoring Model for Assessing the Suitability of Management Science Models." *Management Science*, **18**, No. 10, pp. 526–543 (1972).
2. Anthony, W. P. and Nicholson, E. A. *Management of Human Resources*. Columbus, Ohio: Grid, Inc., 1977.
3. Argyris, Chris. *Integrating the Individual and the Organization*. New York: John Wiley & Sons, Inc., 1964.
4. Gibson, J. L.; Ivancevich, J. M.; and Donnelly, J. H., Jr. *Organizations: Behavior, Structure, Processes*. Dallas: Business Publications, Inc., 1979, pp. 181–187; 341–360.
5. Souder, W. E.; Maher, P. M.; Baker, N. R.; Shumway, C. R.; and Rubenstein, A. H. "An Organizational Intervention Approach to the Design and Implementation of R&D Project Selection Models," in *Implementing Operations Research/Management Sci-*

ence, R. L. Schultz and D. P. Slevin (eds.), New York: Elsevier, 1975, pp. 133–152.

6. Souder, W. E. "Effectiveness of Nominal and Interacting Group Decision Processes for Integrating R&D and Marketing," *Management Science*, **23**, No. 6, pp. 595–605 (1977).

7. Zaltman, Gerald and Duncan, Robert. *Strategies for Planned Change*. New York: John Wiley & Sons, Inc., 1977.

8. Zaltman, Gerald; Duncan, Robert; and Holbek, Jonny. *Innovations and Organizations*. New York: John Wiley & Sons, Inc., 1973.

9. Schultz, R. L. and Slevin, D. P. (eds.), *Implementing Operations Research/ Management Science*. New York: American Elsevier Publishing Co., Inc., 1975.

10. Lockett, A. G. and Polding, E. "OR/MS Implementation—A Variety of Processes," *Interfaces*, **9**, No. 1 (1978): 45–50.

11. Souder, W. E. "Cost/Progress—A Breakthrough in Operational Budgeting." *Managerial Planning*, **17**, No. 1, January/February 1969, pp. 1–9.

12. Souder, W. E. "Experiences with an R&D Project Control Model," *IEEE Trans. on Eng. Mgt.*, **EM-15**, March 1968, pp. 39–49.

15.7 BIBLIOGRAPHY

Keen, P. G. K. and Morton, M. S. *Decision Support Systems: An Organizational Perspective*. Reading, Massachusetts: Addison-Wesley Publishing Co., Inc., 1978.

Souder, W. E. "Achieving Organizational Consensus with Respect to R&D Project Selection Criteria," *Management Science*, **21**, No. 6: 669–681 (1975).

Tani, Steven N. "A Perspective on Modelling in Decision Analysis." *Management Science*, **24**, No. 14: 1500–1506 (1978).

Vazsonyi, Andre, "Decision Support Systems: The New Technology of Decision Making." *Interfaces*, **9**, No. 1: 72–77 (1978).

Zmud, R. W. "Perceptions of Cognitive Style: Acquisition, Exhibition and Implications for System Design." *Journal of Management*, **5**, No. 1: 7–20 (1979).

Index

315